Proper Women

Proper Women

*Feminism and the Politics of
Respectability in Iran*

Fae Chubin

TEMPLE UNIVERSITY PRESS
Philadelphia • Rome • Tokyo

TEMPLE UNIVERSITY PRESS
Philadelphia, Pennsylvania 19122
tupress.temple.edu

Copyright © 2024 by Temple University—Of The Commonwealth
System of Higher Education
All rights reserved
Published 2024

Library of Congress Cataloging-in-Publication Data
Names: Chubin, Fae, 1985– author.
Title: Proper women : feminism and the politics of respectability in Iran / Fae Chubin.
Description: Philadelphia : Temple University Press, 2024. | Includes bibliographical references and index. | Summary: "This book looks at a women's empowerment NGO in Iran that struggled to connect its clientele with global notions of feminism. Clients found that the Western-informed concepts preferred by the center's staff read as upper-class. The author theorizes a sensitive relationship between global and situated notions of feminism"— Provided by publisher.
Identifiers: LCCN 2023033008 (print) | LCCN 2023033009 (ebook) | ISBN 9781439923276 (cloth) | ISBN 9781439923283 (paperback) | ISBN 9781439923290 (pdf)
Subjects: LCSH: Women—Iran—Social conditions—21st century. | Women social reformers—Iran—Social conditions—21st century. | Feminists—Iran—Social conditions—21st century. | Feminism—Iran. | Women's rights—Iran. | Non-governmental organizations—Iran.
Classification: LCC HQ1735.2 .C488 2024 (print) | LCC HQ1735.2 (ebook) | DDC 305.420955—dc23/eng/20231108
LC record available at https://lccn.loc.gov/2023033008
LC ebook record available at https://lccn.loc.gov/2023033009

9 8 7 6 5 4 3 2 1

To maman & baba.

Contents

Introduction	*1*
1 Studying ALLY	*14*
2 Women, Class, and Citizenship in Iran	*24*
3 Glocalizing Women's Empowerment	*55*
4 From Empowerment to Advocacy	*79*
5 The Invisible Class	*96*
6 Oppositional Consciousness and Solidarities	*116*
7 The Symbolic Economy of Propriety	*131*
Conclusion	*151*
Epilogue	*158*
Acknowledgments	*161*
Appendix: Theory, Method, and Politics	*163*
Notes	*169*
References	*173*
Index	*183*

Proper Women

Introduction

"I wouldn't live in this country for a second if it wasn't for my girls,"[1] Marva told me as she recounted her decision to leave Canada, where she had lived for nearly two decades, to take on her current position in Tehran as the codirector of ALLY,[2] a nongovernmental organization (NGO) seeking to empower young, marginalized women. She had decided to return to Iran with the conviction that she could play an important role in the unfortunate lives of the impoverished and exploited young women who had found refuge and hope at ALLY and its women's empowerment program. Marva's confident wittiness and commanding presence solidified her reputation as the mama bear of the organization. As I shadowed her during the first day of my fieldwork, I noticed the close bond she shared with many of the young women, who greeted her with funny anecdotes, random hugs, and spontaneous smiles. Shadowing Marva also meant hastily moving between the two buildings of ALLY, attending multiple meetings, and watching her get on and off the phone every few minutes to manage the crises she faced daily. That day, I watched Marva navigate the unexpected and growing conflicts among the staff, particularly over the recent performances of *The Vagina Monologues* that some workers were resisting as culturally alien. I noticed her compassion for and frustration with the young teenage women in the organization's dormitory whose history of trauma had complicated their relationships with the staff as well as her fears about the court hearing of one the clients accused of adultery following her sexual assault, which had kept everyone on their toes. "This is a labor of love. You get tired, you get disappointed, but you come back the next day full of energy, ready to do it all over again," Marva told me with an exasperated yet hopeful tone.

After a long, hot, and chaotic day, Marva was finally free to sit down with me for a chat and a short break. Before heading up to her office on the third floor, I noticed a wall covered with the pictures of young children and heard the sound of aws and ohs as young women gathered to look back and forth at the pictures and the faces of their teachers. Acknowledging my curiosity with a smile, Marva signaled for me to follow her upstairs, where I knew she would tell me more about the wall that had sparked everyone's interest. When we reached the third floor, Marva dropped the headscarf from her head while airing her clothes, hoping for a breeze from the room's open window. She made us coffee and asked me to join her on the small balcony adjacent to her office, where small plants decorated her humble resting spot. The anonymous baby pictures on the wall belonged to the staff and clients, and the guessing game of which picture belonged to whom had been Marva's idea, she told me as she lit a cigarette and offered me one. Seeing their teachers, social workers, psychologists, managing directors, and fellow clients as children, Marva thought, could help "bring everyone closer and ease the tensions." That day, I had not understood Marva's reference to the tensions in need of remedy, but only a few weeks of my ethnographic study would reveal the complexity of staff/client relationships. While I could tell that the clients felt love and gratitude toward the organization's staff, observing the class dynamics and spending alone time with them had shown me the other side of this relationship—the marginalized clients' growing critique of the privileged views of the middle-class staff, who they did not believe understood the multifaceted challenges of the poverty and ethnic marginalization they endured.

Marva's desire for reconnection was reflected in her game, which demanded acknowledging the child inside, an image seemingly free of the divisive markers of social class and status. But after seeing the wall covered by the staff's pictures and not that of the clients, Marva had realized the game had proven "insensitive." She had not considered, up until then, that many of the impoverished, refugee, or orphaned young women simply did not have a picture of their childhood. "It's a constant struggle," Marva told me, acknowledging the importance of being self-reflexive in spaces like ALLY. Sitting on the balcony floor, Marva pointed to Paulo Freire's *Pedagogy of the Oppressed*, the book she said she was trying to find time to get through. She opened up about the challenges of figuring out how to respond to clients' complaints, how to manage growing conflicts between the staff, and how to incorporate clients' voices in the program when she did not agree with them.

It was a struggle to manage the competing worldviews, unexpected grievances, and unintended consequences of a growing program with limited resources. ALLY's women's empowerment program was developed by a group of highly educated Iranian administrators who lived or had previously lived in Europe or North America. The program implementation was carried out by a more locally grounded middle-class staff who served young, impoverished ethnic-minority and many Afghan refugee women whose definition of *empowerment* did not always align with that of the administrators or the staff. It soon became clear to me that many tensions at ALLY reflected the different subjectivities of the cosmopolitan administrators, middle-class staff, and impoverished clients, whose varying class, ethnic, and national identities had shaped their understandings of oppression and justice.

ALLY struggled not only with its contentious internal dynamics but also with the challenges of running a feminist project in Iran, where the government has long been hostile to feminist initiatives and articulations of women's rights outside the government-sanctioned Islamic framework. As a liberal and secular women's empowerment program centered on gender equality and sexual self-determination, ALLY's program encountered a plethora of challenges in its advocacy. These challenges reflected the contentious and politicized character of feminist activism in Iran, the association of feminism with Westernization, the entanglement of the discourses of progress with class politics, and a societal desire for engaging in the culturally authentic reform witnessed in many postcolonial nations.

While I had initially chosen the organization simply as a fieldwork site where I could gain access to marginalized women, soon ALLY became more than a recruiting site for my research project. Fairly early, I began to see the organization itself as a unique and productive space for examining the intersectional inequality lived by its impoverished ethnic-minority noncitizen clients and the need for political intersectionality as manifested within the program's content and internal dynamics. ALLY, in fact, offered an ideal context to observe how different ideas concerning *zan-e tavanmand* (an empowered woman), the role of religion in women's subordination or emancipation, and the importance of individual autonomy and sexual self-determination for women's empowerment are negotiated by women and men of varying class, ethnic, and national backgrounds. Ally was a *site of contestation* on which various battles about feminism and progress were fought.

My curiosity about the workings of this NGO stemmed from the limitations I had noticed in previous studies on women's lives in Iran that examined either the patriarchal policies of the Islamic government or the heroic defiance of women's rights activists in the face of state repression. This limitation has left open the question of how women of varying class and ethnic backgrounds, with different ties to the global stage, develop and contest feminist discourses. While political Islam and a lack of political opportunities have captured the attention of most studies on gender advocacy in Iran, it is imperative to study feminist activism in relation to class and ethnic politics and activists' transnational connections. Previous studies have shown the role of middle-class and elite women in shaping the feminist discourses of the nineteenth and twentieth century in the Middle East as well as the problematic narratives of progress and emancipation that reinforced elite women's higher social status vis-à-vis other women (see Abu-Lughod 1998). Many studies on feminist activism, however, have failed to consider the voices of non-elite women and their role in the development and the contestation of feminist discourses. While it is important to appreciate the courage and vision of cosmopolitan middle-class feminists, it is critical to examine how their feminist projects entangle with class and ethnic politics and imperialist discourses to produce subjugating effects.

Examining feminist advocacy through this lens can answer important questions concerning how "women's empowerment" is imagined and how efforts to empower women are received: Why do well-intentioned efforts to "empower" marginalized women fail to gain purchase among the intended beneficiaries, even when such programs are formulated and implemented by local women? In any given context, whose voice dominates debates about gender oppression, and how does their involvement consolidate class projects and identities? How do ideas and practices considered modern and progressive and taken up by the local elite usher in emancipation while facilitating other social hierarchies?

Women-led NGOs and empowerment programs across the world grapple with similar questions and contentious dynamics, especially as they seek transnational connections and solidarities. The dualism of local versus Western feminisms has erased the heterogeneity of local subjectivities and has failed to capture the complex relationship between gender, class, and power. Moving beyond these simplistic conceptual frameworks requires asking different questions regarding women's empowerment—questions that consider the unequal social and economic standing of cosmopolitan NGO activists and their marginalized service recipients. These complexities demand that we examine gender politics alongside the axis of class and the dynamic interplay between local and Western discourses through which calls for "women's awakening" has been historically shaped.

In postcolonial contexts where accusations of cultural imperialism and counternarratives of cultural authenticity are hard to escape, attempts to transform women's lives are characterized as either indigenous or foreign. The East versus West dichotomy has left its mark on feminist scholarship when indigenous feminism is seen in stark contrast to Western feminism. However, the origin of feminism cannot be found in a culturally pure location untouched by external elements (Ahmed 1992; Barden 2005). The link between Western and non-Western societies has long been assumed to be a one-way process in which liberal ideas of emancipation and individual freedom originate in the West and are then exported to the rest of the world. This problematic narrative assumes that Westerners are the only actors on the global stage while ignoring the progress and resistance that lie within non-Western societies (Povey 2016). While scholars have studied the marginalizing effects of Western feminism, the local efforts have been presumed to be free from subjugating assumptions and practices. This book challenges the binary of local and global by highlighting the deep entanglement of Western discourses of progress with middle-class and ethnic discourses of respectability in Iran as they shape women's empowerment efforts.

Transnational Feminism as "Justice-Enhancing" Praxis

Any examination of self-proclaimed feminist interventions and initiatives necessitates an assessment of conceptual frameworks tied to feminism, particularly the value placed on individualism, autonomy, and secularism in hegemonic feminist discourses. The global dominance of an imperialist, missionary Western feminism has led many scholars to formulate transnational feminisms that are anti-imperialist. The complicity of feminism in imperialist agenda has been examined in the context of the U.S. invasions of Afghanistan and Iraq and how the feminist framework of women's liberation from oppressive cultural and political structures was used to justify the U.S. militaristic agenda in the region. The complicity of feminism in imperialism has also been discussed in relation to the neoliberal agenda of international institutions and transnational corporations that have co-opted feminism by presenting it in terms of "investing in women." Neoliberal feminism places the responsibility of overcoming poverty and social ills on individuals and claims that women's inclusion in free market capitalism is key to their empowerment (Eisenstein 2017). Given the complicity of hegemonic feminism in imperialist agenda, how can we envision a feminist initiative, activated through transnational connections, that does not reproduce imperialism?

Serene J. Khader (2019b) has argued that key to developing an anti-imperialist transnational feminism is separating universalism from universalist features that result in imperialism. Since dominant conceptions of feminism tie this movement to Western liberal values of autonomy, equality, and individualism (often dressed as "universal human rights"), the challenge is to envision a transnational feminism without the kind of universalism that reproduces imperialism. While feminism requires normative commitment, Khader argues, the types of values that missionary and imperialist feminists embrace (i.e., individualism, equality, and anti-traditionalism) are unnecessary for and unrelated to feminism. As bell hooks (2000) proposed in *Feminist Theory: From Margin to Center*, feminism cannot be a fight for the equality of men and women but is a movement to end sexist oppression without overlooking intersecting systems of oppression such as racism, classism, and imperialism. Gender equality without racial and economic justice can only deliver equality for white bourgeois women. If we define feminism as opposition to sexist oppression and oppression as a social system that subordinates one social group to another (Frye 1983), then we can articulate a feminism that does not need to be tied to the values of autonomy, individuality, or equality.

Individualism, for instance, is often seen as central to both feminism and to neoliberal imperialism. Individualism is tied to feminist objectives when the subordination of women's individual interests to the needs of their family members, community, and nation is concerned. Given that women's value has been historically tied to their relation to others, it is argued that women's liberation can only be achieved by embracing individualism and separation from relations that deny women's personhood. Mainstream Western feminisms emphasize a type of independence individualism that sees women's financial independence as necessary for their liberation from oppressive gender relations. Naila Kabeer (1994), for instance, asserted that women's ability to earn an income reduces their attachment to roles dictated by custom. This argument posits that women's economic independence would undo traditionalism and make women count as persons. This understanding of individualism underlies the structure of many women's empowerment programs, which encourage their clients' economic independence through vocational training.

The necessity of individualism for women's liberation has been critiqued by noting the importance of familial and communal relations for women's well-being. A persuasive argument in American feminist political theory is that the liberal value of individuality devalues women's and men's experiences of dependency and relationship (Jaggar 1985; Mackenzie and Stoljar 2000). Neoliberalism encourages individualism and defines development as empowering individual women, resulting perversely in a "feminization of responsibility" (Chant 2006, 2008; Khader 2019a). As Khader has argued (2019b), feminist assumptions that tie women's emancipation to their economic independence can be traced back to ideological suppositions that associate capitalism with liberation from tradition.

Anti-traditionalism is another contested feminist value. Secular feminism advocates for autonomy through the rejection of the traditional dictates of society. Secular feminists have long argued that loosening women's ties to their culture and religion would allow them to question patriarchal cultural norms as an important step toward ending sexist oppression. This approach implies that living by modern Western cultural norms is the only morally just and ideal scenario for women because the West's association with modernity assumes a lack of adherence to traditions and rituals. Women of non-Western cultures, meanwhile, are seen as "prisoners" of their inherently patriarchal cultures. The "imperialist associational damage" of anti-traditionalism (Khader 2019b) is evident in how it resorts to constructing non-Western cultures as particularly patriarchal and how it justifies imperialist agenda through the imposition of Western cultural norms. By linking sexism to traditional cultural norms, this feminist perspective ignores historical, social, and political contexts as well as transnational structural injustices—such as neocolonialism and neoliberalism—that harm women.

The necessity of anti-traditionalism for feminism is often argued on the grounds that patriarchal norms are frequently justified with claims that they are traditional or religious. Consequently, it is argued that secularism and the adoption of a crude comprehensive liberalism are the only ways of achieving the feminist goals of ending gender oppression. While scholars such as Saba Mahmood (2005) have argued that moral judgments cannot be separated from imperialist concepts of progress and backwardness and suggested that we abandon normative judgments, Khader (2019b) posits that feminism does have genuine normative requirements. She argues, however, that anti-traditional autonomy (rejecting culture and religion) is not required for feminism. While feminism challenges those traditional dictates and practices that promote sexist oppression, it is the content of some traditional dictates that requires opposition and not their source as inherited external dictates. Khader emphasizes that sexism is an effect of social practices and that many sexist practices are new (unrelated to traditions) and are, in fact, justified on anti-traditionalist grounds. Meanwhile, Islamic feminist social movements and other feminist traditions in organized religions show that antisexism *can* be articulated within religious and traditionalist frameworks.

Khader asserts that Western feminists often assume that there is a single standard of justice (justice monism) and that this standard is best expressed in Western Enlightenment ideals and particular conceptions of individualism, choice, and freedom. Khader envisions "transnational feminisms as a justice-enhancing praxis that aims at reducing or eliminating sexist oppression" (2019b: 7) rather than advocating for gender equality or non-traditionalism. She argues for a nonideal universalist approach that examines priorities and strategies for challenging sexist oppression in their particular contexts. For instance, complementarian gender systems in which men's and women's distinct roles are thought to complement each other might not be a feminist ideal for those who see women's liberation in gender equality but might be the best option for increasing women's well-being in some contexts. In this perspective, commitment to "justice-enhancing" feminist practices serves women more than commitment to some just ideal. Feminist activists' commitment to ideals of sexual self-determination and anti-traditionalism as necessary for women's empowerment, such as I observed at ALLY, at times results in interventions that further ostracize and disempower their marginalized clients. Activists' insistence on their feminist ideals in the face of their unintended disempowering consequences reveals the global hegemony of a missionary feminism rooted in justice monism.

Khader maintains that developing a transnational anti-imperialist feminist approach necessitates the acquisition of rich empirical and contextual knowledge and attention to structural injustices. My analysis of ALLY and its women's empowerment program aligns with Khader's anti-imperialist normative framework and makes use of her two epistemic prescriptions. First, this book makes visible oppressive global structures by rejecting culturally reductionist analyses of gender that locate non-Western women's oppression in their culture and religion. Second, I bring attention to context to demonstrate that feminist efforts should be aimed at improving conditions for women's lives rather than meeting some ideal standard of equality or freedom. This approach avoids viewing Western moral judgments as objective and unmotivated by interests to instead advocate for a kind of moral judgment that examines issues as political strategies in which choices are conditioned and constrained by power relations (McLaren 2021).

Margaret A. McLaren (2019) and other scholars (Bunch 1995; Petchetsky 2002) have noted the tendency of feminists from the Global North to emphasize the (lack of) legal and political rights of women in the Global South while ignoring or minimizing their economic and social concerns. Yet women's well-being is inseparable from their economic and social rights and the transnational structures of neoliberalism and militarism. A transnational feminist framework (McLaren 2019) does not isolate sexist oppression from class, caste, racial, ethnic, and religious oppression and therefore recognizes the importance of intersectionality (Crenshaw 1991) for an anti-imperialist transnational feminism. In this view, feminism "is necessarily a struggle to eradicate the ideology of domination that permeates Western culture on various levels as well as a commitment to reorganizing society so that the self-development of people can take precedence over imperialism, economic expansion and material desires.... Feminism as a movement to end sexist oppression directs our attention to systems of domination and the interrelatedness of sex, race, and class oppression" (hooks 2000: 31).

This book offers an intersectional and transnational analysis of feminism in Iran by bringing multiple fields of study—postcolonial feminism, women's development literature, and Iran's gender studies—in conversation with one another. The convergence of these fields in this study reveals an inextricable connection between Iran's contemporary liberal feminism and the colonial discourses of progress that tie anti-traditionalism to women's liberation. This book delineates the challenges faced by well-intentioned activists whose loyalty to feminist principles of independence, equality, sexual autonomy, and anti-traditionalism complicated their objective of empowering marginalized women. Examining Iran's class and ethnic discourses of respectability alongside hegemonic accounts of "women's development" reveals why empowerment at ALLY was linked to embodying anti-traditionalism in lifestyle and fostering a middle-class habitus in impoverished ethnic-minority women. This book demonstrates that, like most feminist NGOs, ALLY was at once both an agent of class discipline and regulation *and* an empowering and enlightening institution.

What Lies Ahead

The title of this book, *Proper Women*, has two meanings. First, it represents the attempts of empowerment programs to cultivate in marginalized and impoverished women a sense of propriety defined by middle-class discourses of proper mannerism, modes of feeling, patterns of speech, and schemes of perception. The cultivation of a middle-class habitus (Bourdieu 1990) was seen as an indication of empowerment at ALLY because it allowed inclusion in middle-class spaces and, hence, class mobility. Yet, it also constructed the poor as lacking proper culture, education, and an enlightened perspective necessary for emancipation. The other meaning of the title references Giorgio Agamben's (1995) theory of biopolitics and the concept of "proper life." Agamben (2005: 2) reveals the construction of the figure of *homo sacer* or "bare life" in modern politics that allows the elimination "of entire categories of citizens who for some reason cannot be integrated into the political system." These groups of people, rendered as bare life, are abandoned due to the incapacity or unwillingness of the state to regulate or police certain types of violence (Pratt 2005). Development and aid programs regard bare life as being on the precipice of potentiality—the potential to transform into a normative way of living, or what Agamben calls the "proper life." *Proper Women* brings attention to the regulatory discourses that constructed ALLY's clients as bare life and the organization's efforts to prove the potential of bare life to become proper.

Chapter 1 offers an overview of ALLY—the different aspects of its women's empowerment program, the feminist sensibilities of the founder and the administrators—and my methodological approach to studying the organization. Chapter 2 places the stories of the organization's clients in the sociopolitical context of Iran and explains the gender, class, and ethnic discourses that render their marginalized lives as bare life. This chapter provides an overview of the history of the development of feminist discourses in Iran alongside colonial and class politics while examining the gender politics of the Islamic government, the immigration policies of the state toward Afghans, and Iran's repressive political climate. I also explain the process of NGO-ization in Iran, where, increasingly, issues of collective concern are transformed into projects addressed by NGOs like ALLY.

Chapter 3 offers a transnational feminist analysis of ALLY's women's empowerment program by revealing the liberal conceptions of choice, agency, and anti-traditionalism that shaped its tenets. The adoption of a liberal and secular feminist framework that emphasizes women's sexual autonomy and anti-traditionalism had unintended consequences for the organization's clients, who reported an increasing sense of helplessness. In this chapter, I show how middle-class activists' liberal conception of agency inadvertently erased the agency of the marginalized clients, and why their rights-based advocacy did not equip the subaltern women with a framework of gender justice that would find currency in their communities. The contentious relationship between the cosmopolitan and local elite over the practicality of advocacy for sexual autonomy among marginalized women reveals that notions of "foreign" versus "culturally authentic" reform are central to feminist debates in Iran and globally circulating "women's rights packages" are always contested in accordance with local norms and the dominant definitions of proper cultural progress.

ALLY's politics of empowerment refused the isolation and abandonment of bare life by providing marginalized women with a level of care that demarcates the potentiality of bare life for becoming "proper." Chapter 4 explores this concept and its place within aid/development zones and empowerment programs. ALLY attempted its advocacy for marginalized women through the framework of capabilities rather than rights. The adoption of this framework reveals three interconnected conditions: The limited political opportunity for rights advocacy in Iran, the perceived need to emphasize clients' capabilities to counter stigmatizing discourses, and the staff's perception of social change, which entailed prioritizing gradual cultural change through a "critical mass" framework (Oliver, Marwell, and Teixeira 1985).

Chapter 5 demonstrates how staff prioritized granting clients the *cultural capital* necessary for inclusion in middle-class spaces. This chapter reveals the ever-present and less acknowledged discourses of class as they shape individuals' definition of success, position the poor (clients) in relation to the economically privileged (staff)—particularly in terms of "lacking" culture, taste, and social skills—and define empowerment as the development of a middle-class identity and cultural capital in the poor. Given the hegemony of middle-class discourses, the organization directed resources toward cultivating a middle-class habitus in impoverished clients through the exploration of various hobbies and vocations. Such training required extending the length of the program—much to clients' dissatisfaction. As staff took pleasure and pride in providing marginalized women with artistic and intellectual opportunities they saw as empowering, the basic needs, vulnerabilities, and susceptibilities of the impoverished women were overlooked.

Chapters 6 and 7 take us to the world of the impoverished, ethnic-minority female clients of ALLY and their responses to the organization's empowerment program. In Chapter 6, class tensions are explored in relation to the middle-class staff's refusal to acknowledge their privileges in a context where the clients insisted on the importance of recognizing class as significant to relationships at ALLY and fundamental to the employees' ability to offer proper help. This class tension also encompassed clients' resentment and resistance toward those feminist accounts that lacked recognition of the interlocking forces of class, ethnic, and gender marginalization. The staff's liberal feminism, cultural reductionism, and inability to effectively problematize class and ethnic privilege, while frustrating the clients, had the unintended consequence of nurturing a strong oppositional class consciousness and ethnic solidarities among the young women. This chapter reveals that the outcomes of women's empowerment programs should not be studied solely in relation to the agenda and objectives set by the administrators and the staff; they should also be examined in relation to the subjectivities and the agency of service recipients.

Chapter 7 demonstrates that, despite their clear oppositional class and ethnic consciousness, many young women emulated the middle-class norms of respectable femininity through their choice of attire, demeanor, rhetorical strategies, and lifestyle in order to develop a dignified habitus in a highly stratified society. Rather than analyzing the young women's trendy and immodest Western-inspired style or their premarital sexual practices as a form of resistance against a repressive moral order (as previous studies have argued) or as an indication of embracing the secular and liberal feminist values advocated at the organization (as ALLY's staff interpreted), I examine these women's transformation in appearance and lifestyle as a performance of middle-class privilege that could grant them "symbolic economies" (Bettie 2014) and facilitate their class mobility.

In the concluding chapter, I argue for the necessity of a glocal, intersectional, and anti-imperialist analysis of empowerment by reviewing the book's findings and examining the definitions of *power* on which women's em(power)ment programs are constructed. I propose potential directions for future research and encourage feminist activists to consider the advantages of a justice-enhancing practice as opposed to justice monism.

1

Studying ALLY

"Come on, stop it and sit up," Minoo, a seventeen-year-old client, whispered with frustration to a group of young women who were playfully yet quietly arm wrestling on the round table around which all were seated. The disapproving glances of others conveyed the same message and brought their game to an abrupt end. Having just entered the room, I was surprised by the calm, serious, and disciplined demeanor of the young women, who often enjoyed loud and playful banter. "We are waiting for Ms. Maryam," Minoo told me to remind me of their scheduled meeting with the organization's founder and to explain the unusual silence in the room. It was clear that the clients took such meetings with Maryam, who traveled to Iran several times a year, seriously. These meetings were meant to allow clients to express freely—without the presence of other staff—their grievances, complaints, and ideas for bettering the organization's program.

I had yet to meet Maryam, with whom I had only exchanged emails thus far. Maryam had established the organization in the early 2000s and had begun her work in a small house with no official permission and with a handful of staff and clients. Residing outside of Iran most of her life had not severed Maryam's strong ties to her home country.

Her considerable financial resources and strong networks in the diaspora had allowed her to envision and later establish ALLY as a space of refuge for young women who had ended up on the streets, in juvenile detention centers, or in the sex work industry due to poverty, neglect, and abuse. Social abandonment, according to Maryam, is the root cause of the young women's problems, for there are no legal, social, or institutional services accommodating these extremely vulnerable women. "The girls who are *aasib dide* [harmed] and especially those girls who have been harmed and are from lower economic classes almost have no place in Iranian people's minds; they don't exist in the Iranian psyche," Maryam told me in an interview about the society that has closed its eyes to the experiences of the most marginalized.

Maryam entered the building with her scarf laying on her shoulders rather than her hair; she wore capris pants and a see-through *manto*[1]—an outfit not even slightly in compliance with the government's requirements of women's clothing in public. Tall and slender, she exuded authority and warmth, and her lack of care for the government-imposed rules of hejab was a clear indication of her fearless and uncompromising attitude toward what she considered her rights as a woman. After entering the room, Maryam quickly opened the floor to clients, asking them to freely share their thoughts. She took notes of their complaints about the quality of food prepared at ALLY, about the social workers they considered to be unprofessional and a psychologist who seemed to encourage clients to get married, and about many more instances when ALLY and its staff had not met their expectations. Such meetings were held periodically for clients to share their suggestions and grievances with Maryam or the managing directors of the two centers. A desire for self-reflection, self-improvement, and welcoming clients' voices was noticeable, especially as Maryam asked the young women to share their ideas for expanding or altering ALLY's program and listened intently and supportively to their suggestions. This inclusive and democratic approach to organization leadership, however, was not always felt as such by clients, some of whom had told me that they did not believe anyone was "really listening." It seemed like Maryam's original plan to run the organization with a nonhierarchical structure had faced serious obstacles. "I used to say that this is a democracy, but now I tell them that it's a dictatorship," Maryam told me as she recounted all the struggles she faced when she approached management with an "inclusive and democratic" style. As ALLY grew over the years to become an official organization serving two hundred young women yearly, with two buildings, a dormitory, and seventy staff members, it had seemed impossible to incorporate the conflicting ideas of staff and clients into the empowerment program. Now, although Maryam says that she hears everyone out, she is the one who makes the final decisions, especially in those instances where staff and clients' suggestions do not align with the feminist values on which she had wished to build the organization. In the following sections, I explain the feminist values that shaped ALLY's empowerment program and my methodological approach to studying them.

Women's Empowerment at ALLY

ALLY's women's empowerment program was designed (and changed over the years) to respond to the multifaceted and complex struggles of its clients. Using recent scholarship on adolescent development and trauma, ALLY's program developer, Raha, worked diligently to bring the organization's program up to par with similar programs across the world. A doctoral student in the United States, Raha had extensive knowledge on women's development initiatives and had utilized her connections in academia and her activist circles to develop ALLY's program. The administrators' social and geographic background had connected them to the global stage and the "global value packages" (Merry 2006) promoted by many international institutions such as the United Nations (UN) and the World Bank. Through trial and error, ALLY's program had grown to have three main components—social work, psychotherapy, and education. The in-house social workers were responsible for helping clients navigate the everyday struggles of their living conditions, such as disagreements with family members that could turn abusive or violent, a lack of access to essential resources such as health care, and the management of work and family demands that complicated these young women's ability to attend the organization. In addition to the services provided by social workers, individual and group therapy was offered to help women recover from the trauma of neglect, sexual and physical abuse, incarceration, or extreme poverty. The third component was ALLY's educational program, which was composed of *vocational training*—with the aim of preparing clients for entry into a more skilled labor market—and a *social program* that would provide them with social skills as well as creative opportunities for self-realization and self-empowerment. Daily life at ALLY consisted of attending a variety of workshops on topics such as sexuality, violence against women, and empowerment and taking computer skills, English, interpersonal communication, painting, creative writing, and other courses designed to provide women with vocational and life skills. During their second year in the program, clients would choose a specialty area and receive more advanced training. In their final year, they worked with the organization to find internship and employment opportunities, prepare for job interviews, and find ways to maintain a supportive relationship with ALLY after graduation.

Throughout the three-year program, ALLY also provided its clients and their immediate family members with a variety of resources including food, hygiene products, health insurance, and medical treatments. Living in extreme poverty, many of the clients could not afford the expense of the daily commute to and from the center. The organization covered any such costs that would deter families from supporting their daughters' involvement in the program. Covering the expenses of clients' health insurance and their medical bills as well as the medical bills of their immediate families helped to defuse families' resistance and provide a healthier home environment for clients' psychological well-being. Family members' resistance often emanated from the importance of the young women's labor at home or at sweatshops as a source of aid and necessary income. Thus, convincing parents to allow their daughters' admission into a three-year program required persuasion and incentives.

In the beginning, ALLY identified and admitted at-risk women by working within underprivileged communities. But after years of establishing itself as a trusted advocate, most of the clients were referred by either women who had graduated from the program or juvenile detention centers or charitable organizations with which ALLY had worked before. ALLY also admitted clients who were dealing with the extreme deprivation of legal and material resources due to immigration, such as Afghan immigrants. While the Iranian clients of ALLY could seek the help of other governmental agencies or charities, Afghan clients heavily depended on ALLY in the absence of alternative resources for undocumented or documented immigrants in Iran. I elaborate on the social and economic vulnerability of Afghans in Iran in the next chapter.

Both ALLY's buildings were located about thirty minutes apart in quiet, narrow alleys close to two of the busiest city centers of Tehran. The rustic and old exteriors of the buildings were not marked by any sign, keeping the identity of the organization concealed. The location of the centers, I later learned, although great for me and the middle-class staff of the organization, required a long daily commute for the young clients who lived in the slums and outskirts of the city. During my fieldwork, clients' participation in ALLY's empowerment program required attendance five days a week from 8:00 A.M. to 4:00 P.M. To get to the organization on time, many of the young women had to leave home as early as 5:00 or 6:00 A.M. Traveling another three to four hours back home in the afternoon rush hour added up to a total of five to seven hours of daily commute. Many of the clients, especially Afghans, got home around 8:00 P.M. only to start work at sewing shops until after midnight. For many of the young women, this was the only arrangement that would allow them to attend the organization while providing financial support to their impoverished families, who depended on the girls' meager income. Most families were hoping that the girls' educational training at ALLY would help them in the future, as their income increased with their skill sets.

Maryam, Raha, Marva, and the remaining members of the directing team regarded their program as a feminist one due to their investment in women's well-being, their commitment to upholding the principles of gender equality, and their objective of challenging patriarchy. Soon after establishing ALLY, they understood that patriarchal attitudes were common among not only their clients but also their growing team of staff. This had become apparent when some of the staff (psychologists and social workers) had blamed clients for their "poor judgment" when they were subjected to date rape or chose multiple partners. To remedy such problems, a variety of workshops on sexuality and women's rights, including a performance of *The Vagina Monologues*, were offered for clients and staff. The workshops and performances, which challenged the cultural gender and sexual norms in Iran, were designed to nurture a "feminist consciousness" that was seen by the founder as necessary for personal and social change. Maryam believed that with appropriate training, the staff would embrace liberal feminist values and transform their patriarchal mindset. Yet, the imposition of such trainings, as I show in Chapter 3, had resulted in growing conversations and conflicts about the feminist values of ALLY, their cultural resonance, and ALLY's definition of *women's empowerment*.

It is also important to note that while some of the staff and administrators openly identified as feminists, many others advocated for the marginalized women's rights and helped with implementing the program without necessarily identifying as such. Except for a handful of staff, no one at the organization had engaged with gender studies or the internal debates within feminist scholarship. I investigated staff's assumptions about feminism, empowerment, and gender oppression by analyzing their accounts of clients' struggles and the cause of those struggles, by asking for their definition of *women's empowerment*, by examining the content of the courses they offered, and by listening to many classroom conversations. As I show in Chapter 3, (sexual) autonomy and individuality were valued at the organization while religion and tradition were seen as limiting women's agency. These liberal and secular feminist values did not appear on the written agenda of the organization, but my data reveals that they shaped the content and approach of the organization's program and the staff's assessment of clients' progress. My analysis of ALLY's program concerns these unwritten and sometimes unspoken measures of empowerment advocated by the administrators and staff.

Nongovernmental and charity organizations like ALLY have been on the rise in Iran since the 1990s and have been successful in achieving their humanitarian goals. Yet, in several aspects, the laws governing the operation of NGOs and their registration have complicated their activities. For instance, according to Article 26 of Iran's constitution, NGOs cannot engage in activities that violate "the principles of independence, freedom, national unity, Islamic standards or the basis of the Islamic Republic." Such restrictions and their ambiguity have allowed the government to restrict and even shut down NGOs for promoting values that are deemed "un-Islamic" or "politically charged" by the state. Thus, it is important to note that ALLY's secular and liberal feminist teachings and programs were not publicly advertised or articulated. ALLY's administrators promoted their secular feminist programs, such as their sexuality training, to foreign donors whose support was implicitly contingent on the alignment of ALLY's values with their own. Yet ALLY's administrators had to emphasize their vocational training when attempting to build relations with governmental agencies such as Behzisti, the state welfare organization, which often collaborated with ALLY over the years. While ALLY had considerable autonomy in shaping the content of its program, it had maintained that autonomy by keeping a low profile, hiding several aspects from state authorities, and relying only on foreign donations. By examining these political challenges in Chapter 4, I offer further explanation for ALLY's approach to advocacy, which promoted cultural reform over organized political activism.

The Ethnography of ALLY

I gathered my data in 2014 through in-depth interviews with ALLY's workers and administrators and eight hundred hours of participant observation of the organization's two centers, as I daily participated in the routines of meetings, classes, and workshops. I first came across the organization when I stumbled upon one of its online fundraising campaigns. After speaking with Maryam, the founder, and Raha, the program director, about my research plans, I gained their permission to conduct my ethnographic study there. I believe it was the administrators' desire for improving their program that facilitated my gaining access as a sociologist who could potentially offer valuable feedback. Maryam was particularly interested in instilling a feminist pedagogical philosophy into ALLY's educational program. During my fieldwork, I shared my observations with the administrators, trained one of the staff members on feminist pedagogy, and recruited the help of my academic colleagues in the United States to develop a workshop on feminist pedagogy for the staff. My contributions, however small, established trust and granted me the continuous support of the organization to conduct my research.

While I interviewed ALLY's staff and administrators, I did not conduct formal interviews with the clients. This was part of the agreement Raha and I came to after many conversations about clients and the ethics of research with vulnerable populations. Many of the young women, Raha told me, would willingly share their stories of sexual and physical abuse if given the opportunity to speak about themselves. Such retelling of the stories, without the presence of a trauma expert, had proven to retraumatize the young women and worsen their mental health. I agreed with only using the method of participant observation and informal conversations to learn about the young women's lives and perceptions. While I was initially concerned that using different methods would pose limitations on my study, soon I realized that many of the classes and workshops were designed to engage clients in discussions and dialogues about their life experiences, values, and perspectives. Whether it was a workshop on violence against women, an art therapy class, a workshop on sexuality, or a community development course, clients were encouraged to and did freely share a great deal of information about their personal lives, their *daghdaghe* (concerns), their experiences of being a woman or an immigrant, their perceptions of inequality and social change, and their thoughts on ALLY. I also gathered data by socializing with the young women in the hallways, participating in their class projects, chatting with them during the breaks, and joining their group conversations when I was invited. While I did not officially conduct interviews, I had ample interactions, conversations, and observations to gain an in-depth understanding of clients' perceptions on many topics relevant to my research.

I similarly observed ALLY's workers and administrators during their staff meetings, as they taught classes, and as they interacted with clients. ALLY's staff were between the ages of twenty-three and sixty years old, college educated, and middle class. In addition to attending meetings, classes, and workshops run by the staff, I shadowed members of the managing team to learn about their daily tasks and was invited by a few teachers to meet with them outside of the organization for a friendly chat. I conducted interviews with sixteen of the employees in various positions at the organization, such as teachers, psychologists, foreign affairs personnel, educational coordinators, social workers, program director, managing directors, and the founder. A more detailed reflection on the challenges of establishing rapport with my participants and ethical dilemmas related to this research can be found in the Appendix.

My research within an organizational setting required that I remain tuned to unspoken tensions or conflicts. Early on in my ethnographic study, I began to see a growing tension between the clients and program personnel as the young women routinely critiqued the staff, their behavior, and their decision-making. It was easy to see how making sense of clients' constant complaints had become an everyday interpretive task for the staff, who were confused about the reception of their efforts among the impoverished women. It also did not take me long to notice the swelling tension between the staff and administrators, whose varying understandings of help and empowerment had caused irresolvable fractions among them. I witnessed and observed daily encounters shaped by resentment, frustration, guile, and puzzlement while attempting to navigate my way through the ethics of research and the friendships I had come to make at the organization. I soon realized that it was necessary to place at the center of my analysis the daily tensions and conflicts I had come to witness at ALLY. These tensions reflected more than individual disagreements; they reflected the contentious character of feminist activism and class politics in Iran and the conflicting perceptions of justice and empowerment. Examining these tensions and relations of power as the *problematic* of my study (Smith 2005) required leaving out of my analysis the stories of cooperation and harmony, the stories of many women who left the organization feeling safe, heard, valued, and empowered. It meant dedicating my analysis not to those lives transformed and the lifelong friendships made at ALLY but to the painful process of connecting and transforming.

Keen to conduct a study capable of offering recommendations for feminist initiatives that aim to empower marginalized women, I had to critically investigate power and privilege in this feminist space. Knowing that I had to represent all aspects of the staff's work—the lifesaving and the problematic—I felt an ethical guilt when faced with the painful task of critiquing people with whom I had built friendships. As I wrote the following chapters on the challenges of the organization and its internal conflicts, my internal dilemmas grew as did my mistrust in the ability of my work to capture the genuine kindness of the staff, who came together daily, despite the unpleasant conflicts and with little reward or compensation, only to support the marginalized women who depended on them. I struggled with the disturbing fear of offering an analysis that presents my research participants in the light of their shortcomings and presents ALLY in the light of its failings. Years after my fieldwork, I still ask myself questions many ethnographers contend with: "Did I 'thank' them enough? Have they reconsidered our time together? Do they wonder what became of me or of my research? How would they feel now about the ways that I represented them?" (Berbary 2014: 1222). Rather than moving beyond these uncomfortable reflexive moments, I reflect on them regularly—not to selectively omit unpleasant data but to do a kind of responsible research that is committed to social justice and offering answers to the questions my participants grappled with. I moved beyond the doubts and fears as I recalled the self-effacement and humility of my research participants and the unrivaled diligence with which they worked every day for self-improvement. I hope my ethnographic research, following the same ethics, has done what it was set to accomplish: Offer an analysis of what lies beneath the everyday conflicts to discover how to move beyond.

2

Women, Class, and Citizenship in Iran

Tehran, the capital of Iran for more than two centuries, has become a giant city in the Middle East, with a population of fourteen million. Tehran's history of urban development and immigration and its high population density make two realities readily apparent when one arrives at the city. First, high air pollution and traffic congestion are most noticeable at first blush. Second, there is a visible divide of class apparent in the architecture and construction of the city as well as the appearance of its people. Class disparity, in fact, has become the most salient expression of the city:

> Because of its location, Tehran grew along a sloping north-south axis. The resulting difference in altitude reflects the socioeconomic hierarchy, making the north-south duality a salient feature of the urban structure. The north, with its green spaces, more moderate climate, and beautiful vistas, is the home of the afflu-

---

Adapted by permission from Springer Nature Customer Service Centre GmbH: Springer Nature, *International Journal of Politics, Culture and Society*, "From Empowerment to Advocacy: Innominate Identity Politics as Feminist Advocacy in Iran" by Fae Chubin, Copyright © 2019 Springer Nature.

ent Tehranis; the south belongs to the lower middle class and poor. Urban morphology in the north is well planned and characterized by wide, tree-lined streets, large houses, and lower density of population.... The class division between north and south has in turn produced a "status division." The rural origins and ethnic backgrounds of the migrant poor in the southern suburbs have set them off culturally and socially from the Westernized urban rich, who stigmatize the poor as *dehaati* (rural/backward), and *hamal* or *amaleh* (literally unskilled construction laborers; see Bayat 1997: 30–32). Stereotypes also represent south Tehranis as traditional and religious. (Khosravi 2008: 59–60)

Understanding ALLY and the class and ethnic dimensions of its women's empowerment program requires understanding the sociopolitical context of Iran. It also demands investigating the modalities of Tehran's urban culture and the growing class and ethnic inequalities that are formative of the subjectivities of ALLY's middle-class Tehrani workers and its impoverished ethnic-minority noncitizen clients.

The process of urban development and modernization (i.e., Westernization) began in Iran in the 1930s with Reza Shah Pahlavi; it was later intensified by his son, Mohammad Reza Shah, in the 1960s and led to the rapid industrialization of Iranian cities. Mohammad Reza Shah's intensive program of socioeconomic development, funded by rising oil revenues, turned Tehran into the destination of many immigrants from rural areas and small towns—a migration process that increased dramatically after Shah's mismanaged 1963 Land Reform program (Bayat 2007). The economic deprivation experienced by agricultural laborers following the Land Reform was the reason for their mass migration to urban areas, where they hoped to gain higher-paying city jobs and greater access to amenities. Most of the immigrants, being ethnic minorities, poor, and low-wage workers, had to settle in the slums south of Tehran (Khosravi 2008). The extensive and rapid demographic growth of cities such as Tehran resulted in the spread of slum areas with substandard housing and a lack of essential services and facilities.

Anti-Shah mobilizations of the 1970s were directed at Shah's poor economic and social policies, the repression of dissent, and his rapid Westernization projects, which were perceived as facilitating imperialism. By 1978, many of the urban poor, particularly young men, had become politically mobilized largely through Islamic revolutionary committees. In his taped sermons, Ayatollah Khomeini, then an exiled cleric, condemned Shah's failure to attend to the housing needs of the urban poor or provide basic amenities for the rural poor. He proposed that Islam represents the *zagheneshinan* (slum-dwellers) and the *mostaz'afin* (dispossessed) and not the *kakhneshianan* (palace-dwellers). The growing wealth inequalities, worsening living conditions, and lack of employment opportunities had aggravated the new migrant urban poor, who were encouraged by Khomeini's populist promises and came to join the opposition forces that overthrew the monarchy and ushered in the Islamic Republic in 1979 (Hashemi 2020).

The establishment of the Islamic government was soon followed by eight years of war with Iraq (1980–1988) and the subsequent shortfalls in oil revenues, which brought on an economic crisis. The Islamic government attempted to consolidate its power by expanding its reach among the poor and those most impacted by the effects of the war economy. Among the measures taken by the state were distributing ration cards, instituting price control, subsidizing basic food commodities such as sugar, rice, and oil, providing indirect subsidies for electricity and piped water to rural and urban poor, and expanding the scope of social welfare institutions. The state also engaged in expanding the infrastructure, building schools, roads, and health clinics in small villages and the countryside, all of which gave the lower classes greater access to basic goods and social services.

The presidency of Akbar Hashemi-Rafsanjani following the end of the Iran-Iraq War in 1988 and the death of Khomeini in 1989 ushered in a new "pragmatic" approach to development that aimed to integrate Iran within the global economy through liberalization policies by requesting technical assistance and credit approval from the International Monetary Fund (IMF). Similar to what occurred in other countries subjected to the structural adjustment policies of the IMF, the neoliberal economic model encouraged capital accumulation, consumerism, and development centered on growth and a reduction of public spending. Iran's move toward a global market economy expanded the urbanization and urban migration process that had already intensified in Tehran due to the settling of refugees from the Iran-Iraq War as well as those displaced by war in Afghanistan. While such policies led to the growth of the war-drained economy, it also led to the rapid growth of highly affluent social groups. A drop in oil revenues in 1991 and a sharp rise in non-oil imports strained the economy, triggered a trade deficit, and increased Iran's foreign debt (Ehsani 1994). The subsequent austerity measures of Hashemi-Rafsanjani, which entailed cutting subsidies to large families, led to rapid inflation and unemployment that particularly impacted the urban poor.

While Mohammad Reza Khatami's presidency (1997–2005) expanded the public discourse on civil society, rights, and social justice, Khatami's welfare expansion and social insurance program remained limited in addressing the needs of the lower economic classes working in the informal economic sector (Hashemi 2020). Following Hashemi-Rafsanjani's footsteps, Khatami implemented economic reconstruction programs that encouraged neoliberal economic policies and the privatization of state-dominated industries such as the telecommunication and power-generation sectors. Despite the economic growth experienced during this time, high rates of unemployment persisted while class inequalities increased. The presidency of a conservative and populist politician, Mahmood Ahmadinejad, in 2005 came with the promise of supporting the poor and upwardly aspirant social groups, who expected that the state development efforts would facilitate their social mobility. Although Ahmadinejad initially supported large-scale state subsidies for gasoline and food, the guidance of the IMF led to a blended populist/private economic model whereby state-owned enterprises were privatized and state subsidies for petrol and essential services were cut, though his administration claimed that the savings would be distributed among low-income individuals (Hashemi 2020). In his second term, the recommendations of the IMF and global financial organizations resulted in a subsidy reform plan according to which all subsidies were to phase out by 2015. The all-time-high inflation and unemployment during Ahmadinejad's presidency and the inadequacy of his plan of monthly cash transfers to households to alleviate the economic burden of the cut subsidies resulted in the increasing indebtedness of people who sought loans from employers or banks to supplement their income (Hashemi 2020).

In June 2010, U.S. Congress passed the Comprehensive Iran Sanctions, Accountability, and Divestment Act, which was signed into law by President Barack Obama to increase restrictions on Iran's oil export and other Iranian-origin imports as part of a campaign against the Iranian nuclear program. These sanctions and even stricter revisions in 2013 had a significant debilitating impact on Iran's economy. Although the signing of the Iran Nuclear Deal in 2015 generated hope among the Iranian population that the war-like economy caused by the sanctions would improve, the U.S. withdrawal from the deal in 2018 led to a significant decline in oil exports, the shrinking of the economy, significant inflation, and a lack of access to necessities for large segments of the population.

The postrevolutionary state's departure from a welfare state critical of consumer capitalism to one that embraced neoliberal integration in the global economy has worsened economic inequalities while promoting a consumerist culture centered on individualistic strategies for economic success. Shahram Khosravi's (2008) ethnography demonstrates that young Tehranis engage in a global youth culture characterized by the consumption of Western products and culture, a trend that began decades ago following Mohammad Reza Shah's modernization project (1941–1979). The wave of Islamization that followed this period in the 1980s, with its critique of capitalist consumerism and the goal of reviving Islamic tradition, created a contentious duality of *sonat* (tradition) and *tajadod* (modernity). While the Islamic government has focused on "protecting" the youth from the "cultural invasion" of the West, transnational connections forged by Iranians in diaspora, access to a globalizing media (satellite and internet), and the increased mobility of cultural products have worked as a counterforce against the Islamic government's ideological agenda. The intensification of transnational connections, increasing wealth inequalities, and Iran's long-lasting class and status hierarchies have consolidated a classist culture in which the middle- and upper-class Tehranis pride themselves on being well educated, egalitarian, and freethinking, with *farhang-e balatar* (literally having a "higher culture," often in comparison to the traditional working class; see Khosravi 2008). These characteristics are often emphasized to embolden the constructed binary between the "cultured" middle and upper class and the "traditional, village-minded," working-class southern Tehranis or *shahrestanis*.[1] While Khosravi interprets the embracing of the Western culture by the youth as a manifestation of their defiance against the imposed order of an anti-Western and repressive government, Iran's history of Westernization and

Iranians' long history of internalized inferiority vis-à-vis the West can best explain the character of this youth culture (Olszewska 2015).

In the following chapters, I demonstrate how Iran's class and ethnic discourses shape assumptions about women's empowerment and progress. I show how middle-class staff and impoverished ethnic-minority clients of ALLY resisted, contested, and reproduced these discourses through their advocacy for or attempts at constructing a dignified self. Before doing so, in the remainder of this chapter, I place ALLY's women's empowerment program in the larger history of the development of feminist discourses in Iran along colonial relations and class politics and in response to changing political opportunities. I also elaborate on the growing trend of the NGO-ization of social movements, the state's immigration policies toward Afghans, and the limitations of the current literature on agency, resistance, and social change.

The History of Feminism in Iran

In *Rethinking Global Sisterhood: Western Feminism and Iran*, Nima Naghibi (2007) demonstrates the connection between the development of feminist discourses in Iran and the history of imperial expansion and class oppression. Her literary study of Western women's writings about their travels to Persia[2] traces the dominance of liberal feminist discourses in Iran to the nineteenth century and the development of the language of universal sisterhood, itself fashioned within the discursive framework of modernization and progress. In their writings, Western women travelers and missionaries contrasted their self-proclaimed autonomous subjectivity to the passivity and oppression of veiled Persian women.[3] In an attempt to carve out a political voice for themselves in the male-dominated imperial apparatus, Western women participated in the reproduction of colonial and racial order. They positioned themselves as the savior of their oppressed, silenced, and veiled sisters, who relied on the civilizing forces of the Empire to break free from the bondage of their backward traditions and cultures. In doing so, middle-class Victorian women constructed themselves as "intellectual and political vanguard at the forefront of history" (Felski 1995: 149).

In the late nineteenth and early twentieth century, economically and socially elite Persian women used the framework of global sisterhood to express solidarity with their Western counterparts. Similar to their Western sisters, elite Persian women presented the practice of veiling as a marker of oppression and backwardness tantamount to imprisoning women. Privileged (unveiled) Iranian women, who wished to close ranks with their Western "enlightened" sisters, participated in the discursive subjugation of their working-class counterparts by positioning themselves as the epitome of modernity and progress while portraying veiled women as the embodiment of subservient womanhood (Naghibi 2007).

By the early twentieth century, a form of secular feminism emerged in Iran. This feminism, however, was not borrowed, derivative, or a clone of Western feminism (Barden 2005). Secular feminism in the Middle East grew within the discourse of secular nationalism, which envisioned a collective identity based on a shared cultural experience. Middle East feminism developed its own critique of colonialism and engaged with its own secular and nationalist discourses in the era of Western domination. The constitutionalist movement in Iran in the early twentieth century occasioned lively debates about modernity and religion, and the school of Islamic modernism argued that there is no contradiction between assuming a modern and Muslim identity at the same time. Women were active participants in the Iranian constitutional revolution from the early stages by facilitating strikes and offering financial, moral, and even physical support to the constitutionalists (Malikzadeh 1992). Middle- and upper-class women of Tehran and other large cities supported the new parliament formed after the success of the constitutional revolution in 1906 and contributed to the intense political debates of the time by forming a network of women's associations, schools, and hospitals and through challenging misogynistic readings of Islam. Within this dynamic context, women of higher social and economic strata created a feminist discourse that was anchored within both the religious reform movement and secular nationalism and saw the liberation of women in the advancement of the nation. Meanwhile, the Western discourse of scientific domesticity was adapted by Shi'a clerics and Qajar aristocrats who advocated for selective progress on gender issues. While highly regulatory, this discourse elevated the status of motherhood by presenting women as educators of the nation (Afray 2011). Other groups of women supported the popular social democratic rhetoric that had spread to Persia from Russia by oil workers and merchants who had experienced the 1905 revolution. These women wrote about the social and economic challenges of the poor, particularly poor women. Both the regulatory discourse of scientific domesticity and the discourse of social democracy allowed women to carve out for themselves a political voice, to challenge the authority of men, and to enjoy increased opportunities for public and professional participation (Afray 2011).

The reign of Reza Shah (1925–1941) brought about a new era of gender and sexual politics in Iran, as he introduced highly controversial modern disciplinary practices concerning bodies that required men to wear Western suits and hats and women to unveil. Raza Shah's reforms were not unrelated to the unveiling and gender reforms unfolding in Soviet Central Asia and the Caucasus in the 1920s. The reforms initiated by the Soviet Union included abolishing the sharia law, decriminalizing homosexuality, legalizing secular marriage based on mutual consent, ensuring the right to divorce for both partners and women's right to vote and abortion, introducing equal pay for equal work, and establishing coeducational schools (Afray 2011). The Soviet campaign for unveiling women accompanied the formation of a government organization for women—Zhenotdel—in which hundreds of unveiled women worked. These reforms received mixed reactions from communist men in Central Asia. Eventually, the resistance of the conservative community resulted in the closing down of Zhenotdel (Massell 1974). The intellectuals in Iran and Turkey were influenced by these gender reforms, and the secular and authoritarian rulers of these two countries—Mustafa Kemal Ataturk in Turkey and Reza Shah in Iran—used gender reforms as a vehicle for nation building and the modernization and Westernization of their respective countries. Although women's emancipation was originally a signature issue for socialists and progressive democrats, it became appropriated by these rulers to disarm Turkish and Iranian leftist forces (Afray 2011). Rapid modernization and secularization from above created a new middle and upper class in Iran who were increasingly Westernized and unable to understand their traditional and religious compatriots. Meanwhile, the urban *bazaar* classes and peasants continued to follow the orders issued by the religious establishment (Keddie 1981).

Between 1919 and 1932, privileged women were responsible for the proliferation of feminist organizations and periodicals. They called for women's educational opportunities in ethics, literature, and science, argued against the imposition of the veil, and advocated for the economic independence of women (Sullivan 1998). Intellectual women such as Taj al-Saltaneh, a princess of the Qajar dynasty, candidly wrote about forced marriages, the unilateral right of men to divorce, the impact of polygamy on women, and the importance of companionate marriage for women's well-being while tying women's education and rights to raising better citizens and building a stronger nation (Afray 2011). One of the best-known nongovernmental women's organizations of the time was the progressive Patriotic Women's League (1922–1932), which sponsored the second regional Conference of the Women of the East in 1932. The conference participants were from a variety of countries and religions and advocated for reforms in marriage and divorce, equal pay, women's education, greater political rights for women, and particularly unveiling (Afray 2011; Salami and Najmabadi 2005). Following the conference, Reza Shah disbanded the Patriotic Women's League and established the government-controlled Ladies' Center (Kanun-e Banuan), which became an important institution that attracted many members. Yet the establishment of such an institution also meant that gender reforms were decreed by the royal family and were to come only from the top (Afray 2011).

In addition to his educational and legal reforms, Reza Shah aimed to create modern Iranian citizens who emulated European culture in appearance and conduct. By the late 1920s, greater interaction with the West had already resulted in slight alterations in men's and women's clothing. Wearing lighter veils, dropping the *rubande* (face covering), and even abandoning the veil were common practices among elite women in Tehran, as ministers and deputies of the Pahlavi government expected to attend social functions with their unveiled wives (Afray 2011). Reza Shah required all men, except for clerics and theology students, to replace their cloaks with European-style suits and hats in 1928 and issued a formal decree that ordered women to unveil in 1936. In doing so, he undermined social, religious, and tribal distinctions based on appearance. The unveiling of women, while done under the name of "women's awakening" and reducing gender segregation, prevented veiled women from attending such spaces as public baths, theaters, stores, and bus stations. The new decree became popular among upper- and middle-class men and women, who eagerly purchased European-style clothing to replace their *chador*⁴ and keenly followed the expectations of the elite society to walk, talk, and interact in a modern Western way. Subsequently, more attention was given to women's gestures and bodily dimensions, as these factors impacted girls' chances of finding a proper suitor (Afray 2011). The forced unveiling did not eradicate the old discourse on women's modesty and chastity; it simply recast it. While veiled women were harassed by the police, who ripped chadors and scarves off their heads, the unveiled women were pestered by men who saw unveiled women's bodies as an invitation to sexual harassment. Now a measure of a women's propriety was the simplicity of her dress, her demeanor in public, and the way she carried herself in relation to men. Without any campaign to equalize laws regarding divorce, marriage, custody, and inheritance and without any democratic debate within which gender reforms would take shape, women's conditions did not change, and unveiling did not result in women's personal autonomy or economic power, as promised.

By supporting the forced unveiling act of 1936, elite Iranian women reproduced colonial discourses by equating unveiling with women's emancipation. This trend resulted in the alienation of rural, working-class, and religious urban women from the mainstream modernization project and the discourses of women's liberation. The forced unveiling of women celebrated by privileged Iranian feminists was directly responsible for lower-class urban women's decreasing public participation and increasing dependency on men for affairs previously conducted by women in public (Hoodfar 1997). While presented as an emancipation measure, the unveiling act was experienced as a restriction and a violation of personal choice by many veiled women. Over time, advocacy for women's rights became associated with an authoritarian state, elite cronies, and imperialist politics as the feminists of this era attempted to consolidate feminism by reducing diversities of class, race, religion, and politics to a common identity of woman. By constructing a universal account of oppressed womanhood and dismissing the intersection of identities, they reproduced inequalities along class and ethnic lines (Sullivan 1998).

In 1941, Britain had taken control of Iran's southern regions while the Soviet Union had stationed forces in the north. Worried about Reza Shah's pro-Germany sympathies, the Allied forces demanded that he abdicate power in favor of his son, Mohammad Reza Shah. The monarchy of the younger Shah brought a degree of democratization to Iran as progressive nationalists campaigned for political reform and revived constitutionalism. As a result, numerous political organizations and trade unions emerged, and the expansion of print media, radio, cinema, and television in the 1940s led to the acceleration of the modernization of gender and sexual norms. Between 1941 and 1953, dozens of political parties and women's organizations were formed. Yet, these women's organizations, like those in many parts of the world, were primarily auxiliary branches of leftist and nationalist political parties. The Stalinist Tudeh (masses) Party, for instance, was the country's largest and best-organized political party and had a progressive social agenda that called for greater educational and employment opportunities for women, childcare centers, vacation time, equal pay, and better working conditions. The Tudeh also recruited impoverished women who broke through centuries of class and gender barriers by fighting for workers' rights and organizing trade unions (Afray 2011). In 1944 and 1945, Tudeh deputies and female leaders of the party called for women's suffrage, although without success. Other left-leaning organizations, such as the Women's Party (Hezb-e-Zanan), also campaigned for women's suffrage. Years later, and after changing its name to the Women's Council (Showra-ye Zanan), the Women's Party eventually became an umbrella organization of several women's organizations. Members of the Women's Council built international ties with women's organizations in Europe, the United States, and Turkey and demanded "complete equality between the sexes" (Amin 2008). The relatively open political climate of the time allowed more women to study at institutions of higher education, become schoolteachers, and work in factories and offices, while a few women were able to enter the male-dominated professions of medicine, law, and the natural sciences (Afray 2011). The abdication of Reza Shah, while allowing for the expansion of democratic and secular groups, strengthened the culturally conservative clerics whose power had diminished under his secular rule. In the 1940s, Ruhollah Khomeini was gradually becoming a prominent conservative religious figure who attacked Reza Shah's secular reforms and his government as corrupt and Westernized, although he endorsed similar plans for industrialization, economic development, and military conscription in his proposed Islamic state. Khomeini and conservative clerics of the era successfully created moral panics over changing gender and sexual relations in Iran and opposed unveiling, mixed schools, and women's employment as changes that could ruin female honor, destroy families, and promote corruption and prostitution (Chubin 2014).

In 1953, the Central Intelligence Agency (CIA) instigated a coup to overthrow the democratic government of Prime Minister Mohammad Mosaddegh, who, in 1949, had formed a political opposition composed of nationalists, liberals, and social democrats—the National Front. The coup was a response to Mosaddegh's efforts to nationalize Iran's oil, which was previously under the control of Britain. The Anglo-American coup brought an abrupt end to a period of relative political freedom by returning Mohammad Reza Shah to more absolute power. The nationalist coalition of Mohammad Mosaddegh, however, was also weaking from inside due to battles over women's suffrage and rights. Opposition to changing gender relations was not exclusive to conservative clerics. Many nationalists within the National Front, cleric or non-cleric, supported progressive economic and political changes but remained conservative on gender issues. Some warned women's organizations that their demand for suffrage was causing divisions at a time when imperialist threats required a united nation, while other progressives opposed it on the grounds that elite men would dictate women's votes and further manipulate the elections. In 1952, the National Organization of Women (Sazeman-e Zanan-e Iran) sent a telegram to the United Nations requesting their intervention on behalf of women. The pressures from both sides weakened the nationalist coalition of Mosaddegh and provided the United States and Britain with an opportunity to exploit such a divide to successfully carry out a coup.

By the late 1950s, various independent women's organizations were controlled by the newly formed High Council of Women's Organizations, run by Ashraf Pahlavi, Mohammad Reza Shah's twin sister (Najmabadi 1991). The council was later replaced by the government-controlled Women's Organization of Iran (WOI) under the leadership of royalists from privileged social and economic backgrounds. This transition accompanied a shift in attitude toward women's rights as a social movement to a form of tokenism, where women's rights were treated as a symbol of the nation's modernity and the monarch's progressiveness (Najmabadi 1991). Subsequently, many of the achievements of women in the 1960s and 1970s, such as gaining the right to vote and to stand for public office and the passage of the family protection laws of 1975, were framed as Shah's "endowments" of rights to women. These tokenist policies primarily affected secular, urban, and middle-class women and were mostly "modernizing patriarchy" (Yeganeh 1993). The association of Iranian feminism with the monarchy posed considerable challenges for Iranian feminists, since their activism was limited by the ideological framework of the Pahlavi regime and the privileged women running the organization. Furthermore, the growing anti-Shah sentiments and mobilizations, which had gained widespread support by the late 1970s, came to associate feminism with imperialism due to the strong ties between WOI, the U.S.-backed ruling regime of Iran, and Western feminists who traveled to Iran with the invitation of elite Iranian women who had sought their leadership (Naghibi 2007).

The anti-Shah movement consisted of men and women of varying class and ideological backgrounds seeking to overthrow the Pahlavi regime. The rapid Westernization efforts of Reza Shah and his son Mohammad Reza Shah, the mismanaged land reforms that exacerbated the economic frustrations of the rural poor, and the repression of political dissident were major grievances of the anti-Shah movement in the 1970s. The feminist agenda of WOI, aligned with the Pahlavi regime's project of modernization, did not speak to the material needs of the rural and peasant women who supplied labor for the growing export market and were negatively impacted by the unbalanced reforms. Those who benefited from the state-sponsored feminism advocated by WOI were primarily urban middle- and upper-class women from privileged and educated classes (Tabari 1980). This resulted in a growing gap between working-class women and their privileged "sisters," who saw "traditional" (working-class) women as in need of their guidance and enlightenment. By the late 1970s, WOI was widely critiqued by Iranian women who did not see their needs and priorities reflected in an organization that was deeply affiliated with the monarchy.

The 1979 revolution resulted in the establishment of an Islamic government, and although their large-scale participation in the movement was paramount to its success, women remained on the losing side of this power transition (Bayat 2013). Since the mainstream feminism of the twentieth century was deeply associated with Westernization, the revolutionary government and its band of clerics opposed feminism and discourses of equality as foreign and imperialist. For instance, since Western and elite Iranian women with ties to the monarchy had associated women's veiling with their subjugation, the revolutionary government's nationalist and anti-imperialist project constructed the veil as a symbol of national and cultural honor and made veiling mandatory. The forced unveiling act of 1936 and the forced veiling of women after the 1979 revolution demonstrate the contentious position of women's bodies in Iran's colonial and postcolonial nation-building discourses. By 1979, the historical association of feminism with the Westernization agenda of the Pahlavi regime and its endorsement and control of WOI had resulted in binary thinking; (imperialist) feminism came to stand in stark contrast to Iranian (nationalistic) tradition. Hence, Iranian feminism was caught between two forces. On one hand, Western feminists and Iran's elite feminists appropriated Iran's indigenous anti-imperialist feminism in the hopes of transforming it into something they could relate to as "international sisters." And on the other hand, the conservative clerics undermined and silenced all Iranian feminist groups by associating feminism with imperialism and by positioning feminism as "counterrevolutionary" (Naghibi 2007).

The newly established Islamic Republic claimed that the state had to be founded on Islamic principles and laws. Khomeini, the leader of the Islamic revolution, and his supporters showed no tolerance toward any political opposition and, much like the secular Pahlavi regime, employed legal and political means to suppress dissent (Tamadonfar 2001). The newly established political institution, as well as the new constitution, embodied an internal contradiction for attempting to simultaneously be a liberal republic based on notions of equality, rights, and the rule of law while being Islamic (and totalitarian). The constitution written by the postrevolutionary regime contained 175 articles and was crafted in response to the political schisms within the ruling elite and a strong will to centralize power (Tamadonfar 2001). The constitution grants all Iranians a wide range of rights, including freedom of religion, freedom of speech and assembly, the right to education and social security, and the right to private property and fair trial, among others. Yet, the contradiction between notions of popular sovereignty and the sovereignty of God had to be reconciled. This was done by restricting all individual rights in favor of the clergy's understanding of "permissible rights" according to sharia, which served the ruling elite's interests. Freedom of press, expression, and assembly, for instance, were protected, according to Article 24, "as long as those activities are not detrimental to the fundamental principles of Islam and the rights of the public." The vague language of the constitution allowed the ruling elite to repress freedom by labeling oppositional activities as detrimental to Islam at will. While liberal principles of the constitution were limited to consolidate the power of the theocratic regime, the democratic elements of the republic, such as popularly elected presidents and parliament and local council members, were structured in ways to allow Khomeini and his band of clerics to openly and effectively exercise authority.

In the immediate aftermath of the revolution, the provisional government and revolutionary forces denied the legitimacy of rights talks for women, calling the discourse of "rights" the tool of "Western imperialist" forces seeking to undermine Iranians' commitment to Islam (Osanloo 2006). The new government rejected liberalism and its emphasis on individual freedom on the grounds that individualism erodes the importance of relational identities (relation to family, community, nation, and Islam) and that communal responsibilities should take precedence over personal rights and freedoms. The new Islamic government rejected the notion of gender equality by claiming essential differences between men and women. They emphasized the complementarity of the sexes, encouraged women's commitment to domestic life, and recognized women's rights only within the confines of a conservative interpretation of Islamic principles. It was under this political ideology that the restriction of rights was justified. Shortly after the revolution, Khomeini made hejab mandatory for women and ordered the repeal of the 1967 and 1975 Family Protection Law that granted women the right to divorce and to custody, among other rights.

Soon after the mandate of compulsory hejab, thousands of women throughout Iran marched in protest of the state's intrusion on their civil and personal liberties. However, their protests were repressed by revolutionary counterprotesters who physically and verbally attacked them. While secular feminism in Iran originally emerged from a religious reform movement, it was particularly at this time that secular feminism was pitted against Islamism and its regressive gender policies. As the new Islamic regime was quick to limit women's rights and liberties, many secular Iranian feminists began to discuss Islam as the source of women's subordination (Naghibi 2007). As secularism became associated with modernity and the West, secular activists began positioning religion as "backward" and "traditional." This contentious opposition was ultimately to the detriment of both (Barden 2005).

The prerevolutionary modernization projects of the Pahlavi government and the growth of the school of Islamic modernism nevertheless had affected the expectations and aspirations of many Iranians, whose sizable middle and working class had relatively high rates of literacy and educational attainment by the 1980s (Moghadam 2002). Meanwhile, the Islamic policies of the state had unexpected consequences for women's liberation that propelled scholars to question the dominant assumptions about the harmful effects of Islamism on women (see Bahramitash and Kazemipour 2006). For instance, Homa Hoodfar's (2007) study demonstrates that Afghan refugee women's exposure to Iran's Islamic government, which mandated women's education as Islamic, provided Afghans with a definition of Muslim-ness that was progressive and empowering. Meanwhile, policies such as the gender segregation of public transportation and educational spaces had the unexpected consequence of increasing women's educational opportunities, freedom of movement, and public participation in Iran (Shahrokni 2019). These studies suggest that contrary to assumptions about the need for abandoning culture and religion, key conditions for Muslim women's empowerment "may well remain within Islam, not only as a force for reshaping cultural, social, and political institutions, which in any case are themselves in flux, but also in terms of legitimizing such changes" (Hoodfar 2007: 266).

By the late twentieth century, secular feminism, although doing important work particularly within NGOs, seemed to have reached its impasse (Barden 2005). During the 1980s and 1990s, a form of Islamic feminism emerged in Iran, as female parliamentarians and civil servants began to advocate for greater opportunities and equality for women within the Islamic framework. Islamic feminism created a progressive religious discourse in response to the growing conservative interpretations of Islam. Islamic feminism did not legitimize Iran's Islamic government but critiqued it and demanded a reading of the religion that was committed to gender justice. Between 1997 and 2005, the "reform period," the administration of President Khatami motivated a vocal women's movement to seek "a hybrid notion of rights informed by both civil legality and Islamic principles" (Osanloo 2012). Arzoo Osanloo's ethnographic research on female Quranic meetings and family courtrooms in Iran demonstrates the presence of "rights talk" among women who, religious or not, use such discourse to articulate their experiences and demands. The reform era was also characterized by the establishment of women's affairs offices in every ministry and government agency, the development of NGOs that addressed women's needs, and a more assertive advocacy for women's liberty and rights by female parliamentarians and activists who mobilized a lively women's press (Moghadam 2002). Women's emergence as right-bearing subjects who challenge the discriminatory policies of the Islamic government, Osanloo claims, is the legacy of hybridized spaces of mediation and negotiation within Iranian Islamic civil courts "that permit the production of right-bearing, individuated subjects that are also Islamic" (Osanloo 2006: 203).

"Rights talk" in Iran, however, was plagued by a setback after the presidency of Ahmadinejad, a conservative candidate who criticized the rights language in favor of emphasizing relational identities (Osanloo 2012). Activists' rights talk fueled a backlash and culminated in mass protests and a clash between citizens and the state forces in 2009 over suspicions of fraud in the presidential elections. The repressive measures of the government toward political activism have increased ever since, and the election of another reformist president, Hassan Rouhani, in 2013 and 2017 did not generate much openness in the political space for rights advocacy.

Asef Bayat's (2013) study suggests that the repression of women's activism in Iran has been accompanied by the collective yet individualized resistance of women in public domains. Through working, playing sports, creating art and music, running for political office, gaining higher education, and simply walking and jogging down the streets, often without respect for the state's policies of hejab, women in Iran have imposed themselves as public players with a sense of autonomy (Bayat 2013). Similarly, Pardis Mahdavi's (2009) research suggests that the youth in Iran see themselves as part of an unfolding "sexual revolution" by opposing patriarchal sexual norms with their bodies and lifestyles. The sexual austerities imposed by the Islamic government, such as the criminalization of sexual relations outside marriage, did not result in the kind of repression assumed to exist in Iran following the revolution (Afray 2011). Gender and sexual norms have changed in Iran, and women's increasing economic autonomy has afforded them more privacy to become sexually active before marriage. However, it is particularly the upper- and middle-class women from Tehran and other big cities who have been able to navigate their sexual autonomy more safely within the societal restraints with the help of their economic resources.

The repressive measures of the Iranian government toward political activism have also moved advocacy toward NGOs and charities. Many female-run NGOs in Iran, in fact, are extensions of women's organizations from the 1990s and have the same objectives of challenging women's subordination by confronting the state and patriarchal institutions (religion, family, and community), encouraging income-generating activities for women, and pushing for policy influence (Rostami-Povey 2004). Yet NGOs have also faced a crackdown, particularly since the presidency of Ahmadinejad, whose administration criminalized the activities of journalists and human rights and women's rights activists. The foreign policy of the United States toward Iran is also responsible for the closing of political opportunity structures and the state scrutiny of NGOs' affairs. In their essay "When Promoting Democracy Is Counterproductive," Haleh Esfandiari and Robert S. Litwak (2007) argue that the United States' $75 million support of NGOs in Iran to promote democracy coupled with loose talks about regime change from members of Congress have fed a sense of vulnerability and paranoia among elements of Iran's ruling regime, who fear NGOs' "soft" plot for a civil society uprising from below. As a result, NGOs in Iran are either subject to censorship or are defensively engaging in self-censorship (Esfandiari and Litwak 2007).

NGO-ization of Identity Politics

The postrevolutionary state of Iran found its revenue from oil insufficient to finance the provision of food, health care, and education it had promised to the poor, who they saw as their main constituents. To address this limitation without allowing any threat to its monopoly of power, the Islamic government has allowed a controlled form of public participation (Hoodfar 2010). By establishing state-sponsored volunteer networks, the state mobilized citizens to provide social services and education to underprivileged groups in low-income neighborhoods and rural areas. NGOs, as another form of volunteer mobilization, have taken on the task of providing social services to those in need of governmental provisions and have been relatively tolerated by the state. Most registered NGOs in Iran, in fact, cater to marginalized populations such as working children, undocumented immigrants, people with disabilities, sex workers, people with drug addiction, the impoverished, and other vulnerable groups. Bayat (2013) argues that states often encourage self-help initiatives as long as they do not turn into oppositional forces and that the unthreatening nature of NGOs is the reason behind their proliferation in Iran. Hoodfar's (2010) study, however, demonstrates that, contrary to dominant assumptions, women working within the state-sponsored volunteer health networks in Iran saw their activities as capable of challenging the state's ideology and policies. By changing their mandate from health activism to social and political activism, many female volunteer workers blurred the boundaries of state and civil society by successfully negotiating a number of cultural and state restrictions on women. Investigating the transformative potential of NGOs is increasingly important because of activists' preference for working within them due to NGOs' participatory model and because activists often fear state agencies' top-down and corrupt approach (Sharma 2008).

But how engaged are NGOs in identity politics in Iran? The term *identity politics* signifies a wide range of political activity that aims to end the injustices experienced collectively by members of marginalized social groups. "Members of that constituency assert or reclaim ways of understanding their distinctiveness that challenge dominant oppressive characterizations, with the goal of greater self-determination" (Heyes 2016: 1). Women and racial and sexual minorities are among marginalized social groups who have engaged in large-scale identity political movements in the second half of the twentieth century. Yet in contexts with limited political opportunities for mobilization, these political and social movements have faced greater obstacles (McAdam, Tarrow, and Tilly 2001). In studies conducted on women's activism in Iran, scholars have documented the impact of changing political opportunity structures on the framing and tactics of women's rights movements and their visibility (Moghadam and Gheytanchi 2010).

Hard-liners' control of the state, the state designation of women's rights advocacy as a "threat to national security," and the rhetorical war on Iran by the U.S. government are among the factors that have bolstered Iran's security apparatus and have given impetus to the persecution, harassment, and imprisonment of many Iranian activists who deployed the frame of "women's rights" advocacy (Moghadam and Gheytanchi 2010; Sameh 2014).

It is in this context of increased state surveillance and limited political opportunities for feminist activism that an organization like ALLY attempts to advocate for marginalized women. The advocacy practices of ALLY, its repertoire of action, and even the content of its program are best understood when placed within this precarious political environment. It is within the larger context of the development of feminist discourses in Iran, its colonial history, its association with class privilege, and indigenous attempts for culturally authentic feminism that we can best understand how the diverse constituents of ALLY contested women's empowerment and defined their own feminist agenda.

Chapters 3, 4, and 5 offer an institutional ethnographic portrait of the educated and middle-class NGO workers who, with varying understandings of empowerment, developed ALLY's women's empowerment program. Chapters 6 and 7 offer an ethnographic portrait of the poor and ethnically marginalized women from the slums of Tehran who came together every day in an upscale organization to simply stay away from the violent realities of their lives and to use the variety of resources provided by the organization to create alternative "symbolic economies" (Bettie 2014). Following Gayatri Spivak (1985), I use the term *subaltern* to refer to these young women, whose marginalization and inability to access the lines of social mobility were shaped not simply by being women in Iran but also by being poor, ethnic minorities, and/or immigrants. Antonio Gramsci (1891–1937) coined the term *subaltern* in his *Prison Notebooks* to refer to groups excluded from society's established structures for political participation and those outside of the hegemonic power structure. In the 1980s, the term gained increased prominence and currency in the work of Spivak and the larger postcolonial studies to denote colonized people and the imperial history told from the perspective of the colonized for the purpose of countering the Eurocentric and elite bias of history. Following this approach, I speak of ALLY's clients as subaltern women whose voices are often occluded by the hegemony of Western theoretical constructs.

Defining the Subaltern

Before beginning my fieldwork in Tehran, I read many stories on ALLY's website about clients' traumatic experiences of violence and neglect as well as their positive transformation after entering the organization. The website encourages the Western audience, as well as Iranians in the diaspora, to read these women's stories as stories of oppression *and* defiance and to consider donating to ALLY, since its independence from the Iranian government has left it with only one source of funding: Donations. I had nothing but these stories in mind when I first entered ALLY's organization in Tehran as my ethnographic research site. I read the website's stories of these girl-women, rightly pictured as victims of a patriarchal society, and of how grateful they are to ALLY for allowing them to transform their lives from that of helpless victim to hopeful survivor. I believed that was the (only) story of these young women—until I entered the site.

Poor and Afghan in Iran

My second day at ALLY, I met Armaghan, a seventeen-year-old Afghan woman who, like many others who had escaped the war in Afghanistan, had sought refuge in Tehran. She was very welcoming of me when we first met, knowing that I lived in the United States. "Oh wow! It's my dream to live in America," Armaghan told me with a big smile and sparkling eyes. Not long after, she began to ask me questions about life in the United States and seemed disappointed when I confirmed the existence of racism there and explained the challenges of being Middle Eastern in America. Similar to many other Afghan clients of ALLY, Armaghan aspired to appear Tehrani and middle class. She spoke Farsi with a Tehrani accent, as many Afghans born and raised in Tehran do, and rarely spoke Dari outside the confines of her group of close Afghan friends. Although similar in style to what young, middle-class women wore in Tehran, Armaghan's clothing was made of inexpensive material. That day, she had dyed her hair purple and was wearing tight black leggings under her manto, a look that I soon found out had become fashionable in Tehran. It was also the look to which the government was reacting with fines and jail time as another attempt to discourage women's clothing that is not aligned with the "Islamic values" of the state. Armaghan, however, wore them persistently and fearlessly despite the threats from the government and her older sister's scornful reaction, which entailed calling her a "whore" for wearing the leggings "to get attention from men." "I'm starting to doubt whether I'm a whore because of how my family reacts," Armaghan said at the art therapy class in which we were all sitting. "But I don't care," she said. "I have to dress nice especially because of what people think about all Afghans as being poor and dirty." She was very fierce but also very conscious of the risks and challenges of being an Afghan immigrant in Iran. That day, she recounted her story of physical confrontation with an Iranian man who had sexually harassed her on the street. "I kicked him and his motorcycle while cursing at him for groping me," she said. The man then attacked her, calling her a "dirty Afghani," saying that he had all the rights to do whatever he wanted to "Afghani whores." The observing police officer did not intervene after he realized her ethnicity—a reaction Armaghan believed would have been unlikely if an Iranian woman had been involved.

The parents of Armaghan and of other Afghan clients of ALLY were among millions of Afghans displaced after the communist coup in Kabul in 1978 and the subsequent Soviet invasion in 1979. Since the 1980s, the civil war, the coming to power of Taliban, and the U.S. invasion of Afghanistan have led to more population movement and a growing Afghan refugee population in the neighboring countries. Among those who left Afghanistan, many sought refuge in Iran, particularly the Hazaras, who are Shia and Persian speaking (Olszewska 2015) and have come to engage in low-wage occupations as a means of securing independence and supporting the needs of their family. However, well before 1978, people of Afghanistan were visiting Iran as migrant workers, pilgrims, or merchants, engaging in trade and cultural exchange.

Although the government formed after the 1979 revolution has employed the rhetoric of Islamic solidarity to claim that "Islam has no borders,"[5] the state has established a regime of national preference regarding social and economic rights. Particularly in the realm of immigration policy, the Islamic republic is a "modern nation-state perusing a rather ad hoc realpolitik, not too different from those of liberal Western democracies" (Olszewska 2015: 8). The Iranian government conferred on demand the refugee status of Afghans in Iran in the 1980s, embracing Afghans as cobelievers suffering at the hands of atheist Soviets. Yet their policy toward Afghan immigrants more likely reflected the need for cheap labor in a country at war with Iraq and in the postwar reconstruction that followed. Receiving residence permits, however, became more difficult in the 1990s, and it was almost impossible for Afghans to obtain a refugee status card or to renew their temporary cards after 1998 (Hoodfar 2004). Without refugee status cards, Afghans in Iran were no longer entitled to "food subsidies, healthcare, access to the labor market and public education for children" (Hoodfar 2004: 149). Without permission to work unless within a subset of low-wage and manual labor and with no financial assistance from the government, Afghan immigrants have experienced extreme financial and psychological insecurity in Iran. Poverty and housing discrimination have resulted in cramped living conditions—a family of eight might live in one room—and the absence of legal protection has left many Afghan women dependent on their families and immigrant communities for survival. As a result, these women are unable to report violence and abuse within their communities.

As scholars of immigration have argued (Golash-Boza 2015; Johnson and Trujillo 2011), the "illegal" status of immigrants is a category developed through lawmaking and enforcement by states worldwide to create a disposable population who can be exploited for their cheap labor. The periods of tolerance, harassment, and expulsion of Afghans in Iran are meant to benefit the country by exploiting their cheap labor without allowing them to feel comfortable and settle there permanently (Monsutti 2005). The government systematically enforces the low status of Afghans in Iran by such policies as the designation of certain cities and provinces as "Afghan-free zones" for the purpose of securing "public safety." The restrictions of movements imposed by the government apply to both documented and undocumented Afghans, who are barred from certain towns and provinces, and any assistance to them is decreed a crime (Ahmadi 2012). Even for those Afghans who are documented, their "legal" status is difficult to maintain or prove and does not guarantee many freedoms. The residence permits are only valid for a short period of time, and extending them entails a difficult process, requiring investment of a great deal of time and money (Olszewska 2015).

In addition to the legal forms of discrimination imposed by the state, Afghans face prejudice and discrimination from Iranian citizens as well as the police. The racialized figure of Afghans in the Iranian discourse is one used to instill fear in children (Olszewska 2015), and the term *Afghani* is commonly used as an insult to imply a low class and ethnic status. Afghans have been continuously scapegoated for all social problems in Iran, including unemployment, drug trafficking, the spread of infectious diseases, and rape and murder (Olszewska 2015). Afghan refugees experience discrimination and hate crimes, and Afghan men are frequently picked up and abused by the police and deported if the family is not able to pay a bribe (Hoodfar 2004). These attitudes reflect the racialized fear of Afghans as dangerous, perverted, and criminal Others, an image reinforced through Iran's long-lasting racist nationalistic ideologies that construct Iranians as a race distinct from and superior to their "backward" neighbors (Maghbouleh 2017). The "inferior" position of Afghans has served as a means of self-identification for Iranians who attempt to raise their own status by distancing themselves from their Afghan and Arab neighbors and through identification with the European culture (Olszewska 2015).

Despite the Islamic Republic's anti-Western propaganda and the twentieth-century search for an authentic, native Iranian identity in the face of Western political and cultural imperialism, "the older admiration for and a sense of inadequacy vis-à-vis the West persist as an uncomfortable and guilty indulgence of many Iranians" (Olszewska 2015: 48). Golnar Mehran (2002) has pointed to a persisting deep-seated sense of inferiority among Iranians toward the West. The perception of Afghans as inferior enables Iranians to reflect the distance they have traveled from their *aghab-mandeh* (backward) neighbors and the *pishraft* (progress) they have made in becoming more modernized and Western (Olszewska 2015). Hence, Afghans play an important role in the Iranian imagination when national identity and citizenship are concerned (Adelkhah and Olszewska 2007). As Zuzanna Olszewska (2015: 21–22) has argued, the presence of Afghans in Iran remains a paradox. "They have been welcomed as oppressed co-believers and yet excluded as noncitizens; appreciated for their cheap, diligent labor and yet blamed for stealing jobs; lauded as fellow Persian speakers and yet mocked as primitive country cousins; allowed to settle in cities and integrate into Iranian society and yet discriminated against in most aspects of public life. As a result, they are an absent presence: living alongside Iranians, yet strangely invisible." While Iranian activists for refugee rights and some NGOs, such as ALLY, have been sympathetic toward Afghans and their struggles in Iran, Afghans remain an invisible group and are treated as problems to be managed.

Olszewska's study on Afghan refugees and their poetry circles demonstrates how Iranian nationalism has led to a sense of exclusion among the Afghan population in Iran. Yet her study also challenges common assumptions about Afghan refugees as helpless and vulnerable with no history, agency, or politics. She argues that the experiences of Afghans in Iran have been a combination of opportunities and exclusion. It is particularly the larger changes in the Iranian society, such as the rising rate of literacy, declining fertility, the increasing emphasis placed on women's rights, and the larger modernization and industrialization trends, that have shaped the opportunities and aspirations of Afghans. The impact of these factors, however, depends on Afghan's economic position and location (for instance, whether they worked as urban dwellers or in rural agriculture). Hoodfar's (2004) study on Afghan refugees in Iran demonstrates that many Afghans who sought refuge in Iran following the Soviet invasion did so in protest against the communist decree of mandatory education for all boys and girls, which they saw as un-Islamic. Yet, they embraced modern education following their exposure to the Iranian government's discourses that promoted universal education as necessary for a Muslim nation.

From the outset, the Islamic Republic placed a great emphasis on education, built schools in poor rural and urban areas, and made education mandatory for boys and girls. The state policies regarding mandatory education and the gender segregation of educational spaces made education accessible to many girls from conservative families who were no longer objecting to their daughters' education under Islamic principles. The Islamization of the public sphere has similarly allowed women from conservative backgrounds to be active in public life, travel, enter various professions, choose their husbands, and appear on television (Afray 2011). These trends resulted in a soaring literacy rate in Iran and public engagement for women. They similarly provided Afghan women with a range of opportunities and the ability to demand women's rights within an Islamic framework. Many Afghans, in fact, remained in Iran during the reign of Taliban in order to ensure their daughters' education. In 2004, when the Iranian government prevented refugee children from attending public schools without paying a substantial fee, the Afghan community faced a great hurdle. Determined to pursue an education, Afghans created semi-clandestine and autonomous schools (*madareseh-ha-ye khodgardan*) run by educated Afghans outside the authority of Iran's Ministry of Education (Olszewska 2015). These schools have done more than offer an education; they have also provided Afghans with a sense of collective identity (Chatty, Crivello, and Hundt 2005). Olszewska's research on Afghan poets demonstrates that many educated Afghans have consistently sought access to the cultural capital of *farhangi* (cultured) or *roshanfeks* (intellectual), which signifies their aspiration to be upwardly mobile and claim a higher status.

Armaghan's aspiration for class mobility was visible in her attempts to appear middle class through her style of clothing and her self-distancing from the stigmatized image of the "poor and dirty Afghani." This self-distancing was achieved by performances of respectable middle-class femininity that, as I explain in Chapter 7, entailed adopting the liberal and secular feminist lifestyle advocated by ALLY's middle-class Tehrani staff. As I show in the following chapters, the responses of Afghan women to the liberal feminism advocated at ALLY entailed two seemingly contradictory responses. On one hand, many Afghan women critiqued liberal feminism's limitations for explaining their unique struggles at the intersection of their class and marginalized ethnic and national identities. On the other hand, they adopted the organization's middle-class feminist rhetoric as a form of cultural capital to create alternative symbolic economies that would grant them agency and dignity. I examine this simultaneous adoption and rejection of liberal feminism as a reflection of marginalized women's strong class consciousness and concurrent desire for inclusion and class mobility.

Poor and Religious in Iran

Unlike many of the clients at ALLY who would considerably transform in appearance after joining the organization, Khadije had maintained her conservative and religious look, covering her hair under her black *maghnaeh*,[6] wearing no makeup, and wearing a long manto under her black chador. She was also more reserved and, unlike most clients, was not enthusiastic about meeting ALLY's guests from abroad or becoming friendly with the staff. In fact, there was a look of detachment in her eyes that drew clear boundaries between her and those she perceived as outsiders. She was among those clients, I later learned, who saw the teachings of ALLY as antagonistic to her cultural and religious values and who would complain about the anti-religion sentiments of some teachers to those staff she saw as sympathetic. Khadije's criticism of the staff, however, went beyond those complaints and encompassed critiques of the teachings she saw as misinformed and reflective of the privileged standpoint of ALLY's workers.

When I met her for the first time at a community development class, her visible frustration with the teachers and her intelligent responses caught my attention. Barmak, Hamid, and Shirin were three college-educated friends in their mid-twenties who taught a community development course with the goal of educating ALLY's marginalized clients on a range of social issues. Although none had a social science degree, their passion for the subject was enough to convince them of the importance of developing a space where the young women could discuss issues relevant to their daily lives. That day in class, soon after the conversation began on the role of technology in human history, the teachers were bombarded with skeptical remarks from the young women, who were unsure about the accuracy of the arguments presented to them. After explaining that the industrial era has been marked with "more leisure time," "more traveling," and a specialized labor market in which people "choose their profession based on their personal interests," the young women exchanged hesitant glances and quickly began to express their doubts about the accuracy of the statements read to them by Barmak.

"There are still many people who can't choose their own job and don't enjoy any leisure time," Khadije said while rolling her eyes and closing the book she was reading in class. I could see that the teachers were quite puzzled by the unexpected objection of Khadije and the other young women. Shirin began to describe the advancements made in transportation technology to demonstrate the increased ability of people to travel far and often in the postindustrial era. "Many people can't travel," Khadije said again to problematize Shirin's privilege and her own poverty. "We don't go on trips. Ask the people in this class to see how many have traveled during the holidays. Don't look at yourselves," she said as she laid her forehead in her palm and looked away, implying that she had no interest in continuing the conversation.

It was easy to interpret Khadije's statement as that of an impoverished woman with limited education who could not see beyond her personal experiences to understand the larger impact of industrialization and technological transformations worldwide. What was not as easy to recognize was Khadije's resistance to a Eurocentric middle-class account of history in which she and the world of poverty and uneven global development in which she lived were missing. I noticed again and again and in different classes the skillful attempts of Khadije and other young women to problematize those accounts of history or any social commentary that did not critically interrogate inequalities of class and status. Khadije's resistance to course content and her determination to maintain her religious appearance despite a larger pressure felt at ALLY for looking and thinking "modern" and middle class were often perceived as reflective of her lower education and religious views. Her *choices* for conforming to religious norms were not seen as agentic, and her *resistance* to certain educational materials was not seen as an empowering act of defying dominant class ideologies. After a few minutes of ignoring teachers' responses, Khadije calmly reopened the book she was reading: *One Thousand Years of Solitude*, by Gabriel García Márquez.

Many ethnographies on contemporary Iran that have sought to study subjectivity and personhood have focused on the experiences of secular and middle-class youth from Tehran. These ethnographies examine the lives of young people who position themselves against the moral order prescribed by the Islamic government and interpret their actions as acts of rebellion and resistance toward the political order. Olszewska (2013) has argued that these ethnographies' perception of subjectivity is undertheorized and that they carry problematic assumptions. Among these works are Mahdavi's *Passionate Uprising* (2009), which reports on an unfolding sexual revolution among Iranian youth who use their bodies as sites of protest by engaging in sexual acts outside the norm of modesty prescribed by the government. In his book *Young and Defiant in Tehran* (2008), Khosravi speaks of a "culture of defiance" among Tehrani youth, who resist the subject position imposed on them by the state by casting themselves as modern, cosmopolitan, and *ba-kelas* (classy). In this literature, "secular, middle-class subjects seem to rise autonomously, and must then busy themselves with resisting an alien subjectivity that a pernicious government attempts to force on them" (Olszewska 2015: 17).

The model of human agency in these studies has been vastly criticized for a liberal assumption that locates agency in moral and political autonomy. In their critiques of this liberal bias, postcolonial feminist scholars have offered more complex views of personhood that recognize the inseparability and continuity of agential and nonagential features of self. According to Soran Reader (2007), endurance, patience, and compassion are not signs of passive victimhood but, in fact, are rational (and at times courageous) responses. Mahmood (2005), similarly, by analyzing the practices of women in the mosque movement in Cairo, has challenged the conflation of agency with resistance to norms in order to argue for a conception of agency entailed "not only in those acts that resist norms but also in the multiple ways in which one inhabits norms" (15). Mahmood questions the normative, liberal assumptions that underlie dominant analyses of agency as well as their allegiance to an unquestioned ideal of individual freedom. Poststructural analyses of subjectivity see the formation of subjectivity as dynamic, shaped through coercion or persuasion, and never as a pre-given state that can later be manipulated and colonized (Eagleton 1985). In this sense, subjectivity is understood as a form of awareness shaped out of the tension between the inner processes and the external imposition of "cultural and social formations that shape, organize, and provoke" modes of affect and thought (Ortner 2005: 31). One must then ask what political forces have constituted those subjectivities that appear as autonomous and in defiance of oppressive politics of the Islamic government. "What forces contribute to the socialization of rebellious middle-class youth in Iran: class or generational awareness? Prerevolutionary memories or cosmopolitan desires transmitted through global mass media and internet? Or perhaps even the unintended effects of state policies themselves?" (Olszewska 2015: 17).

Kevan Harris (2012) has argued that the disaffection and resistance of the middle class in Iran reflect a pattern witnessed in many countries with an upwardly mobile middle class who see the state as blocking their access to social power. "They are educated and cognizant of cosmopolitan habits but lack the political and cultural capital that would allow them to fully enjoy the middle-class lifestyle they aspire to, free of the bureaucratic authoritarian characteristics of the Islamic Republic" (Harris 2012: 451). The Islamic Republic's modernization efforts, in continuation of the prerevolutionary era, its gradual bureaucratization and professionalization, and its biopolitical management of the population have resulted in policies that on one hand centralize power and on the other create individualized self-reflexive subjects of the late modern age with a culture of consumerism and competition (Adelkhah 2000). But Iran's Islamic government was originally a welfare state that got its strength from its economic and social populism and the development policies that particularly benefited the poor (Abrahamian 2009). Those who benefited from the state's policies were a loyal "rentier class" who received privileges and financial incentives for embracing the state's ideology. Among those were less-privileged rural and urban residents, veterans and the families of the martyrs of the Iran-Iraq War, and a group of conservative middle-class citizens. The country's growing population of newly educated youth, however, became disillusioned by an economy and government unable to create jobs for them. These policies—in addition to larger trends, such as rapid urbanization, an increasingly youthful and educated population, growing female literacy and workforce participation rates, and the arrival of new technologies like satellite television and internet—have resulted in "the development of complex and diverse subjectivities that are some combination of Iranian, Islamic, *and* inexorably modern" and can be observed among both the elite and those within the lower economic classes (Olszewska 2015: 19).

The dominant tendency to either overstate the repressive power of the state or emphasize the heroic defiance of (middle-class) Iranians against it has left out the possibility of studying the overlapping space between state and society—to see the Iranian state "as an imperfect hegemony, governed through a mixture of coercion and consent, visible or diffuse" (Olszewska 2013: 844). Depicting the lifestyle of the secular middle class who are cosmopolitan, *badhejab*,[7] followers of the latest fashion, and consumers of Western luxury brands as an expression of defiance against a repressive state leaves out the fact that the cultivation of certain cultural dispositions may indeed reflect norms of middle-class respectability and not merely political resistance. Meanwhile, reducing defiance to the practices of the secular middle-class urbanites leaves out the stories of poor and working-class women, immigrants, and refugees or those who support the political ideology of the Islamic Republic. How would poor women's acceptance or rejection of secular liberal feminism be perceived if our conceptualization of agency were to change and if the discourses of class and ethnicity were to enter our analysis? By answering this question in the following chapters, I argue that any analysis of contemporary feminist dispositions and advocacy in Iran should be conducted in terms of their development out of colonial, racial, and class discourses and within the context of limited political opportunities.

The next chapter offers an examination of middle-class, liberal, and secular feminist discourses as they were translated and contested by ALLY's middle-class staff and cosmopolitan administrators. Through an examination of this feminist contestation, I demonstrate the intersectional inequalities that limited the effectiveness of liberal discourses of sexual autonomy as means of empowerment for marginalized women and the debates around "cultural resonance" versus "universal human rights" that shaped many tensions at ALLY.

3

Glocalizing Women's Empowerment

"Over here! Our class got canceled, they told us we are watching a play!" Nazanin, one of the clients, yelled as she stood on the stairs, directing me to a classroom on the second floor by nudging her head. None of us knew what had triggered that day's change of plans. I could see, however, that the prospect of skipping the regular class schedule had excited many of the girls. Marva, the managing director, was standing at the large classroom door where the play was scheduled to be performed. As I passed her, she gently grabbed my arm. "It's *The Vagina Monologues*, you might want to be here," she whispered in my ear as I leaned toward her. She walked away from me with a cheerful smile and an inconspicuous wink, acknowledging our mutual knowledge of what the promised play was about. As I moved past the front rows, I noticed Reza taking a front seat. Reza was an Iranian Swedish art therapy teacher at ALLY who directed plays for local theaters while staying in Iran. Little by little, it dawned on

---

Portions of this chapter previously appeared as Fae Chubin, "Glocalizing Women's Empowerment: Feminist Contestation and NGO Activism in Iran," *Journal of Contemporary Ethnography*, 49, no. 6: 715–744. © Fae Chubin 2020. https://doi.org/10.1177/0891241620947135.

me that the three actresses sitting on the chairs facing the audience, reviewing their notes, and chatting with Reza might be his theater colleagues and friends. I had heard from the managing team their plan for holding multiple performances of *The Vagina Monologues* for both the clients and the staff. The administrators believed the performance and educational workshops on sexuality, which they had made mandatory for all, were necessary for raising a feminist awareness among ALLY's staff and clients. As I picked a seat somewhere near the back of the room, I wondered about the reception of such sexually explicit language among the young women.

Unlike what I witnessed during my previous experiences watching the play in the United States, the raunchy performance in Tehran appeared to have left a tense feeling of discomfort in many of the audience members. I did not notice any strong reaction from the clients—neither the collective laughter nor the voices of confirmation I had heard during the performance in the United States. While the three actresses offered believable performances, I wondered if the stories of American women simply had not resonated with this group of young, impoverished Afghan and Iranian women. While shame, pain, and pleasure are experienced universally, the tone, language, and mode with which women share their sexual stories and the appropriate context for those stories vary considerably among cultures and social groups. That afternoon, at the center's cafeteria, I met Nazanin, who sat down to have tea with me. Having seen her at the performance, I asked what she and other clients thought about *The Vagina Monologues*. "Most of the girls were OK with it," she said. "It was some of the staff that got really angry after." I probed Nazanin for her view on the workers' reaction to the performance. "I think it's because the male and female staff were all in the same room. They said they were embarrassed to look into each other's eyes after," Nazanin said, shrugging her shoulders. The days and weeks following the performance were tense with conflicts between some of the personnel and the managing team. While I did not witness it firsthand, I heard about the conflicts from the clients and administrators. The conflicts resulted in two male staff members, who clients counted among their favorites, leaving the organization. In the meetings held by the managing team with the distraught clients who were upset about losing their beloved teachers, the details of what transpired were not shared. Clients were only told about the "irresolvable disagreements" of some of the staff with the managing team. Later, in personal conversations with the administrators and the remaining staff, I heard varying accounts of the nature of the disagreements. For the managing team, the workshops and their "radical" content worked as a filtering system through which they could discard those staff who did not "share the same feminist values" and thus "did not belong at ALLY." Maryam, the founder, spoke of the mindset of those staff as being "patriarchal" and recounted how one of the male workers had mocked the program director for "only being concerned with things from the waist down," referring to her insistence on holding workshops on sexuality. Other staff members, however, blamed the tension on the culturally insensitive character of the workshops prescribed by the administrators who lived abroad and were unwilling to consider the point of view of the local workers, who favored programs that were more culturally resonant.

The decision to perform *The Vagina Monologues* was one of many choices made by the administrators that were challenged by the staff. The secular and liberal women's empowerment program of the organization (with its emphasis on sexual autonomy, sex positivity, and freedom of choice), designed by members of the cosmopolitan middle class, was contested and challenged by the local middle-class staff of the organization on varying grounds. This chapter examines these points of tension between the cosmopolitan administrators and the locally grounded staff to reveal the contestation of globally hegemonic discourses of empowerment and agency by actors with varying levels of access to the global stage. I show how the staff were actively involved in contesting certain aspects of the feminism advocated by the organization for lacking cultural resonance and practical value. However, the cosmopolitan administrators rejected constructing resonant frames because of their lower transformative potential and an uncompromising commitment to a liberal and secular feminist framework.

The activities of an organization like ALLY were shaped by forces beyond its national borders. The presence of Western feminist discourses of sexuality in ALLY's programming reveals their movement across borders and actors' responses to globally hegemonic discourses of women's empowerment. Embedded within these discourses of empowered sexuality are the accounts of feminist scholars who have revealed the links between women's status, economic mobility, and sexuality and have related women's liberation to their sexual autonomy. Marcela Lagarde (1990) has argued that the construction of women's sexuality as passive justifies their mandate to serve and please others. Others assert that access to sexual pleasure relates to one's position in social structures that determine who can access resources and respect. These arguments have compelled feminist scholars and activists to emphasize women's sexual liberation as necessary for their emancipation. ALLY's focus on women's sexual autonomy and its development of sexual education programs for the staff and clients were done in the light of this feminist scholarship. ALLY also relied on donations from Iran's diasporic community and its Western donors in Europe and North America. A liberal frame that emphasizes sexual liberation, secularism, and choice resonates with Western donors, whose interest often drives the process. Millie Thayer's (2010) ethnographic study on feminist movements in Brazil demonstrates that access to and dependency on foreign funds have shaped and transformed the agenda and content of many feminist NGOs in the Global South over the years.

Sexual education programs often emphasize the importance of sexual knowledge and "knowing one's body." These narratives around "knowing" as a means of feminist empowerment, however, imply a "valid" sexual knowledge and that the knowledge held previously does not count as valid and is, in fact, lacking (Portocarrero Lacayo 2014). As Ana Victoria Portocarrero Lacayo explains, "Through this exercise of validation/invalidation of knowledges, a particular way of understanding sexuality and pleasure is understood as universal, and the variety of ways in which women construct and negotiate their sexuality in their particular contexts become invisible" (2014: 232). The liberal conception of sexuality and agency, deemed universal, sees sexuality at the center of an individual, open, visible, and out loud, and in so doing "reinforces power inequalities between women based on their access and willingness to embrace this new knowledge" (Portocarrero Lacayo 2014: 232). Portocarrero Lacayo argues that this discourse separates women into a binary of "liberated" and "disempowered other" and justifies efforts for enlightening those who *lack* such knowledge. It is in this process of the colonization of knowledge that Western sexual knowledge becomes "common sense" (Santos, Nunes, and Meneses 2007) and sexuality becomes understood as an experience that some "liberated" women have "discovered" and should transmit to others. "This hierarchal relationship between women who know and those who require instruction continues to haunt contemporary Western and diasporic Iranian feminist discourses that celebrate the universal experience of all women" (Naghibi 2007: xxvi).

The hegemony of the feminist discourses of the Global North, with their emphasis on women's sexuality, is manifest in many empowerment programs implemented in the Global South, including ALLY. The content of an empowerment program does not merely reflect the *intentions* of its developers, as is often assumed. Intentions themselves reflect social and cultural forces that often remain unacknowledged (Sharma 2011). Development experts or feminist activists create and implement programs not in isolation but within the larger global context in which certain hegemonic discourses shape their assumptions and objectives. ALLY's women's empowerment program was a function of nonindigenous interests (e.g., donor interests and the hegemony of the model of empowerment advocated by international institutions) as well as indigenous interests (e.g., feminist discourses in Iran, the interest of dominant classes, and political structures). In any given study of empowerment, the intended objectives of administrators and translators should be studied in relation to the larger unacknowledged discourses that define empowerment, feminism, and development. As Shubhra Sharma argues, "the best of intentions may not produce the best of results and the reason for such infraction lies not in the intentions per se but in the complex social and cultural structures and discourses that such intentions are embedded in and also shaped by" (Sharma, 2011: 3). The discourses, not the intentions, produce effect. Yet, while intentions are often clearly stated, discourses remain hidden, even as they produce structured effects (Sharma 2011).

Glocalization and Vernacularization

Various studies (Merry 2006; Sharma 2008; Levitt and Merry 2009; Thayer 2010; Radhakrishnan 2015) have explored the processes of adaptation, translation, and appropriation of globally generated ideas in local contexts. For instance, Peggy Levitt and Sally Merry (2009) speak of the presence of a "global women's rights package" with loosely coupled elements such as gender equality, autonomy in marriage and divorce, the right to earn income and inherit money, and protection from violence and discrimination. They argue that this global women's rights package shapes the agenda and activities of many local NGOs and national women's movements across the world and "is expressed through a set of national and international laws and practices like the Convention on the Elimination of all Forms of Discrimination against Women (CEDAW), international women's conferences, International Women's Day, and the theoretical work of many women's and feminist studies programmes that have proliferated at universities over the past 30 years" (Levitt and Merry 2009: 448). This package refers to a set of ideas that are promoted and acknowledged globally and derive their legitimacy and influence from the countries and institutions in which they are born (e.g., UN) and the media that broadcast their messages.

While this package is widely circulated across many national contexts, Levitt and Merry demonstrate that in contact with local settings, these notions take on some of the ideological and social attributes of the local context. They call this process *vernacularization* and argue that this process of adaptation varies greatly depending on the context and the character of the channels through which these messages are transferred. "NGO directors and staff are quintessential vernacularizers" (Levitt and Merry 2009: 449), and they determine the frame through which the global value packages will attach to local norms and institutions. In the case of ALLY, the administrators and program developers decided whether *The Vagina Monologues* would be performed and whether its content would remain the same or adapt to local norms. Message framing is a political project decided on by a host of factors, including donor interests, the convictions and objectives of program developers, the appeal to local actors, the desire for a wider audience, the financial resources of an organization, and the symbolic value of certain messages (Levitt and Merry 2009). For instance, a secular human-rights frame is associated with the West, modernity, and progress, which increases the audience of the organization and allows for alliance and coalition building. However, such a frame may not always find resonance in postcolonial contexts and among the more religiously oriented, who resist secular and foreign influences and are suspect of cultural imperialism.

In any given process of vernacularization, intermediators and translators play a key role in negotiating local, national, regional, and global systems of meaning (Merry 2006). This process of translation, however, reflects inequalities of power between actors. The translator's work is influenced by factors ranging from their ethnic, gender, and class identity to the agenda of those who fund them. It was not surprising, then, to notice conflicts between the Western-educated upper-middle-class administrators of ALLY who were tasked with satisfying and impressing their donors and modeling effective empowerment programs tested in other national contexts, and the more locally grounded, college-educated middle-class staff of ALLY, who were more concerned with local cultural norms and the applicability of the program objectives to the lives of the organization's clients. In addition to operating within their class and social positions, both groups worked within the constraint of hegemonic discourses that defined their perceptions of feminism and their interpretive framework. For instance, the global women's rights package encourages "embracing a particular kind of agentic self that is self-interested and rational rather than religious, affective and communitarian" (Levitt and Merry 2009: 448). Many empowerment programs across the world have adopted this notion of agency, which finds rejection of religious and traditional norms essential to women's empowerment and development of an agentic self. As local actors design and define their empowerment programs, the globally dominant liberal and normative assumptions promoted by international institutions shape their assessments of clients' progress.

Thayer's study (2010) reveals that the global flow of funds and donations, often from the North to the South, determines the content of women's empowerment programs. Her research on feminist organizations in Brazil clearly demonstrates that access to and dependency on foreign funds have shaped and transformed the agenda, content, and relations of feminist NGOs over the last few decades. As liberation movements in Europe and America began to place women's bodies, sexualities, and health at the center of their struggles, the content and agenda of feminist organizations in the Global South experienced a similar shift in objective. The material and cultural resources of the Global North transform into global *forces* as they travel to their former colonies. This, however, is not a simple case of "cultural diffusion," where hegemonic discourses of Northern feminists are meekly accepted by women in the "Third World." While the North's economic and cultural resources and travel budgets allow the movement of feminist theories and gender discourses from the North to the South, there are still a variety of actors who engage in the dissemination, selective adoption, translation, or rejection of those ideas (Thayer 2010). Glocalization in this context does not refer to cultural hybridization but to how the global permeates the local. Studying the articulated intentions and interests of program developers and implementers can help us delineate the negotiations between international development imperatives and local cultural, political, and social norms.

The Cosmopolitan and Local Elite

Everyday interactions and relationships at ALLY were shaped by care and camaraderie yet also marked by increasing tensions and conflicts over what constitutes women's empowerment. The administrators of the organization saw education, sexual autonomy, freedom of choice, and inclusion in the market economy as necessary for clients' empowerment. In this chapter, borrowing from Levitt and Merry (2009), I refer to this group as *cosmopolitan elites*—individuals who have ties to the global stage, have often lived or studied abroad, and teach and learn about global value packages. These activists or NGO directors interact with outside ideas on a regular basis and take on the task of translating and transferring those ideas to local contexts of which they are also a part. With their intercultural skills, cosmopolitan subjects negotiate complex global processes and relate in diverse ways to different cultural environments and groups of people (Chin 2013).

Another group of NGO staff—who I call the *local elite*—is more situated within the local culture and is often college educated and middle class. These vernacularizers acquire ideas from the cosmopolitan elite and perform a second level of translation for the clients and fellow staff. The local elite at ALLY saw empowerment in the same light as the cosmopolitan elite, though they rejected certain elements of secular and liberal feminism (such as sexual autonomy and rejection of religion) as culturally alien and practically irrelevant. This group measures the feminist ideals of the organization against the practical realities that govern the marginalized clients' lives and their own gender and sexual norms. As I show in the following sections, vernacularizers also translate the grievances of local constituents and talk back to the cosmopolitan elite. Clients also talk back, resist, and engage in the process of vernacularization by placing the new ideas in dialogue with their own personal experiences and standpoints. The third group—the *local subaltern*, or the marginalized clients of the organization—saw gender oppression as deeply linked to their class and ethnic oppression and resisted those organizational narratives that reduced the struggles of the poor to their "cultural poverty" (I explore the perspectives of the local subaltern in Chapters 6 and 7).

It is important to note that by classifying the Western-educated administrators as cosmopolitan elites, I do not intend to construct them as Western or inauthentic agents or their feminist ideals as "foreign." To do so is to ignore the processes of hybridization central to all cultural contexts whereby the new discursive formations open themselves up to intrusions by various elements in the preexisting intellectual and linguistic practices of a country (Chatterjee 1995: 23). As Margot Barden (1995) has argued in her analysis of Egyptian feminists, cosmopolitan activists who have lived abroad are still part of the vital local culture—even if unaware of its intricacies—through their identification with the local and their commitment to it. The cosmopolitan and local elite shared similar national, ethnic, and class identities and therefore many similarities in perspective (although their transnational connections were vastly different). Hence, this categorization is merely conceptual, and the role and social class of participants did not always place them neatly in one category. This chapter illustrates how liberal and secular feminism is perceived among middle-class NGO workers in Iran and how assumptions about anti-traditionalism as a feminist value created challenges for ALLY's objective of empowering women.

Contesting Religion and Agency

> It was when I saw the girls' issues that I created ALLY's vision. And now I have come to this conclusion that [the girls] can learn all the vocations in the world, but if their perception of themselves and the society does not change, if they don't gain self-esteem, [nothing will change]. You can train them to go to work and make money, but that doesn't change anything. (Maryam, Founder)

Maryam shared this sentiment with me on the fourth-floor balcony of ALLY's second building, where she and other managing staff often took their smoking breaks. The spacious balcony was sparsely decorated with planting pots and separated from the busy management office by a large glass door. Sitting on the balcony stairs leading to the rooftop and watching Maryam share her convictions about ALLY's ultimate objective, I wondered about the significance of the narrative I was hearing so frequently. A few weeks before, Shirin, a college student who taught community development classes with her fellow colleagues and friends, had shared a similar conviction:

> After a few months (of teaching at ALLY), I realized that I need to get more involved. I talked to one of the psychologists and told him about my concerns. I told him I feel like you are giving these girls a series of abilities and skills. But at the end, their perspective is not changing. What changes their lives is not those skills but that perspective that has to change. (Shirin, Teacher)

I wondered about the importance of these narratives for ALLY's staff and administrators and the meaning they gleaned from their work. I had come to learn from the same staff and administrators the structural inequalities that left many young women in need of seeking refuge at ALLY: Extreme poverty, exploitation at sweatshops, living conditions that included sexual and physical abuse by drug-addicted and negligent families, the absence of legal protection or material resources to escape abuse, and the unwillingness of the state to prosecute violence against women, particularly when Afghan immigrants were involved. They had shared these factors and many unsettling stories with me as they explained their criteria for—and the urgency of—admitting clients into ALLY's empowerment program. Despite this shared realization that it was the objective reality of the clients' lives that required transformation, the fundamental objective of ALLY's program was consistently and firmly described by the cosmopolitan and local elite as effecting a "change of consciousness."

This insistence on consciousness-raising did not mean that the material reality of the clients' lives was overlooked. The organization's program emphasized vocational training and equipping clients with necessary skills for participation in the market economy. Yet the strong organizational *narrative* that defined empowerment in terms of clients' subjective transformation was noticeable. In fact, Nasim, a member of the managing team, told me that ALLY's vision had come to change over the years to move from focusing on the material reality of the clients' lives to focusing on their perspective of reality:

> At the beginning, empowerment meant that they would come here to get an education, we work on their behavior and mental health, and then they will get a job. That was the end of it. The end goal was for them to be able to go to work and make money. Of course, this is empowerment. But this is not all that empowerment means. It's great if they could get a job and be independent from their family, their husband, or their boyfriends. But there are other things, in my opinion, that are even more important.... The program has been maturing. Our new goal of wanting to change society and change every girl's consciousness wasn't always there, or maybe the idea was not this mature in the beginning. (Nasim, Managing Director)

I could see that for many at ALLY, consciousness-raising was seen as the most crucial component of empowerment in that it could allow women to construct a sense of self that recognizes oppression and demands change. In many conversations, the cosmopolitan and the local elite shared their belief about the importance of developing in clients an awareness that had the potential to disrupt the cycle of abuse, poverty, and misogyny with which clients struggled daily. "It's so baffling that many of them have no specific definition of rape," Rose, a twenty-four-year-old social worker, told me about Afghan clients, "yet nearly all have been assaulted in so many ways, even the completed rape." The major impediment to change, many of the staff told me, was clients' inability to see their living circumstances as oppressive and to see themselves as worthy of different living circumstances. The newly gained knowledge, they believed, would compel women to exercise choice and separate themselves from the oppressive patriarchal forces that restricted their agency.

The organizational emphasis on consciousness-raising reflected a feminist scholarship that finds emancipation in the recognition and rejection of patriarchal control. Since feminist scholars have revealed the embeddedness of patriarchy in all social institutions, such as family, religion, the economy, and the very fabric of morality, empowerment is understood as a process whereby women exercise autonomy and separate themselves from the patriarchal forces that fetter their agency. Transforming into a liberal, secular, and rational actor capable of exercising individual freedom is defined as empowerment when, for instance, culture and religion are found to be deeply patriarchal. This perception of empowerment is particularly prevalent when Muslim women are concerned. Orientalist feminist discourses have long constructed Muslim women's rights in opposition to local familial, communal, and kinship structures of Muslim societies (Kandiyoti 2005) while approaching these structures as the mere reflection of Islam rather than a complex product of social, economic, political, colonial, and historical processes (Khurshid 2015).

While education and knowledge are empowering forces, I wondered if the staff's narratives reflected the growing problem identified by Shenila Khoja-Moolji (2018) in her analysis of the dominant rhetoric of international agencies concerned with the empowerment of Muslim women. Khoja-Moolji demonstrates the dominance of an Orientalist image of Muslim-girl-in-crisis whose salvation depends on her education rather than the decolonial restructuring of the political and economic conditions of the Global South. She questions the emancipatory capacities of educational campaigns that are assumed to be able to "miraculously empower [young Muslim women] to confront historical and structural issues of gender-based violence, poverty, and terrorism" (Khoja-Moolji 2018: 4). While the effects of dominant discourses that prescribe education for Muslim women as the ultimate means of empowerment were seen in ALLY's programming goals, I further explain this focus on social education in Chapter 4 in relation to the organization's strategic measures of advocacy that required emphasizing clients' capabilities and, in Chapter 5, in terms of the perceived need for developing a middle-class habitus in clients. Regardless of the multifaceted motivations behind ALLY's social education program, developing an agentic self through self-realization was understood as an important indicator of empowerment among ALLY's staff.

In ALLY's narratives of empowerment, practicing autonomy was commonly discussed as a significant indicator of having developed an empowered/agentic personhood. Choosing one's own spouse, job, clothing, or values was the most discussed signifier of agency. In my interview with Hamid, a twenty-six-year-old college graduate from Tehran who taught a community development course with Shirin and Barmak, the importance of granting marginalized women the ability to exercise choice was clearly discussed as the central component of empowerment:

> [ALLY] tries to help those who were subservient and at their family's feet and those whose needs were ignored to not feel suppressed, to overcome this feeling of suppression, do some serious work, study, go to work, and choose their spouse and their job and their path not from that place of feeling suppressed. But to think for themselves, to choose their path according to their own will, and make decisions for themselves. (Hamid, Teacher)

Like Hamid, many other employees saw autonomy as the most significant indicator of *tavanmand shodan* (becoming empowered), as it requires separating oneself from the forces that bind one's agency. This separation was especially discussed in relation to religion and culture when empowerment was defined as resisting the norms and values that limit choice and govern action.

> I personally believe that religion is very limiting and binding. I mean, it closes off your mind. It doesn't allow you to think. It's like you think and you want to do something but then you hear certain Imam has said you can't do it and so you don't. But that Imam lived like fifty million years ago! That holds people back and won't let them grow. And that is how we see things here. . . . I've heard that some of the girls have complained about this . . . but it is what it is, whether they like it or not. (Nasim, Managing Director)

Nasim shared her view about religion in her interview with me as I asked her to comment on the growing complaints of clients who believed some of ALLY's employees were mocking or disparaging their religious beliefs. I had witnessed firsthand those class conversations in which teachers spoke of religious moral norms as antiquated and most religious beliefs as superstition. The personal convictions of ALLY's teachers shaped those classroom discussions, not an organizational agenda to oppose religion. Yet, the values and belief systems of those working at ALLY were intentionally and unintentionally defining the hiring process, creating a nearly homogeneous group of staff with secular views.

In the same interview, Nasim also shared her view of empowerment and the impact ALLY has left on clients:

> How do I say this? In this social group, the perspectives are much narrower because the girls come from dogmatic families. So when she comes to [ALLY], a new world opens up to her.... For example, today I saw one of the girls saying that she has a boyfriend. I was so shocked; mostly because she comes from a very religious family. She was saying that "my brother doesn't understand anything. He is so religious, he can't even comprehend this." This is huge! It's so little, I mean it's not really anything, or it might even seem wrong by some. But to me, it's a big jump in that girl with that religious view from such a religious family. The mere fact that she says she has a boyfriend and that her brother will kill her if he finds out means that she has made a choice.... This is a huge jump that you can choose for yourself. You can have this kind of life or the other; but we are showing the way: That you can choose. Which one do you want? (Nasim, Managing Director)

For Nasim and many other staff, a client's decision to engage in premarital relationships in a context where such practices are taboo was a strong indicator of the development of an agentic personhood. Having a boyfriend, not wearing proper hejab, and refusing arranged marriages were discussed by many workers as small yet important instances of exercising choice by defying the dominant discourses of ideal womanhood with which the young women grew up. The cosmopolitan elite's emphasis on choice in clothing, marriage, and sexual relations reflects the global women's rights package that is often adopted by NGOs and carries a liberal bias in its definition of agency. For instance, while Nasim defined *choice* as one's autonomy in deciding for herself, only the instances of *rejecting* religion or tradition were recognized as acts of agency. *Choosing to comply* with the dominant norms and values were never discussed by the staff I interviewed as being instances of practicing autonomy. This bias in feminist theorizing of agency carries a liberal assumption that conflates agency with resistance to norms and not in many acts that inhabit norms (Mahmood 2005). Under these normative liberal assumptions, the religious compliance of clients who chose to wear their hejab or follow religious or traditional guidelines of sexual behavior was not seen as agentive or as a form of patriarchal bargaining (Kandiyoti 1988) with which clients could gain currency in their environments or communities. The lack of data here is a strong indicator of such bias toward certain displays of choice as agentic, which reproduces assumptions about religious women's lack of agency if liberal ideals are not embraced.

These accounts of sexual liberation and personal autonomy also fail to account for variations in the discourses of sexuality and love between people of different economic and ethnic groups. The authority of the patriarchal family and the value placed on female virginity are different across class and ethnic lines in Iran. Lower-class women in Iran who seek boyfriends and engage in premarital sexual relationships might do so not for the purpose of flouting authority but due to their aspirations for social mobility. Many of these women have long used *sighe* (temporary marriage) to access financial resources through a higher-status husband, though such relationships often turn into a nightmare of sexual exploitation (Olszewska 2013). Meanwhile, having a boyfriend might have been perceived by clients as being a means of accessing the worldly and cosmopolitan lifestyle lived by the organization's staff and claiming a higher social status. Romanticizing the sexually licentious behavior of the marginalized clients as a signifier of feminist empowerment or a hard-won freedom overlooks the fact that the risks and benefits of extramarital sexuality are not evenly distributed across class lines and that most women remain ambivalent toward those very practices (Olszewska 2013: 855).

The emphasis on consciousness-raising and a conception of agency rooted in liberal notions of resistance to cultural and religious norms were shared by the cosmopolitan and local elite, reflecting the hegemony of the mainstream liberal and secular feminism among middle-class Tehranis. This brand of feminism assumes that women's struggles are shared universally and ignores the effects of the structural inequalities experienced by women marginalized at the intersection of their class and ethnic identity. Despite this shared perspective, certain elements of this liberal and secular feminism were a source of contestation between the cosmopolitan and local elite at ALLY. In the following section, I demonstrate the contestations over the role of religion in women's oppression or liberation, the importance of sexual education for women's emancipation, and culturally authentic versus culturally alien reform.

Contesting Sexual Autonomy as Empowerment

Liberal feminism's allegiance to individual freedom did not go unchallenged at ALLY. My conversations with the local elite revealed an *inner conflict* around aspects of ALLY's empowerment program that emphasized sexual autonomy in a context where women did not have the ability to implement the newly raised consciousness in their lives:

> Social work is about teaching fishing rather than giving fish to people. But I sometimes wonder if we are teaching them fishing because we are teaching the girls things that are averse to society. We are giving them sexual definitions, but how much can they talk about these definitions at home? If they want to say that we are free to choose our sexual partners, can they really? You know, I feel like it's incompatible with society.... If they listen to what ALLY tells them, they will be kicked out of home and they will be ostracized, and honestly, what can they hold on to in this society if they don't have the support of their families? (Rose, Social Worker)

As Rose's statement suggests, ALLY's teachings centered on an understanding of feminism that advocates for women's recognition of their rights as autonomous individuals, with sexual freedom symbolizing that autonomy. However, Rose questioned the practical value of advocating for sexual autonomy among the clients' social group. While such sexual education would be sought after by secular upper- and middle-class youth in Tehran and other big cities who have been able to navigate their sexual autonomy more safely within the societal restraints with the help of their economic resources, clients' poverty, refugee status, and dependence on their families would not allow them to demand autonomy or have an independent and safe space for their sexual practices, particularly in a country where government has criminalized premarital sexual relationships. Other local elite shared Rose's inner conflict about the personal and social impact of ALLY's sexual education program. Some even questioned the outcome of teaching clients about sexual boundaries and violence, noting that such education had only heightened young women's awareness of their surroundings while they remained unable to escape sexually abusive situations when, for instance, abusers were family members on whom they depended.

> There was a case when the girl did not know what had happened to her was sexual abuse. When she found out, she became extremely sensitive to the extent that if anyone at home touched her, she would think that they wanted to abuse her. She had become restless and had lost her peace at night. When you think about their living circumstances you need to realize that they don't have much space. It's not like they have separate bedrooms. All family members that aren't usually less than five people live and sleep next to one another in a place that is like a studio. Now in these circumstances, for a person that has become extremely sensitive to these sexual matters . . . we haven't given them peace; we have taken that peace from them. (Azar, Social Worker)

Clients' distress and helplessness were the *unintended and unanticipated consequences* of sexual education for impoverished women in a context where women had no power to interfere with the conditions of their living circumstances and where ALLY's program remained limited to consciousness-raising. This posed serious challenges for the young women's mental health, and some reported an increased sense of anxiety and helplessness following this education. In this context, teachings centered on sexual autonomy, while in demand for the middle-class urbanites, were found incongruent with the realities of subaltern women's lives. Moreover, other staff spoke of the dangers of emphasizing individual freedom without attending to the consequences of acting outside of social norms:

> They are given a lot of information about how you have the right to have relations with your boyfriend, you have the right to have

sex, or have the right to wear a certain kind of dress. OK, you have the right, all of us have the right to go out wearing shorts, but we will get arrested. They don't teach what having a right means. You gotta say you have the right to have relations with the opposite sex, but how can you maintain your status in this culture and social context, how can you keep yourself safe? This education isn't done with respect to the other person's beliefs. It's done with an attack on them. (Arezo, Psychologist)

ALLY's clients were encouraged to articulate and actualize in their lives the feminist values of autonomy and equality. Such liberal articulations of rights, however, not only provoked a backlash among clients' families but also lacked translatability between the two contexts. Women would often report that they were mocked and silenced at home when they spoke like their teachers for "using words that are too big for their mouth" or acted middle class in poor communities, where middle-class manners and modes of speech appeared suspicious, at best. Right-based conceptualizations of empowerment, which are popular among many international NGOs, if not translated into local ethical and religious norms might not gain traction among constituents (Ong 2011). Translating and recasting gender rights ideals into local politics and ethics (e.g., through the Islamic feminist framework) may have given the organization's discussions of gender justice more social legitimacy in clients' communities. But those teachings of ALLY that emphasized liberal and secular conceptions of rights and autonomy did not equip the local subaltern with the necessary symbolic tool to carve out for themselves a powerful voice that could meaningfully influence the environments in which they were living. This conflict was also a source of concern for the staff, who worried about the repercussions of the lack of conformity in the context of clients' families and communities.

> Our girls come from very religious and traditional families and from a particular cultural context, and then we bombard them with a series of information, which is a good education, it's not a bad education but . . . the problem is that we don't pay attention to their cultural context and that the girls have to go back to the same context. . . . Many of the girls get excited about what

they are learning and talk about what we teach them at home, and then their father comes here and is like, "What are you teaching my daughter? What's all the talk about homosexuality?" (Barmak, Teacher)

I just tell the girls to think about what you are learning and where you are talking about it. For example, you tell your mom that my virginity isn't important for marriage, and your mom is like [says with angry mom voice], "Your virginity is all that you are! If you say it doesn't matter, it means that you're not a virgin!" And then how are we going to fix this? The problem is not ALLY. It's just that education must be adjusted. (Rose, Social Worker)

Clients differed in the way they responded to the teachings of ALLY that conflicted with their norms and values. While some clients ignored the sexual education offered in favor of their internalized system of morality, others embraced the change at the expense of losing status, credibility, and acceptance within their families and communities. The latter group of women discussed in detail and in various classes a serious feeling of alienation and lack of belonging as well as various instances of confrontation with family members who would not accept the women's new transformed self. In the face of the shortcomings of secular and liberal conceptions of empowerment, a group of local elite argued that religious teachings, rather than being an impediment to women's empowerment, are the only effective tool for an organization like ALLY to secure the well-being of its clients and their communities:

If I really believe in human rights, if I *really* believe, human rights are for men, women, children, a Muslim, and a Jew alike. I don't have the right to speak against anyone's religion.... If one day, hopefully, I teach this [women's empowerment] workshop in Afghanistan, what kind of weapon do you think I'll use? Do you think I'll have these pictures [of women on my PowerPoint]? I will reap the Quran. Don't doubt this! I'll reap the Quran. I'll read it and read it and read it until I can take out facts that I can use for my work. I'm not going to attack their beliefs; I'll trap them with their own trap. (Alborz, Psychologist)

These secular and nonreligious staff members did not mean to leave religion intact. Their goal was to challenge those aspects of religious beliefs that were tainted by patriarchal motivations:

> In this journey [of being at ALLY], anything that is important for them is going to be questioned. They see that hejab is being questioned.... But the [important] thing is to ask "why." If someone says your hair shouldn't show, why? What's the deal with that? Is it about a belief or is it a masculine controlling thing? [It's different] if you say I *want* to fast or pray, whereas someone is forcing you to dress a certain way. (Omid, Managing Director)

Separating religion from patriarchy is the central theme of Islamic feminism (Moghadam 2002) and the scholarship and activism of feminists who strategically critique religion, whether it be Islam, Christianity, or Judaism, without intending to step outside of those traditions (Israel-Cohen 2012). Omid's and Alborz's narratives suggest a similar understanding of religion, where dominant interpretations of religious texts or practices are questioned for their patriarchal motivations. These workers perceived a different relationship between religion and patriarchy, arguing that ALLY's feminist activism should entail developing in clients the ability to separate religion from patriarchy and to utilize a resonant religious discourse to advocate for women's rights. Yet, it is important to note that these employees were not Islamic feminists in that they did not have any religious inclination or necessarily identify as feminist. These local elites were simply doubtful of the practicality of a secular and liberal education in a social context where ALLY's clients lived. Many of the teachings, according to this group of staff, were disconnected from the practical realities of the clients' lives and were merely a reflection of the desire and values of the cosmopolitan administrators of ALLY.

The disagreements between the cosmopolitan elite and the local elite at ALLY in many cases reflected the dilemma of resonance identified by Levitt and Merry (2009). While the cosmopolitan elite emphasize the universality of human rights to increase the power and legitimacy of their frame, the local actors often emphasize localization to increase the resonance of the human rights frame with existing ideologies or the practical realities that govern the lives of their constituents (Levitt and Merry 2009). Unlike the cosmopolitan elite, the local elite believe in a mode of feminist teaching that is context-specific, practical, and culturally sensitive. Teaching clients grand and uncompromising values of freedom and equality, they argue, has little practical productivity in a context where women lack the power to intervene and their communities value a different system of meaning. Their solution was bridging the gap between ALLY's feminist ideals and the belief systems of clients and their communities.

> We are searching online every night to see what kinds of work are being done around the world similar to ours. For example, I saw a [white] woman working in Africa wearing a headscarf, why? So that the society would accept her. The target population that is being educated accepts her like this. So she wears a headscarf. It doesn't matter! What matters is exchanging information. In another context, I will have to wear a (revealing) top in order to say what I want to say. We shouldn't be dogmatic toward anything. The more we bring ourselves closer to the target population's context in terms of their religion, beliefs, and culture, the easier they will accept our words. . . . We need to create some kind of a common language so they would trust us. (Fatemeh, Foreign Affairs Personnel)

On various occasions, Fatemeh expressed her concern over the decisions of the cosmopolitan elite, who refused to take into consideration the symbolic meaning of self-representation as helpers. The local elite understood the importance of acknowledging the target population's values, culture, and belief systems and were pessimistic about the impact of ALLY on clients if the young women could not see themselves in the women they were asked to model. The contentious character of interactions between the cosmopolitan and local elite and the discrepancy between their perceptions of empowerment became particularly evident after a sexuality workshop series and the performances of *The Vagina Monologues* described in the beginning of this chapter. Alborz, a middle-aged male psychologist, for instance, believed that much of the sexual education offered at ALLY was developed and designed for a Western audience and, without proper adaptation, was simply inappropriate for the Iranian cultural and social context.

> [Sexuality] is a very sensitive topic. It's not that *we* are sensitive, humans are sensitive to it. The world is sensitive. The fact that they [administrators] don't see the cultural context is sometimes really bothersome to us. Even when you are working in America, background and social context are very valuable factors. You can even see that Jennifer Lopez dresses like a nun when she goes to certain places. It's just so great to see how much they care about and study the context . . . sometimes these are big concerns for us. We can't take a pre-made package and just take it from one context to another. (Alborz, Psychologist)

The staff's call for adaptation and cultural resonance shows the perceived importance of choosing approaches that are deemed credible and salient by the target population. The closer the content of the program to the essential values and beliefs of a target population, the more likely they will be to embrace the new ideas. However, the call for cultural adaptation was not always perceived as credible by the cosmopolitan elite, who rightfully worried that some staff's desire for "cultural resonance" meant they did not want to be challenged on their (patriarchal) views. The cosmopolitan elite believed that challenging dominant beliefs required aggressive methods and that the power of feminist programs lay in their radical quality. Shiva, a twenty-seven-year-old female employee and a former women's rights activist, had a similar view, believing that the transformative quality of ALLY or any feminist initiative lay in its willingness to "courageously break social norms." For this group of staff, remaining true to one's feminist ideals and values should take precedence over people's convenience or comfort. In response to my question about the perceived "radical" character of ALLY in clients' communities and the subsequent backlash they have experienced, Maryam responded:

> I don't know how radical it is. ALLY *is* radical. You don't even have to be radical. In the context of Iran, this is radical. But in my mind, it's not. The girls always say here is like heaven. I tell

them: This is not heaven; this is normal! That [life you live] is abnormal. In a normal life, they respect you and you can speak and criticize, and this is nothing extraordinary. What can I do if everything in Iran is radical? This might cause a problem at home, so what? What are we gonna do? Stop because of it? Eventually they have to learn that, like any family, you have to handle tradition and modernity, if you want to call it that. I don't think it is modernity. I'm very radical compared to my mom too. She is my mom, and I'm living with her. She took a step forward and I took a step forward, and we finally met somewhere in between. We tell the girls not to hold a microphone and yell all the things you learn here because it will be bad for you. But at one point, we can't really control it. She has to learn to handle this. In the meantime, some will perish too. It's a way of life. (Maryam, Founder)

Although resonance with local norms is significant for the acceptance of new ideas, Myra Marx Ferree (2003) argues that resonant discourses are not as radical as nonresonant ones, and it is the desire to induce greater social change that compels some activists to adopt nonresonant frames. A resonant frame, in fact, can limit the possibility of long-term change due to its less challenging character, which often entails sacrificing ideals. The cosmopolitan elite's insistence on their sexual education program, however, reflected their assumptions about the universality of liberal values of individualism, autonomy, choice, and bodily integrity. The cosmopolitan elites' proximity to the global stage, where "universal" frameworks for women's empowerment are developed through a lens that sees religion and tradition as fettering women's agency, shaped the content of ALLY's program. Moreover, a religious framework for gender justice might not have appealed to ALLY's foreign donors, who valued liberal feminist ideals and traveled to Iran to witness the organization's program firsthand. The local elite, grounded in the local context and in daily interaction with clients, noticed the impracticality of espousing uncompromising values of sexual autonomy for a target population embedded within a different cultural, economic, and political reality. However, in many cases, the local elite reproduced Orientalist and middle-class discourses that emphasized poor religious women's false consciousness, reflecting the history of the development of Iranian feminism out of colonial discourses and class politics.

The administrators and the staff navigated competing demands and realities, which complicated their decision-making regarding the framework and scope of their educational program. While the cosmopolitan and local elite acknowledged the never-ending struggles created by poverty and structural inequalities in Iran, they did not always critically challenge their own assumptions about gender oppression and liberation. During the sexuality trainings at ALLY, the belief that sexual liberation is necessary for women's empowerment stood in contrast to the local elite's perception of the practical realities that governed Iran and the lives of marginalized women. These conflicts nevertheless generated important and vibrant conversations about gender oppression and liberation that are absent in government-sponsored organizations and initiatives in Iran. Despite its challenges and shortcomings, ALLY played an important role in revitalizing feminist debates while offering life-saving social services to marginalized women.

4

From Empowerment to Advocacy

From the first day of my fieldwork, a common narrative about clients' talents was repeatedly shared by the administrators and staff as they introduced me and other guests to ALLY's program. The desire to showcase the young women's achievements was noticeable, as their paintings, sculptures, photography, and writings decorated all the walls and spaces in both buildings. During our tour of the organization, Marva, a managing director, stood before each piece and passionately shared stories about the young women who had created the art. "It's mind-blowing how talented these girls are," Marva told me as she explained the meaning behind each painting and the creative journey of the female artists. "When you think about it, you realize that these girls are more talented than most people. The only thing they didn't have was the opportunity," she said with heartfelt conviction. I heard similar narratives from other administrators, who

---

Adapted by permission from Springer Nature Customer Service Centre GmbH: Springer Nature, *International Journal of Politics, Culture and Society*, "From Empowerment to Advocacy: Innominate Identity Politics as Feminist Advocacy in Iran" by Fae Chubin, Copyright © 2019 Springer Nature.

insisted on the unique capabilities of the women who had sought refuge at ALLY:

> The talent you see in these [women] you can't find in [the rich]. I don't know why. [Maybe] money ruins talent; or [maybe] they haven't suffered or experienced the [same] need to develop the same feelings and thoughts. There is so much talent in these girls. So much! Anyone would be delighted to see it. We got a piano teacher who told us he can't believe how good the girls play the piano only after six months. Because they don't have a piano [at home]. . . . We thought what a great teacher. He said, "It's not me, it's them." (Omid, Managing Director)

It was not hard to believe the many tales of accomplishment and success the staff shared about ALLY's clients. The proof was on the walls, in the provoking and deeply intimate artwork that captured the eyes and hearts of curious onlookers and was exhibited in galleries, having won numerous prizes. Staff members not only shared prideful stories of clients' blossoming artistic talents, they also invited me to listen to them play musical instruments or to hear readings of the poetry and essays written by them since joining ALLY. As I listened to many stories about clients' talents and capabilities and overheard them as they were repeated to other guests, I wondered about the significance of these narratives for ALLY's organizational objectives or for staff's perception of their work. In this chapter, I speak of the organization's emphasis on clients' capabilities as a practice of advocacy for marginalized groups—an advocacy shaped by the constraining cultural discourses and the political climate surrounding identity politics in Iran. I suggest that the potential of an NGO like ALLY for advocacy should be examined through a contextual analysis of cultural and political discourses that may redefine and redesign identity politics itself.

The term *identity politics* describes movements with a wide range of political activity that demand recognition for the rights of stigmatized and marginalized groups. The feminist movement, civil rights movement, and LGBTQ movement in the United States are examples of identity politics practiced through large-scale political movements in the second half of the twentieth century. Unlike movements organized around belief systems or party affiliations, identity political formation aims to emancipate marginalized groups, often through consciousness-raising and legislation. While identity politics is often explained and theorized based on the examples of political struggles in Western capitalist democracies, many nationalist projects and indigenous rights movements worldwide use similar arguments (Heyes 2016).

In contexts where social movements face grave challenges for forming, organizing, and recruiting members, identity politics are often practiced in unconventional ways. Bayat's (2013) work on "social nonmovements," for instance, challenges dominant assumptions about the absence of a strong women's movement in Iran by demonstrating the presence of a distinct form of resistance intertwined with mundane daily practices in public domains in a context where organized political activism by women is often subject to political repression. Mahdavi (2012) has similarly demonstrated that the absence of a visible LGBTQ movement in Iran does not signify an absence of activism and that the Iranian youth see themselves as part of a sexual revolution by using their bodies as a site of protest.

In this chapter, I demonstrate the presence of a mode of advocacy for marginalized groups that I call *innominate identity politics*. This form of identity politics departs in framing, strategy, and organization from the conventional practices of identity politics prevalent in Western societies, where identities are invoked, deployed, and tied to a universal conception of "rights" for the purpose of changing institutions and transforming the mainstream culture. As I show in this chapter, ALLY's advocacy for its marginalized clients was done by using the rhetoric of "capabilities" rather than "rights." Rather than invoking young, impoverished women's unalienable rights as women or ethnic minorities, ALLY's staff insisted that clients were deserving due to their *capabilities*. Rather than organizing their contentious politics around group identity formation, they invested in cultivating the talents and capabilities of their clients. ALLY's emphasis on marginalized women's capabilities was the effect of social and political processes that determined the modes of identity politics available to ALLY's workers. For one, intersecting discourses of gender, class, and ethnicity had rendered organization's marginalized clients as bare life (Agamben 1995). Second, the inaccessibility of the rhetoric of rights in the political climate of Iran had required creative rethinking of alternative frameworks of advocacy. And third, the perceived limited success of large-scale protest movements in Iran had generated among my participants a collective desire for identity politics focused on grassroots cultural change.

Innominate identity politics, as examined in this study, represents a mode of activism that is visibly formed around advocacy for marginalized social groups, yet the possibility of advocacy rests on denying group identity formation and rights-claiming. Identities are innominate (unnamed) yet fought for. It is important to note, however, that while I speak of the organization's *framing practices* (Goffman 1974; Benford and Snow 2000), the extent to which the staff's framing was done consciously or strategically is not a concern of this analysis. Instead, the goal of this institutional ethnography (Smith 2005) is to uncover the larger institutional relations that necessitate certain practices of advocacy as opposed to nonresonant or costly ones. Particularly, I ask: How did the workers of the organization perceive the means and effects of their advocacy for the organization's marginalized clients? And what were the cultural and political discourses shaping and constraining their attempts for identity politics?

Advocacy for Bare Life

> Some of the girls come from Behzisti.[1] When we talked to one of the social workers at Behzisti, she said these girls are society's residue. People who work at Behzisti think that society is working and is creating some waste or leftovers. Like when you build a table and there is some wood or paint leftover, you have to dispose of them somewhere so you don't see them, so they won't bother anyone, like disposing garbage so you don't have to smell it.... The outlook of people who come here, even the educated ones, is that these are street girls, they think runaway girls are spoiled and roam on the street and we have picked them up. They don't have a good social status. (Omid, Managing Director)

Omid shared these remarks with an indignant expression on his face as he recounted how the stigmatized social status of clients as "runaway girls" or "prostitutes" had introduced numerous challenges to ALLY's advocacy and fundraising practices. The stigmatization of sexual relations outside marriage, sexual victimization, and sex work reflects patriarchal discourses that often shame and blame women. Yet, the stigmatization of ALLY's clients was not solely due to their marginalized gender and sexual identities but also to their lower economic class and, for many, their ethnic and national identity. This matrix of domination (Collins 2000) experienced by ALLY's young clients, marginalized at the intersection of their class, gender, and ethnic identities with a stigmatized sexual history, had assigned many the status of bare life.

In his theory of biopolitics, Italian philosopher and political thinker Agamben (1995, 2005) argues that the figure of *homo sacer* in modern politics allows for the elimination of those social groups who for some reason cannot be integrated into the political system (2005: 2). These groups of people are abandoned due to the incapacity or unwillingness of the state to regulate or police certain types of violence (Pratt 2005). The growing number of refugees not claimed by any state, missing sex workers whose cases often remain uninvestigated, and the unprosecuted violence against undocumented workers are all examples of *states of exception* as gendered and racial processes (Pratt 2005) in which certain lives are abandoned. Those constructed as bare life, stripped of their legal status and political life, exist in a state of deprivation (of legal rights as well as material resources) where cultural and political discourses define their exclusion as legitimate and their lives as *unworthy of living*.

With the operation of sanctioned and institutional relations defining ALLY's clients as bare life, the organization's advocacy required attempts for identity construction to transform clients' status from *zoë*, a mere biological life, to *bios*, a qualified and proper form of life (Agamben 1995). The staff's attempts to showcase and recount clients' potential and capabilities find meaning in relation to the cultural and political discourses that define belonging and worth. Rather than engaging in rights advocacy by drawing from universal conceptions of human rights, the staff organized efforts and resources toward providing clients with tools and opportunities for artistic, intellectual, or literary self-expression. Their emphasis on clients' capabilities (both in practice and narrative) were strategic practices of identity politics that aimed to challenge clients' stigmatized identities with an organized effort toward portraying them as capable and endowed.

As you can see, we have many capable girls that are doing great in clothing design. We have girls who have shown so much potential in [mastering] the English language that they have become teaching assistants. We have girls that are operators, with such competence. This shows that we wanted to discover talents, and this is a talent agency. (Fatemeh, Foreign Affairs Personnel)

Something interesting is that I didn't used to appreciate the Afghan society the way I do now. Many people harass and offend them. But I realized what a talented and hardworking group of people they are. One of the things that happen for the girls in this journey is that they discover their talents. This is the biggest gift you can give someone; look how much talent you have, and you didn't even know! (Omid, Managing Director)

These narratives, commonly shared by the staff with ALLY's guests and potential sponsors, suggest two things. For one, they show ALLY's attempts at problematizing subjugating cultural assumptions about impoverished minorities that paint them as unskilled, unqualified, talentless, and indolent. Second, they provide a picture of ALLY as an intervening organization that transforms clients' lives by simply providing them with opportunities for self-development that the clients were previously deprived of due to their unjust social locations.

Emphasizing marginalized groups' potential for *becoming* can turn them into "the object[s] of aid and protection" (Agamben 1995). "Bare life (as defined in conflict or emergency aid/development zones) is life in the precipice of potentiality—as a living corpse 'in need' of rebirth to bios through outside intervention" (Fluri 2012: 40). ALLY's politics of empowerment was an attempt to reject the isolation and abandonment of bare life by providing marginalized women with a level of care that demonstrates the potentiality of bare life for becoming "proper." Yet, such intervention efforts are not free of criticisms. Jennifer Fluri (2012), for instance, has demonstrated how international workers at aid agencies and NGOs in post-Taliban Afghanistan justified receiving aid dollars by reducing Afghan lives to bare life and pathologizing them as incompetent, childlike, and lacking capacity. By creating rescue narratives about the suffering of helpless Afghans if foreign intervention did not exist—and at times accumulating capital with "best-selling" books about the trauma and abuse of Afghan women—international aid workers continued to position capitalist modernity as a prime method for rescuing bare life. They constructed Afghan lives as being in need of transformation into proper life while defining proper life by their subjective claims and politicized perspectives (Fluri 2012). Here, I recognize Fluri's critique of NGOs that transform marginalized women's bodies into symbolic sites of protection that are in need of saving. But I argue that ALLY's politics of empowerment, while subjectively defining bios (as explained in Chapter 5), did not reduce clients to bare life. By emphasizing the transformation of the clients (into artists, teachers, fashion designers, and poets), they could argue for the potentiality of rebirth through aid, thus justifying their fundraising practices. Their claims for the necessity of social intervention, however, were also a critique of unjust social structures that had left clients in need of intervention. By attending to the needs, desires, talents, and passions of the clients, who were socially and politically abandoned, they had engaged in the radical and political task of *caring* while recognizing the agency of the women who relied on their resources. To support, honor, and empower the vulnerabilities of the clients was to protest the socially and historically constructed discourses of gender, ethnicity, class, and sexuality that portrayed clients as devoid of value.

While identity politics in the West is also characterized by showcasing the capabilities and worth of marginalized groups (the feminist movement has emphasized women's equal capabilities, and advocacy for refugees has entailed discussions of their social and economic contributions), conceptualizing the marginality of ALLY's clients as *bare life* allows us to better envision the necessity of insisting on their capabilities above all. Using the rhetoric of capabilities to challenge clients' stigmatized social status was a form of identity politics capable of challenging multiple and intersectional systems of gender, class, sexual, and ethnic inequality without reducing identity politics to advocacy for one stigmatized identity. Theories of intersectionality, in fact, were constructed to reject practices of identity politics that had failed to consider the variations of the struggles of their constituency along the lines of their multiple marginalized identities. Advocacy for social groups subjugated at the intersection of various systems of inequality required repertoire and framing practices distinct from those practiced by large-scale political movements, which often emphasize one identity at the expense of others. By moving from a *human rights* approach to an *empowerment* approach to advocacy, the staff could challenge public assumptions about clients and problematize the injustices suffered by them without drawing from the rights framework that often emphasizes a singular identity.

The Inaccessibility of Rights

> Women's rights and children's rights are political in Iran. Always remember this! Whenever there is a discussion of rights, it becomes political. So, we can't easily work on these issues, neither women's rights nor children's rights. But considering the external obstacles, we can create an education plan that won't cause us any trouble even if it leaks outside. But [it can only work] slowly.... I always say right is something you take, no one gives it to you. I have always taught people that you have to go and take your right and don't give up. But keep in mind that you don't have to die taking it either. [Do it in a way] so you don't end up in jail or you don't have to emigrate. (Fatemeh, Foreign Affairs Personnel)

In our interview, Fatemeh, who identifies as a women's rights activist, recounted stories of her activism and her numerous quarrels with state officials before joining ALLY. Wary of government repression if ALLY's program leaked out, she approached me the first day of my fieldwork to ask about the nature of my research and caution me about the implications of my writings. That day, I met Fatemeh in an orientation class, where she told a group of newly admitted clients about the importance of knowing and demanding their rights as women. "This is a country where they have impinged on your rights," she told the young women. "You need to speak loud and clear with your chin up, so you can take your right," she said, standing tall in front of the class, with a fierce and commanding posture. After the session, she asked me if the content of my work could be read by her before being published. Behind ALLY's closed doors, the staff and clients freely spoke of their rights, criticized the government, and critiqued a multitude of inequalities shaping Iran's social and political life. These conversations resembled the *contentious talks* and *oppositional speech acts* identified by Hank Johnston (2005, 2006) as common in repressive states and in spaces away from the surveillance of authorities (such as coffee shops, book clubs, small circles of friends, or informally structured groups and organizations). In particular, *resistant contention* is common to repressive states where actor constitution requires innovative actions for claims-making to open spaces for the formation and emergence of collective action.

While contentious talks were common at ALLY's women's empowerment program behind closed doors, the organization's public image was nonthreatening and apolitical; its focus was on providing impoverished women with opportunities for self-realization and personal growth. It was thus logical for ALLY's staff to caution me about the implications of my writings if they were to make public what was meant to remain behind closed doors. Encouraging women to know and demand their rights, several employees told me, is perceived as "dangerous business" by the government. The implications of engaging in identity politics by the evocation of women's rights were also described by Fatemeh as imprisonment or forced migration. Her remark about the necessity of creating an educational program that would not "cause trouble" demonstrates the perceived need for taking an approach to advocacy that refrains from using the politicized rhetoric of "rights."

The concept of political opportunity structure (POS) (McAdam, Tarrow, and Tilly 2001) in the social movement literature emphasizes the importance of *context*. By identifying factors exogenous to social movements, POS points to the dimensions of the political environment that affect the methods and strategies employed by movements (McAdam 1982; Kitschelt 1986; Tarrow 1994; McAdam, McCarthy, and Zald 1996) as well as the framing strategies available to activists (Snow et al. 1986; Snow and Benford 1988). In studies conducted on women's activism in Iran, scholars have documented the impact of changing political opportunity structures on the framing and tactics of women's rights movements (Moghadam and Gheytanchi 2010). The increasing political repression as hard-liners take control of the state, the imprisonment of women's rights activists on charges of spying for Western governments or spreading propaganda, and the bolstering of the Iranian state's security apparatus resulting from the U.S. government's rhetorical war on Iran have limited the opportunities for women's rights advocacy in Iran.

ALLY's purposeful dismissal of the rights rhetoric in favor of emphasizing clients' capabilities reflected the absence of political opportunities for rights advocacy in Iran. Identity political movements often link marginalized identities (e.g., women, sexual or racial minorities, etc.) to a "universal" conception of human rights. And in most humanitarian work, these universal conceptions of rights are called on to transform "victims into sites of 'humanitarian' biopolitics" (Fluri 2012: 12). But this repertoire of identity politics—group identity formation and rights-claiming—has faced backlash in contexts where liberal discourses of individual rights conflict with national political norms. In the context of Iran, the liberal discourse of rights-seeking has been subjected to state repression when seen as an ideological threat to political Islam.

As explained in Chapter 2, in the immediate aftermath of the 1979 revolution, the provisional government and revolutionary forces denied the legitimacy of rights talk for women as the tool of "Western imperialist" forces (Osanloo 2006). By the 1980s, a form of Islamic feminism had emerged in Iran that motivated a vocal women's movement to use the framework of rights-seeking, "but now a hybrid notion of rights informed by both civil legality and Islamic principles" (Osanloo 2012). Osanloo's ethnographic research demonstrates the presence of "rights talk" among Iranian women who utilize this discourse to articulate their experiences. Rights talk in Iran, however, experienced a setback with the presidency of conservative candidate Ahmadinejad (2005–2013), who criticized the rights language in favor of emphasizing relational identities (Osanloo 2012). Within this historical and political context, "knowledge about rights in Iran is dynamic, intersubjective, and relational, while it is also politicized by the state" (Osanloo 2012: 503).

Unlike the frameworks of human rights or women's rights, which were politically charged, presenting ALLY's intervention in terms of discovering and managing talents would paint its work as benevolent and unthreatening. By focusing on capabilities as inherent to marginalized women and empowerment as a process whereby such capabilities are actualized, ALLY depicted its clients as worthwhile recipients of social services and its own activities as carrying the potentiality of rebirth. Hence, the organizational narrative of capabilities reflected the opportunities and cultural discourses available to ALLY for advocacy and identity politics.

The framing practices utilized by ALLY's staff did not merely reflect the limitations imposed by cultural and political discourses; they also reflected a shared set of beliefs about the effectiveness and desirability of certain advocacy practices as opposed to others. Many of my interviewees distinguished ALLY's work from the activities of the larger women's movement in Iran to explain their deviation from conventional practices of identity politics. Investing in clients' intellectual and social growth and educating the public about the impoverished women's potentials and capabilities, they believed, were effective measures for a gradual yet guaranteed transformation in the mainstream culture. ALLY's workers prioritized gradual and grassroots "cultural transformation" carried out by NGOs over top-down legal and institutional change demanded through large-scale protest.

Mobilization of Culture

> [We are] not like the women's movement in the sense of holding banners and talking about taking your rights, because I think that doesn't make sense. Because it's just an action, and if that core belief is not behind it, nothing will change. Even if the law changes—OK, for example, look at Egypt. It's been a hundred years, not really a hundred years, but it's been a long time since the female circumcision law was put in place, but it's still prevalent because there has been no attitude change. It's correct that law is very important, but the law is not useful without a core change inside and in your consciousness; otherwise, it will all continue [to remain the same]. So we decided to start at the grassroots level and build a foundation, to work with kids in their teenage years. And everyone was asking me why don't you bring little kids instead? I said no, because these girls are very capable and I really believe in them, and why [should I abandon them] if this group of people has already been marginalized and no one cares about them? (Maryam, Founder)

I had asked Maryam to share her thoughts on ALLY's place within the larger women's movement in Iran. Her response demonstrates her vision for ALLY as an instrument of social change while distinguishing its work from conventional practices of protest movements. By deemphasizing the importance of top-down legal and structural changes, she advocated for a grassroots cultural change through empowering marginalized women. "If Iran is to change," she told me in the same interview, "women play a key role.... If you want to change a patriarchal society, mothers must be empowered." Her belief in the young women's potential for transforming Iran was also evident in her quick rebuttal to those accounts that rendered as inconsequential ALLY's investment in those who were imagined as already past their prime age for change. Quick to deploy the rhetoric of capability, she spoke of ALLY's clients as worthy recipients of aid when confronted with the idea of investing in children as better conduits of social change. Other staff at ALLY similarly criticized society's desire for quick, forceful, and top-down social change while insisting on the power of gradual cultural transformation:

> I always say change is like a drop of water in a pond, it has a ripple effect, and the impact expands from the person to family and from the family to society. You can definitely make a positive impact on social trends by changing perspectives. It won't happen quickly. Look! I was reading about women's history in Europe; it took three hundred years before women could get into the Vienna Philharmonic Orchestra only twenty years ago.... We don't have any voice today, but our voice will come out tomorrow when our girls stand up and say 'We are here!' Then you will see [the impact of] our work. Cultural work is like running water, it infiltrates slowly. Cultural work is not a one-night thing. (Fatemeh, Foreign Affairs Personnel)

I heard similar stories and analogies from other administrators, who remained hopeful about the social impact of ALLY if it were to be seen as a gradual and long-term approach to cultural change. In a way, they envisioned a future possibility of collective action and social change should a *critical mass* (Oliver, Marwell, and Teixeira 1985) develop. First used as a loose metaphor by social movement activists and scholars, critical mass theory has become central to theories of social movement, explaining change as emanating from the activity of "a small segment of the population that chooses to make big contributions to the collective action while the majority do little or nothing" (Oliver, Marwell, and Teixeira 1985: 524). Investment in ALLY's clients as "agents of social change," seen through the framework of critical mass theory, meant that wide social change could occur if a significant number of marginalized women internalized and embraced the feminist values of the organization and passed them on to the larger community. Clients were explicitly spoken of as "agents of change" and "mothers of the next generation" who carried the potential of disrupting the cycle of patriarchal control:

> What I understand about ALLY's objective is that we don't concern ourselves with the past generation. Our focus is on maintaining the girls' mental health in their families. Our emphasis is on the next generations, since these are the future women and mothers of this society or whatever society they live in. [Our goal is to stop] these views . . . [from being] transferred linearly to their children or in their marriages. . . . We teach them that this is a vicious cycle. If you get trapped in it, you will be just like your mom and your daughter will be just like you. . . . The focus is on the next generation. (Mina, Social Worker)

Social change, according to ALLY's workers, was a slow and gradual process carried out through investment in the knowledge and consciousness of marginalized groups. The impact of clients on the next generation was seen as a force capable of impacting the larger community and society in due time. This investment was also discussed in terms of reducing the cost of the social abandonment of marginalized groups and their subsequent manipulation by the state apparatus.

> I don't think it's good that there are some people in society who have no opportunity or chance for growth and they become the elements that the society has to pay for later. For example, I strongly believe that here and in Karamooz[2] we are reducing [the number of] those who are subject to governmental manipulation . . . groups such as Basij[3] often manipulate and use those

groups who are economically suffering [to do their dirty work] in exchange for little money . . . to have a better society, it's absolutely crucial to not have a radicalized social group, people who hate other social classes due to no exposure to them. (Hamid, Teacher)

Hamid's statement reveals the intention of ALLY's workers—whether to empower women as mothers or to protect the impoverished from political exploitation—to invest in marginalized groups who otherwise would be subject to control and exploitation. They envisioned social change as emanating from consciousness-raising in the context of NGOs. Trust in their ability to create long-lasting cultural change was evident in Hamid's statement:

Because of the activities of NGOs and other groups and individuals over the last few years, society's outlook to issues of working children, minorities, or women has gotten a lot better. There is still a long way to go, I won't deny that, but it's gotten better. For example, I remember in the past when you saw a father beating his child, this was seen as a normal thing. But it's not like this anymore, people who are aware will say, "What are you doing? It's your child but you have no right to beat them!" Or when it comes to working children on the streets, now disrespectful or insulting behaviors have lessened a lot. . . . I think a big part of it is due to NGOs and their cultural work. (Hamid, Teacher)

The narratives of ALLY's workers reflected an optimistic outlook toward NGOs and their impact on cultural trends as well as on the governmental institutions with which ALLY's clients often dealt. Through tireless advocacy for its clients, ALLY was favorably known among the police forces and judges who were responsible for handling clients' cases. Prior to ALLY's advocacy, the cases of juvenile delinquents were referred to correctional facilities, where they were often mishandled, but now, the prosecutors and police were quick to refer such cases to ALLY, Fatemeh told me in her office as she ended a positive phone conversation with a prosecutor handling a client's case. This, according to Fatemeh, revealed a significant attitude change and growing respect for impoverished and abused young women among officials and responsible agencies.

While many of the staff at times spoke despondently about the social impact of a small NGO, they continued to construct narratives of hope in which gradual cultural change cultivated by NGOs such as ALLY would transform the future of the Iranian society when enough people formed a critical mass. The inability of the organization to engage in rights-claiming or to form organized protests did not prevent employees from envisioning change as emanating from alternative strategies. My participants believed in the impact of NGOs, however gradual and small, on governmental institutions such as law enforcement agencies or the judiciary system. ALLY's investment in clients' talents was also seen as critical to helping clients develop an agentic self, one that is capable of demanding change in the absence of expected cultural shifts:

> When their talent blossoms, the person who used to get beaten up going down the street, when she learns how to play the piano, she is not the same person. No matter what you do, she won't go back to that old mindset. Because she has changed, and she has self-confidence. She will change from a beaten-up person to one that says, "I am a human, I have something to say, I am an artist!" (Omid, Managing Director)

Identity Politics and Political Context

Rather than assuming the absence of identity politics when rights advocacy is repressed, this study demands that we trace social actors' desires, perceptions, and actions to methods of identity politics that defy our conceptual frameworks. Emphasizing or investing in the capabilities of marginalized groups is not placed at the center of identity political advocacy in the West (while capabilities are surely discussed within these movements, the rhetorical emphasis remains on recognizing marginalized groups' "equal rights"). ALLY's departure from conventional identity political mobilization tactics demonstrates a creative utilization of frames, resources, and opportunities for identity construction.

In this chapter, I have argued that limited political opportunity for rights advocacy in Iran, among other factors, has resulted in the emergence of a distinct form of identity politics carried out by NGOs that adopt unique advocacy frames to avoid surveillance and repression by authorities. Since this chapter examines the availability of political opportunities for identity politics under the authoritarian state of Iran in comparison to "liberal democracies," where identity political movements have grown substantially over the last few decades, it is important to complicate this comparison by noting the limitations of the democratic/authoritarian binary often reinforced in such discussions. While Western countries are often labeled as democratic, Martin Gilens and Benjamin Page's (2014) study has demonstrated that average American citizens and mass-based interest groups have little to no independent influence on public policy, even though Americans enjoy regular contested elections and freedom of the press. The control of the economic elite over American politics and elections represents an oligarchical political system rather than a democracy by most measures. Authoritarian practices are not unique to those governments labeled as "authoritarian." The increasing militarized response of the police in the United States and Europe toward mass protests, the arrest and imprisonment of whistleblowers, and the enactment of laws that criminalize anti-pipeline and environmental activists as ecoterrorists are clear examples of how political activism is not free of consequence in Western "liberal democracies."

Constructing Iran as an authoritarian country where democracy is absent also has its own limitations. Liberal principles and democratic practices in Iran are simultaneously present and highly restricted. High public turnouts for presidential elections in which the ruling elite exercises a great deal of power, citizen participation in associations, volunteer networks, and nongovernmental organizations, and the presence of a courageous and harassed press demonstrate a public engagement with democratic practices for building a civil society under an authoritarian government. Hence, democratic practices can exist within authoritarian contexts, as Lisa Wedeen's (2007) study on qat chews as a form of deliberative democracy in prewar Yemen demonstrates. Wedeen also reveals that democratic practices are not inherently liberal. In Iran, while many of the public's demands are liberal in nature—demands for freedom of choice, freedom of expression, and gender equality—not all are articulated within a liberal framework. While the Islamic Republic of Iran rejects such liberal principles as individual right and liberty in favor of Islamic principles, it has not been repressive of all liberal values and rights talk. Osanloo's (2009) research points to the formation of legitimized rights talk in the postrevolution state because of the state's blended Islamic and civil institutions. The "West versus the Rest" dichotomy is therefore inadequate for understanding the great diversity of political conceptions of personhood and rights across cultural contexts.

5

The Invisible Class

After a few weeks of fieldwork, I had come to see the daily complaints of clients and their arguments with the staff as part of everyday life at ALLY. Eye-rolling and side conversations in classrooms were common methods of expressing discontent. On a rainy afternoon, in a community development class designed to increase clients' sense of social responsibility, the escalation of arguments between the clients and the teachers brought to the surface many of the previously unspoken tensions. Crossing their arms and looking away while sitting around a table, the clients stayed silent after the teachers, Barmak, Hamid, and Shirin, asked them to read their proposals for the community development project of their choice. This was the third week of refusing to do the assignment and assigning the blame on lack of time or the difficulty of coming up with ideas. The teachers' last resort was a warning they hoped would do the trick. After being advised that not completing their class assignments could affect their grade and their progress in ALLY's program, the clients' relaxed and uninterested attitude transformed into a mode of rebellion I had not seen before. After all, finishing ALLY's program successfully and on time was clients' ticket to gaining employment and achieving their goal of independence. "You can't force us to do anything!" Mahsa, one of the clients, said loudly as she straightened her back and looked the teachers in the eyes. "I have a thousand problems, and 'doing something good for society' is the last thing I care about," Mahsa continued as she passed a glimpse on everyone's face in class, waiting for others to chime in with their support.

Clients' lack of interest in completing the assignment had become apparent to me weeks prior to this event. I often heard the young women, outside the class, mocking the content of the course and the assignments in front of me for being *chert o pert* (useless), hoping to get the same reaction from me. Inside the classroom, they often kept such comments to themselves in order to, I assumed, maintain a respectful relationship with their teachers. That day, the clients were especially blunt: "I don't know why we are wasting time doing things that will take us nowhere," Afsoon, another client, said in support of Mahsa to object to the inclusion of a community development class in ALLY's program. Soon, arguments between the clients and the teachers extended to arguments among the clients over the fairness of some complaints and the benefits of certain classes, such as the one they were all sitting at. The escalation of arguments in a class of twenty and the teachers' inability to gain control of the room left teachers with what they saw as their only choice: Dividing the class into three small groups based on the amount of work the women had completed. Each group was to be guided and run by one of the teachers in an effort to regain control of the room and respond more effectively to clients' grievances.

I moved to the second floor with a group of clients who had firmly refused to complete the class assignment and were known for their "naysaying attitude." This attitude, Barmak told me later, was the reason for their separation and why the class was at times "unproductive." From those clients, I heard complaints directed at the content and the structure of ALLY's program: "We sit here and play with this mud that the sponsors are paying for. It's such a waste of time, money, and resources," Afsoon said as she questioned the necessity of taking a sculpting course at ALLY while having more pressing needs for finishing the program and finding employment. I had heard clients in monthly meetings with the managing team similarly questioning the logic behind taking classes that they saw as irrelevant to their immediate needs and goals. Clients took seriously classes such as computer, English, accounting, Microsoft, and clerical skills, which were part of ALLY's economic empowerment program. The goal of such courses was to provide the young women with the necessary skills and certificates for acquiring jobs and alleviating their poverty.

ALLY's social education and art therapy program, while enjoyed by many clients, was not always received with the same level of commitment. The necessity of workshops and classes on community development, reproductive rights, sexualities, painting, and sculpting, which were held for informative and therapeutic purposes, was often contested among the clients. This does not mean that these classes were not beneficial or enjoyed by the young women. Clients often told me that, prior to attending ALLY, they had dreamt of attending painting or dance classes and that such experiences brought them an exhilarating sense of achievement. Some had gained considerable skills in painting and photography, exhibiting and selling their work at art galleries in Iran and abroad with the patronage of the organization. Others had used art, dance, or martial arts classes to heal from past traumas. But the inclusion of such workshops and classes was the reason why finishing ALLY's program would take clients a total of three years and require them to attend the organization five days a week, eight hours a day. Dealing with extreme poverty and often the family's abuse if the clients could not establish themselves as contributors to the household through housekeeping or paid labor, many young women saw ALLY's three-year program as incongruent with the demands of their daily lives. Meanwhile, clients' efforts to render as legitimate their concerns in the eyes of the staff had proven difficult. "You might not see the benefits of these classes right now, but you'll see them later," was the response of the teachers and the managing directors, who wished to assure clients about the unforeseen advantages of the classes they saw as useless. "We get the same response over and over again. It's as if we are talking to a wall," one of the clients told me in a private conversation, expressing resentment toward a response she deemed patronizing.

I was not sure how to make sense of staff's uninterested attitude toward hearing clients' complaints as legitimate concerns. I had difficulty understanding why many staff insisted on maintaining ALLY's program as is despite the growing complaints of the clients and their own admission of its impracticality, which had become apparent due to the increasing dropout rate. At times, I thought the staff's behavior represented the power struggle between the privileged middle-class workers and their marginalized clients, as many scholars have argued in their analysis of beneficence or philanthropic paternalism.[1] Yet, in any given state or NGO-led program, there is a diversity of motivations among hierarchically positioned actors and the variety of discourses operating simultaneously (Radhakrishnan 2015). NGOs and empowerment programs witness tensions between the stakeholders and clients who are often of varying class and ethnic backgrounds. Thayer's (2010) study reveals how collaborations between urban middle-class feminists in Brazil and their rural sisters created tensions and conflicts due to each group's different class composition and standpoint. While urban feminists emphasized body politics and reproductive rights, the rural women prioritized land rights, employment, and establishing a voice for peasant women. The unequal class and ethnic position of stakeholders and clients and the varying structural opportunities to exercise their voice (Rao and Sanyal 2010) shape the dynamic of relationships within NGOs. In spaces fraught with inequalities of power and privilege, where all are invited to equally participate in decision-making, "we have a case not of deliberative democracy but of discursive competition that requires individuals and groups to declare their demands in the hopes of being heard" (Rao and Sanyal 2010: 167).

Here, I shift the question from why ALLY workers ignored clients' complaints to ask about the institutional discourses that necessitated maintaining ALLY's program as is despite the growing dissatisfaction of the clients. I do so by emphasizing the larger institutional texts that coordinate the actions and consciousness of social actors (Smith 2005). In this chapter, I show how the daily decisions made by the staff, such as weighing the legitimacy of complaints and assessing the necessity of changing or maintaining the program, were shaped by class discourses of success and class-based social processes of inclusion and exclusion, which in turn shaped organizational narratives and definitions of empowerment. I also explain the everyday conflicts between the staff and clients as a class tension that was formed by conflicting middle-class and working-class discourses of privilege and justice.

More specifically, I argue that in class-based systems of privilege and marginalization, the social processes of exclusion render the working class and the poor as *lacking* what the middle class *have*. With embodied cultural capital being one of those elements that are lacking, empowerment programs are compelled to help their clients develop the cultural capital necessary for class mobility. Following this logic of empowerment, ALLY's program had transformed into one where empowerment had come to mean skillfully *performing* middle class. With a great deal of organizational efforts directed toward granting clients a middle-class *cultural capital* necessary for gaining and maintaining employment in middle-class work environments, clients' immediate need for employment and financial gain was deprioritized. The class-based discursive articulations of success and empowerment embedded within ALLY's program had resulted in equating *performing* middle class with *being* empowered. This chapter offers a critical analysis of the highly invisible class discourses and middle-class subjectivities that shaped ALLY's empowerment program and resulted in clients' growing dissatisfaction and contentious relationships with staff.

Being Poor and Performing Middle Class

Escaping poverty and gaining financial independence through vocational training were the core objectives of ALLY around which most organizational planning and structuring was done. This structuring applied to the arrangement of spaces (where most building rooms were designated as classrooms) and time (when the everyday and weekly schedules separated courses based on subject) and the division of responsibilities (when an "educational unit" monitored the clients' progress at the organization closely). In fact, when entering the organization, it was easy to assume that one had entered a *moasese amoozeshi* (an educational institute), a title many of the staff and clients themselves used to refer to ALLY.

Despite concerted efforts toward preparing clients for the job market, the prospect of finding gainful employment with which clients could acquire a sense of independence was not hopeful. With the high rates of unemployment in Iran, even for the college graduates (Amuzegar 2004), and the high costs of living due to the neoliberal economic policies of the state and the inflation exacerbated by global sanctions, "housing poverty" (Sheykhi 2007) has been a condition with which many clients and their families struggled. Living on one's own and separating from an abusive or unhealthy familial environment were therefore not practical outcomes for which clients could strive. Despite such discouraging circumstances, the possibility of making more money than what clients earned at sweatshops was a promising opportunity for which the young women were willing to strive. Any form of financial gain, ALLY's staff had come to believe through interacting with clients' families, could protect the young women from control and abuse at home by providing them with the status of breadwinner. "When they get older and gain financial independence," Mina, a social worker at ALLY, told me, "they become the helping hand of their families. And their family is not going to bother them as much."

The objective of gaining financial independence through vocational training might appear as the most straightforward aspect of ALLY's women's empowerment program. Yet, the practical realities of providing such training to ALLY's target population had proven more challenging than initially thought. The original program was only half as long as it was during my fieldwork. A twelve- to fifteen-month program was originally designed to cater to the dire financial needs of the young women. At that point, art, dance, and similar classes were being held, but they simply served as recreational activities that could help with women's mental health and, thus, their capacity to learn. That program, however, soon proved ineffective:

> The problem was that they had no communication skills. Their behavioral and communication skills were so weak and so low that they would get fired from their jobs. So, we forced them to pass a two-and-a-half-year program and then decide what specialty they want to choose, decide where their talents are, and after they finished that program and got their certificate, we would see if they were ready or not. (Mina, Social Worker)

> When the girls come to me for their [job] briefings, how much can I teach them in that one session [about the techniques of doing interviews]? I tell them some general things; the things you can find in many of the books out there. Things like you need to look polished, how to speak, how to respond to some common questions. It depends on the girls too, if they get it in the

first interview or if they have to screw up five interviews and find out what it's all about in the sixth one. (Ava, Foreign Affairs Personnel)

Over the years, the perceived lack of behavioral and communication skills among clients had resulted in multiple changes in the length and the content of the program. After noticing the inability of the clients to acquire and hold jobs due to a lack of "interpersonal skills," administrators decided to lengthen the program to a three-year one in which women would go through intensive therapy while attending multiple workshops on communication skills in addition to their social education and vocational training. The management believed the new program was more effective in preparing women for the job market. ALLY's focus on the subjective transformation of the clients as a central element of their empowerment was also partially done in the same light. The understanding was that coming from the strict and limiting environments in which they were raised, most women had not developed the necessary skills for representing themselves in ways that their future work environment would demand. Some women, for instance, especially lacked the ability to work in the public sphere alongside men who were unrelated to them.

> One of the girls that I was working with as a coordinator wouldn't look me in the eye in the beginning. She used to say there is no way she can talk to a man. But now she is getting better slowly. She couldn't say a word. (Barmak, Teacher)

> During the first year, none of them wanted me as a male therapist because they weren't comfortable with me. But I give people chances. [One of the girls] used to come here and would sit on that chair [pointing to the chair furthest away from him] and wouldn't look me in the eye. But now that client sits here [pointing to a nearby chair] and is very comfortable with me. This is an opportunity for them to meet people of a different kind. (Alborz, Psychologist)

The problem of being present and comfortable in public spaces and around unrelated men, I was told, was mostly an issue with the most impoverished Afghan women. It was also the history of sexual abuse and trauma that would deter many of the women from seeking proximity to men, who they associated with potential abuse. ALLY's founder and the team of directors as well as many of the staff, however, saw the presence of the male staff as a necessary component of empowerment.

> What is really great for the girls at [ALLY] is that they see men that don't have a sexual gaze. It's a safe space. I myself wear chador but see how comfortable I am when I come to [ALLY]! It's because [ALLY] is a safe space. This is awesome. The girls can see that people don't look at them as women or as someone to take sexual advantage of. They have male teachers, male therapists, male psychiatrists, male managing directors that eat breakfast and lunch with them. This says that you are a human. Doesn't matter what your gender is, you are a human. Even if you're a girl, I can be a man just sitting next to you. This is really good for the girls. It changes their criteria for friendships and relationships. (Rose, Social Worker)

Gaining financial independence and becoming empowered depended not solely on vocational training but on a variety of unforeseen circumstances to which the staff had to respond. ALLY was responsible for modeling the typical space of future work, and it had to be an ideal space in which the organization's principles of equality, respect, and human dignity were upheld. ALLY was regarded as a transitory space for class mobility; it not only offered job skills, it also provided impoverished clients with the opportunity to learn how to function in spaces from which they were previously excluded. Gaining employment as accountants, hairdressers, secretaries, or graphic designers would require women to shift spaces—to leave the slums and to enter spaces dominated by the middle class. Being present in such spaces and maintaining employment, the staff soon realized, required the ability to "perform" middle class by maintaining the appropriate appearance, speech, manners, and self-representation. The organization refused to provide assistance with finding jobs to those clients who, after three years, had not yet embodied this middle-class cultural capital. The "reputation of the organization could be harmed if we recommended girls who couldn't keep a job," Ava, a foreign affairs staff member, told me in an interview. In a conversation with Barmak, one of the teachers, I learned that the need for changing one's mannerism and speech was at one point expressed by the young women themselves:

> BARMAK: We used to constantly have meetings with other teachers and other people and a couple of psychologists to write our lesson plans. We had a meeting with the girls too and asked them, "What would you want to add to the program? What is lacking in ALLY? If we were to add a class, what do you want it to be about?" We asked for help from the girls, and the need for change came from the girls themselves. For example, having classes on "building relationships" was the girls' idea. Then we realized that these needs exist.
>
> FAE: Do you remember some of the other needs that the girls were talking about?
>
> BARMAK: Yeah, they were so interesting. The girls were saying them in very simple terms. For example, one of them was that [chuckles] we want to speak *gholombe solombe* [yuppie and uppity] because people care a lot about how we speak. Another thing was their appearance that was important to them.

Barmak spoke of clients' desire for learning "big words" and the "uppity" speaking style in the context of a conversation about the changing programs of ALLY and clients' participation in the new design. And he related the women's desire for change in their style of speaking and appearance to their low self-esteem—an organizational narrative often used to explain clients' actions and attitudes. Here, I argue, however, that the clients' request for learning and using "big words" demonstrates the larger social processes of inclusion and exclusion that are especially class-based. Pierre Bourdieu (1986) explains *cultural capital* as a set of symbolic elements acquired through being part of a particular social class. Taste, clothing, mannerisms, posture, and credentials are all different elements of cultural capital that determine one's position within the social order and chance for experiencing class mobility. Objectified and institutionalized forms of cultural capital are seen by one's material possessions, credentials, and degrees. Embodied cultural capital, such as one's accent, dialect, or interpersonal skills, also designates one's social status. What Bourdieu (1990) calls *habitus* is the embodiment of the habits and manners developed by being located in a particular social position. The need to grant ALLY's clients the cultural capital necessary for inclusion in middle-class spaces was recognized by both the clients and the staff. Class-based systems of inclusion and exclusion are strongly present and their presence is recognized, but discourses often do not allow their own articulation. The dominant organizational narratives about raising clients' self-esteem by improving their interpersonal skills point to the staff's recognition of the importance of developing such skill sets without articulating them as effects of unequal class systems and exclusionary social processes. Class inequality and its effects hence remained unexplored, while clients' inability to maintain employment was commonly discussed.

Due to these challenges, ALLY's empowerment program had changed to an extensive three-year process of cultivating middle-class taste and persona in impoverished women. *Empowerment* had gradually shifted in convoluted ways; rather than entailing equipping clients with a substantive skill, it became about helping them appear middle class. Since many of the women lacked a high school education, the emphasis of a number of classes was on expanding their vocabulary and helping them articulate their thoughts in ways that gave the impression of having higher education. "If you had heard the girls a year ago, you couldn't believe they are the same people," Barmak told me proudly, explaining how the creative writing classes had expanded women's vocabulary and ability to express their views. The organization had also recognized the need for taking women to museums, restaurants, movie theaters, and on short vacations that would allow them to acquire cultural capital through experiences that are exclusive to the middle and upper classes. Similarly, cultivating a sense of interest and appreciation for art, music, and philosophy was part of the empowerment process, as it granted clients linguistic or artistic symbolic capital. The presence of these classes for women whose primary struggles were poverty and the accompanying violence demonstrates that for the middle-class staff of ALLY, the ability to appreciate a "higher" culture—as the middle class does—was an empowering goal for which women should strive.

What I really want to see is for the girls to have art workshops and not art classes. Not classes for learning how to paint or how to play the music, but to gain a social understanding of art. For example, the girls feel very alienated from philosophy or poetry, although their creative writing class compensates for that a bit. I would really love it if ALLY would do something so that the girls would reconcile with art and not think that artists are of such a different caliber that they can't relate to them. Because it's really not like that. From a social perspective, we can see that the texture that artists create is the same as the masses of people. (Hamid, Teacher)

Why would Hamid speak of appreciation for the arts or connecting with the world of poetry and philosophy as his ultimate hope for ALLY's clients? Why would the staff not take seriously the complaints of the impoverished women who repeatedly questioned the necessity of such programs for their well-being and success? In my formal and informal interviews, it was easy to see that, for the staff, clients' mastery of literature or passionate interest in art were indicators of having developed an empowered personhood. As they bragged about clients developing vocabulary and conversational skills, I realized that for many of the staff, acquiring middle-class cultural capital was empowerment itself. However, it is important to note that many young women also experienced their new skills as empowering. As I show in the next chapter, they particularly used organizational resources to articulate their own critique of class inequality and the staff's class privilege. Yet, the deep entanglement of the discourses of empowerment and the discursive class-based articulations of well-being had resulted in a common perception of empowerment as one's ability to display a middle-class persona.

When women's empowerment initiatives are implemented in poor rural settings, the focus is on their economic independence through making crafts, sustainable farming, and managing livestock. When empowerment programs are implemented in large urban areas like Tehran, the indicators of success are similarly shaped by cultural discourses of class and prestige commonly found in urban class-based economic and social settings. ALLY's program and the staff's perception of empowerment thus reflected the institutional texts that mark success by employability, type of occupation, education, and one's embodied cultural capital. Class, however, is a dynamic process, a site of political struggle, and more than a set of static positions filled by indicators of employment and housing (Lawler 2005). In fact, class is better understood in relational, rather than substantive, manifestations of class existence. This is to say that middle-class identities rely on "othering" the working class and envisioning a position of superiority. Stephanie Lawler (2005), in her analysis of middle-class identities, demonstrates how the poor are often described in terms of *lack*—of culture, of class, of taste, of ethics, and sometimes of humanity itself. "This constitution of working-class existence in terms of 'lack' is now so widespread as to be almost ubiquitous. It informs social policy ('social exclusion' presumes a deficit model, as do discussions of 'widening participation') and is present even in some (though by no means all) analyses which are sympathetic to working-class people" (Lawler 2005: 434).

Discourses of empowerment are activated by the daily activities of social actors who engage with those discourses through retelling of cultural narratives of success and performing class as a relational construct. While ALLY's employees were particularly critical of class inequality and those cultural narratives that depicted their clients as less than worthy, the larger class discourses of success determined their assumptions, actions, and decisions. They envisioned vertical class mobility for the poor as an ultimate goal for survival and well-being not simply by obtaining employment and wealth but also by embodying the "higher" culture and enjoying leisure activities that accompany economic success. Empowering the poor thus became a process whereby clients mastered middle-class performances by cultivating their cultural capital.

ALLY's workers often expressed their heartfelt commitment to providing clients with opportunities similar to those they provided for their own loved ones. I appreciated greatly, as did many of the clients, the staff's kind and diligent efforts to furnish clients with learning and leisure opportunities. Educators and researchers have long focused on adolescents' brain development and cognition and searched for ways to increase their productivity and ease their transition to adulthood. These narratives recommend providing children and adolescents with opportunities for exploring vocational interests within educational settings. The role of educators is explained as helping adolescents with building career awareness and preferences (Wadlington, Elizondo, and Wadlington 2012). Leisure activities and opportunities to explore new interests are discussed as elements that are central to adolescent identity and occupational development (Vondracek and Skorikov 2011). ALLY's educational program, designed based on relevant research on adolescent development and trauma, emphasized the exploration of vocational interests and leisure activities as central to young women's empowerment.

The middle-class staff of ALLY imagined teen years that could be spent exploring the "finer points" of an education. They thus invested resources and energy into providing the young women with an education that would allow them to explore their talents and interests. Their efforts, however, were often criticized by the impoverished clients for whom this was considered a luxury, as their teen years were simply a point of time connecting an unlived childhood to a forced adulthood. The young women, who had been obligated to work and take responsibility as children, often rejected the plausibility of self-care through participation in ALLY's art, dance, and social education programs. This is not to say that the clients did not enjoy or benefit from those efforts. As I mentioned previously, I spoke with many clients for whom learning to sing, dance, or paint was an unachievable yet salient dream before joining ALLY. The clients expressed a great deal of interest and appreciation for such opportunities but often found themselves struggling with navigating their daily realities within the world of possibilities now known to them. These possibilities, they knew, were temporary opportunities that would be out of reach soon after leaving ALLY. During this three-year program, clients showed continuous and consistent "growth," according to the staff. Many went from having few interpersonal skills to being able to present themselves linguistically, in appearance, and in interests as middle class. During this process, however, as I showed in the beginning of the chapter, clients' dissatisfaction with the program was also continuously growing, resulting in everyday tensions and conflicts at ALLY. Adding courses and programs that helped with clients' development of life skills or interests had involved extending the length of the program, as the process of embodying cultural capital is a lengthy one that requires continuous rehearsals.

Although remaining poor and performing middle class could be seen as an achievement by the staff, who saw empowerment as developing the proper mannerisms, modes of feeling, and patterns of speech, being poor and only performing middle class had proven extremely unsatisfying for the clients, who desired some immediate financial gain and were under extreme pressure by their families to contribute to the household either as breadwinners or housekeepers. The experiences of social workers had proven that attending ALLY required constant negotiation with women's guardians, whose conditions of poverty required family members of all ages to contribute to the urgent needs of the family.

> The families, because they are poor, expect their kids [to work] instead of going to classes ... [they ask them] "What money are you bringing home? If you are there every day, all day, how are you helping the family?" Because of these kinds of pressures from the families, many of the girls decide to quit, especially in the first three months.... We work a lot on this [mentality] by telling them that dear mom and dad, if your daughter keeps doing menial work at a shop right now, she will remain a worker forever. Give it two years, and she will be running the shop! But they are right too. How can someone who is worried about their food for the day even think about waiting for two years for their kids to get a degree and find a job? (Rose, Social Worker)

I heard from social workers about the never-ending struggle of ALLY to convince clients' parents to allow their daughters' participation in a three-year program. Many of the clients I spoke with also complained about the length of the program and the impossibility of pleasing both ALLY and their families. Young women's initial excitement about attending ALLY was gradually replaced by resentment and complaints. "What happened to that Mona who was so hopeful and energetic in the beginning?" Mona, a senior client at ALLY, said with teary eyes at the end of the community development class that had gone sour. Mona had found it impossible to comply with the demands of the program while working toward her goals and maintaining peace at home. Many staff members were aware of clients' dissatisfaction and unhappiness:

They complain a lot about how long [the program] is, and it really is. One of my clients was telling me "I understand! I see that my relationships are much better, my communication is much better and I have better relations with people and I have less problems. But I had a friend who started this with me. I came to [ALLY] and she went to learn sewing and working with machines; now she is making two million tomans [US$700 at the time] a month. I can see how awful her relationships are and that I'm doing so much better, but she is making two million a month!" (Arezoo, Psychologist)

The workers who recognized clients' complaints as legitimate would often speak of this problem as a dilemma for which they had no concrete solution. Designing and implementing a program that provided clients with ample time for recovering from past traumas and developing social skills while immediately equipping them with vocational skills capable of producing income had proven extremely difficult, if not impossible. Ava, the foreign affairs worker, told me about ALLY's limited options:

On one hand, if the program is shorter and less than three years, the changes that we expect [to see] don't happen, and it's not like we have reached our goals this way either! On the other hand, when it's three years long and you are in a tough situation, I have even seen this among middle-class girls, they see marriage as the solution. . . . When you are in a tough situation, you start thinking about detours! (Ava, Foreign Affairs Personnel)

As a result of the growing tension between the clients and the staff, the necessity of implementing a new program that would be more conscious of clients' needs was recognized and prioritized by the directing team. Raha had proposed changes in the length and the structure of the program that could allow clients to attend ALLY while engaging in entrepreneurial work such as handicraft making at the center. However, this could only be done if the number of art and social education courses that the clients were required to take was substantially reduced.

The Invisible Class Discourse in Program Development

"My father expects me to decide if I'd marry a suitor after a couple times of speaking to him. There's no way I can go on the many dates you say is going to help me get to know him better," Parisa, a sixteen-year-old Iranian client, said with a frustrated voice in a premarriage counseling workshop in which clients were advised not to jump into marriages with men they did not fully know. "It all comes down to the skills you will have to learn to use to negotiate with your father and make him realize the negative effects of a rushed marriage," the teacher responded.

"Talk to him?" Parisa asked with a derisive tone. "What are you talking about? My dad's brain is on vacation! Besides, I can't be a *noonkhor* [dependent] forever! That's why he keeps mumbling 'marriage is the prophet's tradition,'" Parisa said disdainfully, mimicking her dad's voice.

Early and forced marriages were common problems among clients who lived in poverty and in families for whom early marriage of their daughters meant lessening their unbearable financial burdens. Some young women, on the other hand, would jump into marriages with their abusive partners or suitors they barely knew, as they saw marriage as a quick way out of their current miserable living conditions. ALLY had gone to great lengths to hire well-established counseling experts to hold workshops that could provide clients with life-changing advice. ALLY would consistently offer workshops on marriage and premarriage counseling with the hope that the information offered by counseling psychologists about the necessary conditions for a happy marriage would deter many women from making bad choices. The young women often expressed a great deal of interest in any opportunity to discuss dating, romantic relationships, or marriage. Many clients had boyfriends, were engaged to be married, or were sexually active outside of marriage, which made talking about boys and dating even more exciting. While they showed a great deal of interest in these workshops, what they could take from them was fairly limited. For Parisa, the dating advice offered in the workshop was a source of frustration for two reasons. For one, it demonstrated the secular middle-class teachers' lack of awareness of the cultural norms within clients' communities, where a long period of dating, while secretly practiced, is not permissible. Second, it showed teachers' lack of awareness of how practices such as forced and early marriages persist due to the poverty and meager resources of the families of the young women. Unable to provide the basic necessities for dependent family members, particularly girls who could not contribute to the household financially, families reluctantly found the marriage of their young daughters to be the only option. As Parisa clearly stated, her father's attempt at upholding the prophet's tradition was the result of his inability to provide for a dependent and not of a religious or misogynist mindset that could be reasoned with.

The content and the structure of the workshops that were formed based on academic research (often conducted on love-based relationships) showed little compatibility with the conditions of the poor in Iran. Various governmental organizations and private counseling centers across Iran offer premarital counseling and dating workshops for the upper- and middle-class youth who live a cosmopolitan lifestyle and can afford such services. Yet the same dating advice offered at ALLY had little practical application for the clients who lived in fundamentally different material and cultural circumstances. This problem was also evident in workshops on health and nutrition as well as classes on communication skills. While catering to clients' health and interpersonal skills was necessary for having a holistic women's empowerment program, the information offered in such classes had little practical value for clients who could not afford nutritional food, choose to date before marriage, or use words with tones and manners prescribed as "good communication" with their poor or working-class family members, who, according to clients, saw such speech as "snooty" and "deplorable." While Raha was aware of the impracticality of such classes and workshops for many of the young women, addressing the larger economic injustices the clients experienced was out of ALLY's sphere of influence. Parisa, therefore, like many other clients, showed a great deal of frustration and disruptive behavior in classes in which she felt alienated.

Similar concerns and complaints were directed toward other aspects of ALLY's program that reflected a class bias. I learned through my observations of courses such as community development that there was a strong organizational emphasis on cultivating in the young women the desire and ability to engage in social activism. In these courses, clients learned about the coconstitutive relationship between society and individuals and were introduced to creative grassroots initiatives. Clients were expected to envision, design, and carry out small community projects (building neighborhood libraries, running literacy classes for community members, cleaning the neighborhood, etc.) as part of the course requirement. ALLY's larger educational program had mandated that clients volunteer at nonprofit or nongovernmental organizations after passing their specialty courses. This volunteering experience and the community development courses were designed, I was told, to nourish in the young women a strong sense of "social responsibility." "Some of the girls are very self-centered," Shirin, a teacher, told me. "We designed these courses to tell them that they have responsibilities too."

> [We ask them] now that you are here and have learned things, what do you want to do for your society? We teach them the concepts of sustainable development, social activism, and social responsibility, and we tell them that you are responsible. If you are doing something for your society, you are not doing anyone a favor. It's a responsibility. (Barmak, Teacher)

ALLY's goal of showing marginalized women that they could be "agents of social change" capable of disrupting unjust social systems was an exciting one. I participated in community development classes dutifully and joyfully to uncover the impact of such education and to understand how these women perceived the mandate of taking responsibility toward a society that has turned its back to their struggles. I heard and saw a great deal of selfless decisions by the impoverished women who wished to help those less fortunate than themselves. During the first week of my research, I heard that following the devastating earthquake in the Philippines in 2013, the young women made a collective decision to forgo one month's supply of the daily fruit they received at ALLY so that the funds could be donated to those affected by the earthquake. While such collective and humanitarian efforts were common, I also came to witness a strong resistance to the idea of engaging in community service or doing unpaid volunteer work from many of the clients. While some of the women embraced the idea and the opportunity, many others rejected the necessity of engaging in community services on the grounds that their effort and energy must be channeled toward overcoming their daily and personal struggles.

The extreme poverty, long working hours, and chaotic households with which clients struggled daily did not allow them to envision engaging in a selfless social service as an empowering activity the way their middle-class teachers did. For many of them, activism was a middle-class leisure activity they simply could not afford. Some had encountered difficulties when implementing a community project for their previous classes. This experience had left them feeling that activism was less than empowering. While the teachers perceived themselves and their clients as equally responsible and capable of impacting their communities, the young impoverished ethnic-minority women found that their marginal status meant their voice and actions had little impact. As the women continued to resist the course content and assignments, the teachers insisted on developing in clients, who they saw as "self-centered," a sense of social responsibility deemed necessary for becoming agents of social change. Ava told me about how the often-ignored class dimension of volunteering services had hindered the development of this program:

> When we send them for volunteer work, they keep telling us that we live far away, do we have to go there? In all these years, only one or two of the girls did this passionately, and I think they were those living in our dormitory. The rest nagged and complained the whole time. This is the reality . . . the meaning of this work isn't really clear for them. We had briefing sessions to explain why, [and they kept asking] "Why should we work for free and pay for the commute too?" The reality is that in all societies, those who do volunteer work are [financially] secure, are of a particular social class, or are concerned for their society. Those who do volunteer work mostly do it for a line on a résumé or maybe they want to go to heaven or something. (Ava, Foreign Affairs Personnel)

Ava's statement suggests her awareness of the class dimension of volunteer and activist work, even though her job required explaining the importance of developing a sense of social responsibility to clients. For many of the young clients, however, community service and social activism were less than empowering. Doing unpaid work when their labor has been exploited and sacrificing their energy in a society where their well-being has been systematically overlooked were counterintuitive, especially when such work was done in the name of "self-empowerment." Moreover, subjecting oneself to rejection by one's community was less than empowering for many of the already marginalized clients, who faced serious obstacles in implementing their community projects. This is not to say that the clients were not interested in or did not see as valuable the act of service. In fact, I witnessed clients' compassionate and collective efforts to help those suffering by sacrificing their little share of resources. What they objected to was the demand placed on them irrespective of their status and outside the realm in which service could remain meaningful and empowering.

It is also important to note that while many clients showed disruptive behavior and refused to participate in community development projects, some others experienced a great sense of agency by envisioning themselves as capable of impacting their society though community service. This group of clients, inspired by the ideas learned at ALLY, wished to share the newly gained awareness with close family and community members. Many of the Afghan clients spoke hopefully about the day they could return to Afghanistan and run similar classes for women. Others had already begun communicating the new ideas with their close family members. In any case, it was apparent that most women found their circle of influence limited to intimate settings. The middle-class conceptions of agency and morality promoted by the middle-class staff, which entailed taking up larger and more ambitious projects, were rejected by impoverished women, who could not ignore the relation between class privilege and social efficacy.

6

Oppositional Consciousness and Solidarities

I walked behind everyone with Barmak as the class quietly moved from the second floor to the backyard, where Shirin had promised a game was awaiting us. Barmak, Shirin, and Hamid, all college-educated, middle class, and in their mid-twenties, taught a community development class at ALLY and believed in the importance of educating the young women on a range of social issues. Barmak began explaining the activity to me as we walked down the stairs. He was excited about implementing a pedagogical technique his colleague had discovered by searching for effective in-class activities online. "Everyone forms a straight line with an arm's length between them. We read a series of statements, and you step forward if the statement is true about you," Barmak enthusiastically explained. "Oh, I know what you are talking about!" I exclaimed. "We do this activity in our sociology classes." Barmak's description had reminded me of the "privilege walk" activity in which students are forced to confront their class and racial privileges by taking a step forward each time a statement about a priv-

---

Portions of this chapter previously appeared as Fae Chubin, "Glocalizing Women's Empowerment: Feminist Contestation and NGO Activism in Iran," *Journal of Contemporary Ethnography* 49, no. 6: 715–744. © Fae Chubin 2020. https://doi.org/10.1177/0891241620947135.

ilege that applies to them is read. Our conversation broke as we reached the backyard, and I began to wonder how such an activity would be useful or doable among a group of marginalized women who surely did not need a lesson in privilege. I soon found out that Shirin had made a few important changes. She walked past all of us standing in line and whispered a random character in our ear. I got a "thirty-four-year-old female doctor living in Tehran." Negar, an Afghan client standing next to me, told me that she got "a rural girl in poverty with illiterate parents." We were instructed to step forward if any of the statements read were achievable by our characters. The statements were about our ability to live alone, to choose our career based on interest, to date or marry for love, to travel alone, and other scenarios that reflected the hopes and dreams I had often heard the young women express.

At the end of the game, with some of us in the front and others many steps back, Shirin asked everyone in the back to share what they felt toward people standing in the front. "Revenge and anger," Saeede, one of the Afghan clients, said, standing all the way in the back near the wall of the small backyard. There was a sadness and a sense of resentment in her eyes and in those of the other clients for whom the activity seemed to have brought up a range of unpleasant emotions. Shirin, Barmak, and Hamid invited everyone to sit in a circle on the ground to have a conversation about the activity. "Some people move forward in life because of the conditions in their lives, and those who are left behind tend to judge them and have ill feelings toward them," Shirin said to problematize Saeede's feeling and discuss what we should take away from the activity. "Those who have more in life might have worked harder, it's not always because *haghe kasi ro khordan* [they have impinged on someone's rights]," Hamid said to add to the point Shirin was trying to make. Shirin pointed out that during the activity, two clients who were assigned the same character had ended up in different places and that this difference reflected their varying perceptions of their abilities and that perception alone—and believing in oneself— can determine how far a person can go in life.

I sat there listening to the conclusions drawn by Shirin and Hamid, disappointed with where the conversation had gone. While I had previously seen the activity played out in the United States to counter meritocratic assumptions about advancement, I was shocked to hear the activity used to ask impoverished women to pull themselves up by their bootstraps and to lose their anger over inequalities they witnessed and lived daily. I was not, however, completely unaware of why Shirin and other teachers had chosen an activity to deny the importance of their own privileges. Their decision to appropriate the activity, in fact, can be better understood in the context of larger class tensions at the organization between the impoverished ethnic-minority clients and the middle-class Tehrani staff. Having paid particular attention to the contentious interactions between the two groups, I had found that clients were increasingly losing patience with the staff, whose point of view often reflected their privileged social positions—privileges the young women were now quick to bring to the attention of their middle-class teachers. As clients continued to problematize staff's privileged standpoint, the staff had found it necessary to further deny their own privilege to legitimize their role as "helpers."

In this chapter, I show how the tension between the marginalized clients and the middle-class staff of ALLY was shaped by the growing oppositional consciousness of ALLY's clients and the unwillingness of the staff to problematize their own privilege. By doing so, I demonstrate the agency of marginalized women, who are often assumed to be passive recipients of services within the context of empowerment programs. Instead, marginalized women can play an important role in shaping the dynamics, the organizational narratives, and the outcome of women's empowerment programs. While the impact of such programs are often discussed in relation to their content, the processes of program development and implementation can be contentious and changing due to varying and conflicting approaches to empowerment by staff and clients. Given that the role of the marginalized clients of these programs in shaping organizational dynamics is rarely explored, this chapter pays particular attention to the oppositional narratives and the disruptions created by clients in the process of service delivery. Faced with the staff's growing resistance to recognizing their own privileges, clients used ALLY's organizational resources to develop their own critique of class and ethnic inequality.

Classless Comrades

Shirin, Hamid, and Barmak were not oblivious to the middle-class privileges they enjoyed in comparison to the impoverished clients of ALLY.

They were critical of social inequalities of gender, class, and ethnicity and passionately advocated for the young women, who they believed were victims of an unjust economic and social system. They were also aware that their contentious interactions with the women were due to the wide social and economic gaps that separated their worlds. This awareness explains the position taken by the staff in the "privilege walk" activity described earlier. Hamid, for instance, had explicitly referred to the growing tension between the clients and the staff as emanating from their different social standings:

> For a while, the girls' view of ALLY was not good. Their view was that these are a bunch of rich people and we are all poor. So [they thought to themselves], "It is their responsibility to help us. The organization must give us money and support us." This was a common view. (Hamid, Teacher)

Hamid's understanding of clients' negative perception of the staff was shared by Shirin and Barmak, who had taken it upon themselves to "help" clients abandon their "negative" views. Shirin told me that the girls carry a deep-seated sense of hostility toward the upper and middle class, as they believe those who are rich must have impinged on someone's rights. I had also noticed that a lack of trust toward the intentions and the advice of the staff had shaped many of the contentious relationships at ALLY. The teachers believed trust could develop between the clients and the privileged staff if friendships grew and the similarities between the struggles of the two groups were seen.

> One group of the girls . . . had a very negative view of society, and their perception of us was that you are a group of people who don't know anything about our pains, who have never had any problems and don't know where we live. But this got a lot better [after they took our classes]. You can kinda see the big distance between the girls and the staff at ALLY. They see that a lot of the staff don't live in Iran, and traveling abroad is a really big deal for the girls. I think some change happened in the groups we worked with, and this feeling has lessened in them. One of the reasons is that we tried to be friends with the girls, and they saw that we're not people who have no problems, and we are not working here

because we are bored with our carefree lives. Sometimes we share our issues with them intentionally. Sahar [one of the teachers] was saying that she doesn't have a TV or laptop at home; she was telling them that she lives in such a circumstance, and the girls couldn't believe it! They were like, "How is it possible for anyone to live like that?" One of the good things that came out of these friendships is that the girls' views changed. . . . They see themselves as separated from the society and see everyone in the society as their enemy. But this gets better by being here and by being friends with the staff. (Hamid, Teacher)

Like Hamid, many of ALLY's employees believed in the importance of changing the negative views of the subaltern women toward the upper and middle classes, who they saw as *bach-e pooldar* (rich kids, or born in wealth). Since the staff members were often challenged and undermined by the young women, who pointed to their privileged standpoint, many began denying their own privilege and demanding to be seen as equally struggling with daily life. For example, Ava told me that she found it necessary to tell the clients that as a woman, she also suffered from many inequalities, otherwise the clients would not give her advice any legitimacy if they saw her as privileged. I was told many times about the need to make the young women realize that "everyone has problems" and that the staff is not bad for having it good.

The collective narrative of the organization that insisted on the goodness of the ordinary middle and upper classes, however, was continuously challenged by clients. Although misfortunes experienced by the staff were shared with the clients, the women rarely acknowledged those instances as legitimate struggles. While Sahar did not have a TV or laptop at home, she was often absent due to her long vacations in Europe, about which stories were often shared with clients. When I was alone with the young women, I found that the staff and their efforts to undermine their own privileges were often mocked. One such source of humor was Hamid's usual reference to the hardship he endured during *sarbazi* (two-year mandatory military service for young men in Iran) to claim that he understood the poverty and harsh living conditions of the young women. The women were frustrated with such remarks, as they believed that temporary deprivation and poverty were two distinct experiences that could not be compared. "Aww, whatever we say, you bring up *sarbazi*!" one of the young women said to Hamid as he once again mentioned *sarbazi* to argue that he understood the harsh living conditions of an Afghan client who was speaking of the challenges of growing up in rural Afghanistan during war. I could see that many of the young women were trying to hold back laughter as they exchanged playful glances with one another. While at times clients responded to such stories of "struggles" with kind yet sneering smiles, they also sometimes problematized the staff's class privilege out loud and in their presence.

I spent a great deal of time in Hamid's class with a group of clients who seemed to have formed close and meaningful friendships over the years. Negar and Sepideh were two of those friends. While both struggled to study for *konkoor* (Iran's competitive university entrance exam), Sepideh had to deal with the extra pressure of not knowing whether she would ever be able to attend college; as an Afghan, she would have to pay quite a lot for the education that is free to Iranians. Like many other clients, Negar, coming from a poor and conservative household, had asked me once or twice whether I could help her figure out a way to leave Iran. Being "tired of everything and everyone," she said she "just want[s] to get away from this life."

When I entered the class that day, the two were flipping through an old issue of *Vogue* and discussing the outfits they believed they might be able to sew if they could get their hands on the right fabrics. I sat across from Sepideh and watched her eyes move from one page to the other as she scanned the glamorous images of beautiful women in expensive clothes. I noticed a growing sadness on her face.

> SEPIDEH: I cannot believe that God is just! When I look at what others have and what I don't have. We [my family and I] have had so much bad luck in the last few years, I just can't believe that this is a just world, and I can't figure out why things are like this. I mean, some people have so much that they don't know what to do with, and then there are those who have nothing! Nothing! A healthy body doesn't satisfy me. I think people should have more than that. When you don't have money you don't have anything!

NEGAR: You know what? I don't buy what people tell me here [about inequality]. When you ask the *roshanfekr* [intellectuals], they say bright stars come out of the darkness. When you ask the religious people, they say God gives you suffering to hear you call him, or some say he's testing your faith!
SEPIDEH: Some say you see bad if you have done bad! Everyone is trying to *tojih* [justify] this for us, and I don't accept any of these!

It was difficult not to notice the strong *us* versus *them* divide in the way Negar and Sepideh were describing the accounts of the powerful *other* to which they would not succumb. Sitting on the other side of the table, it was also easy to see that Hamid and I were positioned in the camp of the other. Aware of such dividing practices and not willing to accept them, Hamid felt compelled, as he told me later, to undermine the clients' account by speaking of suffering as universal and classless. "We might think some people don't have any problems, but we really don't have any idea what others are struggling with," Hamid said after he shared the story of the time his younger brother was left in critical condition at the hospital for a month following an accident. "At that moment, it didn't matter what economic class we belonged to, I was willing to give everything to have my brother back."

"This is not what I meant," Sepideh responded with an irritated voice. "The people I'm talking about have these kinds of problems too!"

I knew I was witnessing yet another familiar give-and-take between the clients and the staff, with the former group forcing an acknowledgment of privilege and the latter fighting it with universal accounts of human suffering to legitimize themselves. "I think everyone is asking us to *kenar biyaym* [be OK] with injustice," Sepideh concluded, refusing to accept that all humans suffer the same and that the problems of a middle-class Tehrani man like Hamid could be compared to hers.

The clients showed a solid awareness of the class divide present at ALLY and believed that the staff's privilege was the source of their inability to comprehend the complexity of the struggles they endured. Staff members, including Hamid, were not oblivious to the devastating daily struggles of the young women. Their refusal to acknowledge their privilege stemmed from their collective assessment of "appropriate" response to those clients who did not trust or value their advice. The clients' suspicions about the intentions of the staff added to their very Marxist analysis of power in which the ruling class (the rich and the religious) justify inequality had made the upper- and middle-class staff determined to have a sense of legitimacy in the eyes of the clients. That is why they shared their own personal struggles, although they often looked rather petty in comparison. While employees were occupied with legitimizing their position, the clients were successfully developing class-based solidarities and oppositional standpoints. Daily conversations and interactions with the middle- and upper-class employees at ALLY, where inequalities (albeit mostly of gender) were commonly discussed, had sensitized clients to social inequalities that deprived them of the relatively dignified life their privileged teachers were living. To develop an articulated critique of such inequality, the young women utilized organizational resources, such as creative writing, community development, or poetry classes as well as workshops on women's rights and effective communication.

Resisting Cultural Reductionism and Building Oppositional Solidarities

> Afghan girls have experienced sexual abuse a lot more than the Iranian girls. Because in the context of their families, they think that relationships can be this way, that my brother can touch certain parts of my body, or that my brother-in-law can look at me a certain way or can make sexual innuendos. (Mina, Social Worker)

> The depth of the problems is not different for the Iranian and Afghan girls. Rape is in both populations, but the perspectives are different. An Iranian girl would react to this experience much faster than an Afghan girl.... Afghan girls, to the contrary, have the same issues but have never had any space to dare to speak and argue with their family members.... Iranians are more active because of their living circumstances. If their life circumstances or the social norms do not allow them to do something, they still do their shenanigans and fight with their families; but not Afghans. Because the patriarchal conditions governing the lives

of Afghans are very different.... If an Afghan girl says that she has a boyfriend, the reactions might be very severe, but not as much in Iranian families. They are not that sensitive. Even if the argument escalates and there is some physical fighting, it will be fighting on both sides, the Iranian girl is going to physically fight back. But in Afghan families, it's very one-sided. One does the beating and the other one just takes it. (Azar, Social Worker)

ALLY's middle-class staff often explained gendered social problems such as domestic violence, sexual violence, and child marriage as a reflection of *faghr-e farhangi* (cultural poverty), which the poor and ethnic minorities struggled with. This cultural poverty was seen as especially severe in the Afghan culture. Azar, Mina, and other Iranian workers explained the widespread problems of sexual and domestic violence in Afghan communities as being rooted in Afghan's deeply patriarchal culture. While no doubt many aspects of Afghan (and most other) culture(s) are patriarchal, dominant accounts fail to explain the persistence of patriarchal control among Afghans due to the country's long history of colonial violence, war, and political instability or the material, educational, and legal deprivation that Afghans have long grappled with in both Afghanistan and Iran. Azar's and Mina's comments reflected the hegemony of cultural reductionist explanations of gender oppression in the Middle East (Bahramitash and Kazemipour 2006), where culture is assumed to be overdeterminist and unchanging and have an independent existence from other social institutions. Without references to these interdependencies, remarks such as those of Azar and Mina inadvertently reproduce discriminatory ethnic discourses that find Afghan culture as fundamentally violent and misogynist and Afghan women as particularly passive and oppressed. Under the hegemony of cultural reductionist discourses, many of ALLY's staff and administrators interpreted problems such as domestic violence and sexual violence as the effects of cultural poverty rather than as the *structural effects* of poverty and social exclusion. Numerous studies have demonstrated the effects of economic and social inequalities on behavioral violence (Garbarino 1999; Gilligan 2001; Crenshaw 1991). Violence in men's immediate social environment, frustration by the inability to provide food, poor living conditions and overcrowding, substance abuse, low levels of schooling, and other effects of poverty have been found to aggravate violence (Gonzales de Olarte and Llosa 1999; Evans 2005). This is not to suggest that the problem of violence against women will be resolved by the eradication of poverty; rather, the effect of poverty and precarious masculinity should be understood as intersecting and not separate categories of analysis.

While staff and clients often agreed on the patriarchal character of many cultural norms and ideologies, in many other instances, the employees' cultural reductionism resulted in tensions between the two groups. My field notes documenting the classes and workshops at ALLY were filled with contentious dialogues between the teachers and the clients over the analyses of gender oppression provided by the staff. The clients expressed resentment toward those accounts in which gender oppression was reduced to matters of culture while intersecting class and ethnic inequalities remained unchallenged. In one workshop, the clients were given the chance to discuss a topic of their choice. "Which matters the most—knowledge or money?" was the topic proposed by Kobra, a sixteen-year-old Afghan client, and most requested by the class. Considering the organizational narratives that emphasized knowledge and education and the reality of clients' daily life, in which money was the defining factor, the women's interest in this question was less than startling. "Why do you think money is such a pursued value?" Reza, ALLY's art therapy teacher, asked to facilitate the conversation. "Dominance," Armaghan, an eighteen-year-old Afghan client, responded assuredly. "Money allows some groups to dominate others," she continued.

"I personally don't care much for money," Kobra chimed in. Her response appeared to me to be an effort to separate herself from those who wished to dominate others. Hearing her remark, Reza probed Kobra to concede if she would marry a poor man knowing that he might not be able to afford to take their sick child to the hospital in the future. "My father has said he'll not marry off his daughter for less than twenty million tomans [US$5,000 at the time]," Kobra said to point to the relatively firm financial status of her future husband. An artist in his forties who had lived most of his life in Europe, Reza was quite puzzled by Kobra's remark. Reading the apparent confusion on his face, clients jumped in to explain Kobra's statement as a reference to the tradition of *shirbaha*.[1] While this tradition is mostly abandoned and primarily entails providing a small and symbolic gift to the bride's family in Iran, the practice persists in the Afghan culture and often requires the groom to give a large sum of money to the bride's family in exchange for their blessing.

Following the organizational agenda of problematizing the patriarchal character of traditions and culture, Reza used this opportunity as a teachable moment: "So what we are doing here is treating women as goods that can be sold. And the gray-bearded sheep make those decisions about how much a woman's worth is." While some of the clients laughed at the reference to the "gray-bearded sheep," others' faces soured in offense upon hearing a disparaging remark about the men in their lives. Still others were unhappy about what they saw as a simplistic account of gender oppression. "A father who is a worker with a wage barely enough to keep his family alive cannot afford to disregard this money or the tradition. Rich people can, but we can't!" said Zahra, an eighteen-year-old recently engaged Afghan client, rejecting the dominant assumption that traditions such as *shirbaha* persist due to men's misogynist views rather than the necessity of maintaining such economic transactions for the survival of the poor.

Following the heated debate that ensued, Reza wrote the word *Agahi* (awareness) in bold letters on the board and turned toward the class to further argue that ignorance is the ultimate cause of women's suffering. "I *have* the awareness," Kobra responded with an irritated voice, "but I'm facing bigger struggles in society." For Zahra and Kobra, the economic struggles of the families who continued to follow the tradition remained the main culprit, and to them, Reza's comments represented the economic privilege of the middle and upper classes, who disregarded such traditional practices for their patriarchal character while vilifying the impoverished Afghans for not as easily surrendering their misogyny. Reza was not unaware of the economic challenges of ALLY's clients and deeply sympathized with their struggles. Yet culturally reductionist discourses that emphasize education and consciousness-raising can be especially appealing when NGO actors feel helpless in addressing structural inequalities that fall outside their circle of influence. As the exchange between Reza and the young women suggests, the subaltern women demonstrated a strong class consciousness and an intersectional understanding of inequality in which their gender oppression was deeply linked to their class and ethnic oppression. They did not leave the mainstream feminist accounts of their own oppression unchallenged and continuously offered their own understanding of gender inequality, which prioritized economic justice.

Solutions to social problems such as child labor and child marriage were other points of contention between the two groups. Staff often spoke of such issues as *moshkelat-e farhangi* (cultural problems) and suggested that educational campaigns about children's human rights would deter families from sending their children to work. The young women, however, rejected these accounts, which vilified the poor by portraying them as ignorant and in need of lessons in morality. In one class on community development, for instance, the teachers described women's unpaid labor at home and child labor as instances of slavery. While clients happily agreed that women's unpaid labor at home is an example of exploitation, they strongly rejected children's work as an instance of abuse. Barmak, Hamid, and Shirin pointed to children's inability to consent and the fact that the money earned is collected by their guardians to solidify their argument. "You can't really say that! The father might know better how to spend the money," asserted Neda, one of the Iranian clients. Others insisted that children's work might be the only way for families to survive. While working children were spoken of in the third person by both groups, the clients' comments in different classes had revealed to me that many had worked as children or had young siblings who were currently working. It seemed that clients' rejection of these arguments was an effort to restore the dignity of their own families and social class, who are often vilified for making choices the middle class are not forced to make. Clients, both Iranian and Afghan, insisted that child labor and child marriage are the problems of the impoverished not due to lack of awareness or morality but due to lack of choice. The economic necessity of sending children to work, even as beggars, or the financial necessity of marrying off one's young children because of an inability to provide for them were problems emphasized by many of the young women.

While a number of the Afghan and Iranian women were vocal about the class privilege of the staff and often mocked them behind their back for not recognizing their privileged views, Afghan women also saw ethnic marginalization as deeply interlinked with their gender oppression. The interaction of a group of Afghan and Iranian clients in a workshop revealed the Afghan women's growing oppositional ethnic solidarities at ALLY. As often happened in such workshops, clients were asked to suggest a topic, and the topic with the most votes was chosen. Among the suggested subjects of discussion were love, jealousy, discrimination, bigotry, and freedom of choice. The topic of immigration was also brought up and sparked huge interest among Afghan women. Maryam, a seventeen-year-old Iranian woman, however, protested the topic with a dispassionate voice, claiming that she was tired of discussing a topic she knew nothing about. While the teacher vouched for the importance of discussing immigration and reminded Maryam of her privilege, Maryam's comment seemed to have dampened the Afghan women's excitement. With one more vote than "immigration," the topic of *tahghir shodan* (being degraded) was chosen.

The teacher asked clients to share an instance of being degraded to begin the conversation. Soheila, an Afghan client who had suggested the topic, began to uncomfortably recount the ways her sister and boyfriend spoke to her in a degrading way. It was not long before many Afghan clients jumped in to share their own experiences of degradation and being disrespected as Afghans in Iran. "They tell us we're only good for washing toilets," Zahra, one of the Afghan women, said. "They always tell us: 'Shut up, who do you think you are to open your mouth?'" Armine, another Afghan woman, said of the time she participated in a heated debate on the subway. One by one, Afghan clients chimed in and shared their own experiences. Nooshin said angrily that each time she objected to men who sexually harassed her on the street, their answer was, "Shut up, you dirty Afghani, we can do whatever we want to your kind." Narges told the story of the day she and her friends refused to take the numbers of a group of boys who were flirting with them. She recounted that their refusal was followed by the boys' loud verbal harassment, which included racial slurs. "People who were watching wouldn't have stayed silent if the boys were doing that to Iranian girls," Narges said; others nodded their heads in her support. Other Afghan clients suggested that the police never investigated rape and sexual violence when the victims were Afghan, unlike when Iranian women were concerned. While two Iranian clients disagreed with the Afghan women's statements by claiming that they themselves had been subjected to degradation in public, the Afghan clients were quick to remind them that while women were subjected to many forms of discrimination, Afghan women's oppression was compounded by their ethnic oppression.

By demarcating their experiences of gender oppression from those of Iranian women, Afghan women insisted on the intersectional character of their victimization. The interaction I just described also demonstrates the development of an ethnic oppositional consciousness among ALLY's Afghan clients in interaction with their middle-class Iranian staff and fellow impoverished Iranian clients. My observation of clients' conversations around family dynamics revealed that this ethnic consciousness did not always represent the view of the Afghan communities the clients came from. Afghan women at ALLY often talked about their never-ending conversations with their families about Afghans' human rights and the difficulty of convincing them that they are as rightful and deserving as Iranians. The decades-long history of xenophobia against Afghans and nationalist propaganda has resulted in the internalization of oppressive ethnic ideologies among Afghan communities. ALLY's organizational discourses, while focused on women's rights and gender equality, had provided clients with the opportunity to develop a well-articulated oppositional and intersectional gender, ethnic, and class consciousness.

In many cases, the staff did a great job of engaging clients with a range of topics concerning community involvement, social inequality, gender and ethnic discrimination, and other social problems. It would be wrong to suggest that the clients' experience at ALLY was that of marginalization by workers who were oblivious to their own privileges. While the clients were critical of certain aspects of ALLY's empowerment program, they had used the organizational and educational resources to develop and articulate their own critiques. In fact, it appeared that their oppositional class consciousness and commitment to ethnic equality were developed as they began to apply the framework of women's rights and gender equality, widely discussed at the organization, to other forms of inequalities they were experiencing. As they developed and articulated their opinions of class and ethnic privilege, the staff and the organization got the brunt of the critiques.

Lauren G. Leve's (2007) ethnographic study of the rural revolution in Nepal demonstrates a similar dynamic. Leve's study reveals that rural women's support and large-scale involvement in the Maoist movement was the result of their politicization through their participation in development programs that had a neoliberal agenda. The literacy and development courses offered, however, contributed to women's political awareness and their eventual opposition to neoliberal policies. This book's study, similar to Leve's, demonstrates that the content of development or empowerment programs is not uncritically adopted and that the oppositional consciousness of subaltern women is formed "based on morally grounded ideas about social personhood . . . not the culturally disembedded valorizations of autonomy, agency, and choice that most models presume" (Leve 2007: 127–128).

7

The Symbolic Economy of Propriety

"The government and the law are *mardsalar* [patriarchal], we have got to stand against them," Noshin, one of the newly admitted clients, said decisively during a creative writing class. "We have to start the movement from inside the smaller societies that are our families," she continued. The discussion Hiva had started on wanting to be a boy had let to a lively discussion among the young women, who passionately shared their views on the relation between Hiva's rejection of femininity and patriarchy. Only a few months into ALLY's three-year journey and living at its dormitory, Hiva had changed considerably in appearance and style. Hiva began wearing loose shirts over their[1] baggy jeans and caps rather than a scarf to cover their newly cut short boyish hair. Wearing bold red lipstick that day during class, Hiva said they did not care that they wanted to be a boy and wear lipstick too. "I'll be whoever I wanna be!" Hiva said indignantly. As I sat there and gazed at Hiva's new look, I recalled our interaction during their first week at ALLY. I remembered Hiva's long hair, their pink and glitter phone case, and their discomfort with revealing their ethnic identity when I asked where they came from. Looking away uncomfortably, Hiva had said they were from Mashhad. Mashhad is a city in the province of Khorasan, which borders Afghanistan and has a large

Afghan population.² I later learned that Hiva's response is a common one among Afghans living in Iran who fear revealing their stigmatized ethnic and national identity. Hiva's Tehrani accent, commonly used by them and many young Afghans who were born and raised in Iran, was enough to stop anyone from further questioning. That day during class, I could see Hiva's new confident attitude as they identified as "*pesar nama*,"³ explaining how their "eccentric character" had caused them a great deal of pain over the years. The other young women, however, had strong ideas about why Hiva felt trapped and ashamed in their female body: "You think being a girl is so horrible because of what our society is like," Nasim, one of the clients, said confidently as she noticed the approving nods of the other women who began sharing different instances of women's oppression. "Boys have a lot of freedom, but we can't even choose to go on trips with our friends," Mona said in support of Nasim's claim. "We have to be home by a curfew when our brothers do whatever they want," another client said before Noshin chimed in to argue that it is in fact the laws and the government that are *mardsalar*.

The young women's analysis of Hiva's rejection of femininity as being associated with patriarchy reflected the absence of larger social debates on the fluidity of gender identities and expressions. Hiva, however, did not reject any of their claims and got furious when one of the young women claimed that "being a woman is not that bad." By that time, Noshin had begun, rather heatedly, to respond to classmates who were sharing their experiences of gender discrimination. "I'm not talking about any particular person, so please don't take it personally, but we are all just big mouths, we protest verbally but don't do anything about it."

Noshin performed middle class exceptionally well. From her stylish clothing to her highlighted hair to her eloquent speaking, which reflected a strong sense of efficacy, she appeared to be a college-educated middle-class woman. Noshin's remarks in class, however, did not sit well with Hiva. "I didn't take what you said personally, but I'm not just a big mouth," Hiva said while explaining that they act nonconforming "in spite of it all," pointing to the challenges of stepping outside normative performances of femininity. For Hiva, their gender-bending practices—dressing in masculine attire and wearing lipstick—were already political acts of protest. For Noshin, however, protest meant an old-fashioned collective organizing of women against patriarchal laws; she recounted a recent women's protest at a soccer stadium to lift the ban on women's presence as an example of a *real* protest.

I use the heated conversation in the creative writing class between Hiva, Noshin, and the other young women to draw attention to a few important and interrelated modes of self-representation common among ALLY's impoverished young clients. First, just like Hiva and Noshin, many clients transformed swiftly in appearance and style after joining the organization. The early morning routine at ALLY entailed a rather quick makeover for many of the young women; they replaced their black chador with colorful scarves, styling the hair that was now to be revealed from under a loose headscarf, and applied makeup and nail polish, all of which would come off before they left for the day. The inclusive and nonjudgmental atmosphere of ALLY allowed many clients like Hiva to show their nonnormative gender expressions in a space where they felt safe and enabled young women like Noshin to diverge from the conservative norms of ideal femininity that emphasize modesty. But the transformation I speak of here reflects more than the freedom to express one's deeper personal desires. The longer they stayed at the organization, the more the young women resembled ALLY's middle-class and secular staff in terms of the style of clothing, makeup, demeanor, lifestyle, and modes of speech. Was the new, secular appearance reflecting the young women's adoption of the feminist ideals of the organization and their "enlightened" self or an aspiration to class mobility in a city characterized by class tensions and social exclusion?

Olszewska (2013) has critiqued a common trend in Iran studies—particularly the anthropology of urban youth culture—in which most social phenomena, such as lifestyle, style of clothing, and consumption patterns, are generally conceptualized as "resistance" to and "defiance" against an oppressive and Islamic regime. Olszewska warns against this trend of theorization, given that lifestyle and consumption patterns are endowed with symbolic values as status attributes in societies with shifting class configurations. Khosravi's (2008) ethnography, while critiqued by Olszewska for carrying the analytical flaw of privileging resistance as a theoretical frame, clearly demonstrates that middle-class norms of respectability in Tehran are characterized by attempts to appear cosmopolitan, chic, ba-kelas, and open-minded, all through the consumption of expensive Western brands and the mockery of the working class for their *bi-farhangi* (lack of culture), being *dehati* (rural or village minded), or *javad* (an epithet that implies lack of taste). Given this larger social context, how can we best explain the efforts of this group of marginalized and impoverished young women to look like their middle-class teachers?

The second noticeable feature of the conversation that ensued in the creative writing class was how the clients' modes of speech reflected an aspiration to the status of *roshanfekr*, or intellectual, which "involves projecting oneself as a sensitive but alienated observer, critical of what they may see as oppressive social convention" (Olszewska 2015: 186). As Hiva and Noshin's debate in the creative writing class demonstrates, ALLY's clients willingly participated in many discussions on gender oppression as critical observers of subjugating social norms. The figure of the intellectual emulated at ALLY was that of a liberal thinker concerned with a society's cultural backwardness that leaves no room for personal autonomy. This mode of speech entailed heavy reliance on the discourses of gender oppression as explanatory of women's life chances while purposefully withholding references to class and ethnic marginalization. The young women's critique of gender inequality and the lack of personal autonomy and their call for mobilization and protest (bodily or collective) resembled a middle-class sense of efficacy that many of ALLY's workers demonstrated. While Noshin's reference to the women's "big mouth" and "lack of action" might reflect their compounded agency, given their marginalization at the intersection of salient social categories of gender, ethnicity, class, sexuality, and citizenship, could their aspiration to the status of a critical intellectual with social efficacy reflect an aspiration for a symbolic capital and a dignified habitus?

Another noticeable change in clients was their adoption of a more secular lifestyle, which included having boyfriends and engaging in sexual relations outside marriage, despite the consequences of these practices in their conservative communities. While this was partly the result of the organization's emphasis on sexual autonomy as empowerment, Olszewska argues that for lower-class women, premarital sexual relationships might not be an expression of resistance, as Mahdavi's (2009) research suggests was the case for the Iranian youth who used their defiant sexual lifestyle as a means of protesting the regime. For the poor and the working class, sexual practices might also reflect a desire "to appear more worldly and cosmopolitan, or to tap into the perceived pleasures of a lifestyle that is seen as higher status, and which may be otherwise inaccessible. For girls from impoverished families, making themselves sexually available may be part of a strategy to access material goods or to find a higher status husband, a dream that so often turns into the nightmare of sexual exploitation" (Olszewska 2013: 853).

In this chapter, I reveal class and ethnic discourses that shaped young, impoverished clients' self-representation in a middle-class space where their social mobility depended on performing middle-class respectability. This respectability, rooted in the history of the development of Iranian feminism alongside colonial relations and class politics, demands a defiant attitude toward norms of hejab and sexual modesty as well as conformity to the latest fashion trends. Iranian middle-class feminism, which primarily grew in the Pahlavi era, positioned the liberated woman in opposition to the veiled and subjugated *zan-e sonati* (traditional woman). Elite Iranian women's self-alignment with Western cultural norms has historically occurred to claim an enlightened status and to situate themselves against the "backwardness" of the traditional and religious poor with lingering patriarchal attitudes (Naghibi 2007). Discourses of middle-class respectable femininity were manifested at ALLY in teachings about patriarchy where male domination was reduced to traditional cultural norms from which some societies and social groups have yet to escape. The figure of *zan-e sonati*—stuck in her traditional religious beliefs, veiled, prizing her virginity, and subjugated by her male relatives—was the one in need of empowerment and transformation into a liberal unveiled woman critical of oppressive cultural gender and sexual norms.

While previous studies have explained Iranian women's badhejabi (improper hejab), sexual relations outside marriage, and high fashion in public as a form of resistance against the moral order defined by the government (Khosravi 2008; Mahdavi 2009; Bayat 2013), this study borrows from Olszewska (2013) and Manata Hashemi (2020) to add that the adoption of fashionable and secular lifestyles can also be attempts at upward class mobility and developing a dignified self in a classist society. Hashemi's ethnography demonstrates that the practices of the working-class youth in Iran for the purpose of "saving face" help with increasing their stock of moral capital, which they can subsequently exchange for social and economic opportunities. While the transformations in the young women were commonly interpreted by the staff as a reflection of their newly empowered self, arguments here and in previous chapters aim to complicate this assumption by exploring a multiplicity of motivations in order to move past reductive dichotomies of empowered/subjugated or secular/religious in our analysis of gender in Muslim societies.

By utilizing Bourdieu's (1997) concept of "symbolic capital," I analyze clients' transformation as an effort to construct "symbolic economies." Bourdieu argues that "the structures of the social space (or of fields) shape bodies by inculcating in them, through the conditionings associated with a position in that space, the cognitive structures that these conditionings apply to them" (1997: 183). These cognitive structures are a form of *practical knowledge* that emerges bodily between the players in the field. Bourdieu argues that people have practical and bodily knowledge of their present and potential position in any given social space, and this governs their sense of placement and experience of the place occupied. This also determines their efforts to behave in ways that would allow them to maintain their relational position ("pulling rank") or to stay within it ("knowing one's place") (Bourdieu 1997: 184). In her ethnography of white and Mexican-American working-class high school students in California's Central Valley, Julie Bettie uses the concept of "symbolic economy" to show how hairstyles, clothes, shoes, and the color of lipstick and nail polish were "employed to express group membership as the body became a resource and a site on which difference was inscribed" (2003: 62). In cultural contexts stratified by class and race, the symbolic economy of youth culture is undoubtedly marked by race and class exclusion.

Given that I did not interview clients about their transformed style and speech, this chapter does not aim to investigate individual motivations behind these transformations. Instead, I place my observations of clients' changing self-expression in their social context to reveal the intersecting gender, class, and ethnic discourses of respectability that coordinate people's everyday actions and are reproduced through them. Rather than examining women's secular or conservative look merely as a reflection of their gender ideologies or a defiant subjectivity, I show how constructing a dignified self for women marginalized at the intersection of class and ethnic inequalities requires constant self-editing and embodying conflicting systems of meaning. Arguments in this chapter do not supplant but supplement data provided in Chapters 5 and 6, where I demonstrated that clients' clear awareness and harsh critiques of middle-class privileges shaped ALLY's program through a visible class consciousness. Here, I simply reveal the other side of the coin—clients' attempts to navigate conflicting and exclusionary social and cultural systems through self-expression in the hopes of increasing their stock of symbolic capital.

The Symbolic Economy of Style

The summer heat rushed us down the stairs and into the basement of the building that was commonly used for art workshops. Allocation of our regular class space to a two-day workshop had brought our community development class to the basement, a space kept cool by two large fans around which clients had quickly gathered to drop their scarves and enjoy the breeze. The walls of the large room were covered with sketches by the young women and the floors with clay sculptures, many still in the making. Before getting the chance to settle around the large rectangular table in the middle, Zahra, a seventeen-year-old Iranian client, began to tell Barmak, the teacher, that she could no longer work on the community project she had chosen for the class. Worried about an area in her neighborhood that was frequented by children and had recently become the dumping site of the neighbors' waste, she had planned to take on the task of making her neighborhood cleaner and safer for children. The municipality's closest trash bins were located a few alleys away. Concerned about the health of the young children playing in the area and done with its pungent smell, Zahra had planned on dragging one of the trash bins from another alley and placing it at the dump site in the dark of the night. After learning of her plan, her mother and brothers were quick to forbid her, as they were concerned about her safety in a bad neighborhood late at night. Disappointed, she turned to Barmak and the girls for help. Barmak's suggestion to call the municipality and report the problem was quickly dismissed by Zahra. However, she seemed to like a classmate's suggestion that she talk to the clergy of the mosque in their neighborhood, as his words would likely be taken more seriously if he were to instruct the community to find a solution. Mina, another classmate, expressed her concern about Zahra's legitimacy as a nonconforming teenage girl in the eyes of the Imam: "If she goes to the Imam looking like this, the first thing he's going to say is, 'You fix your hejab, young lady!'" The girls laughed at the way Mina mimicked the Imam as having a thick voice, holding his head down, and frowning while refusing to look at Zahra.

Mina was pointing to Zahra's new look at ALLY; like the appearance of many other young women at the organization, Zahra's had changed considerably over time. This entailed abandoning the more conservative norms of modesty in favor of a look that was more fashionable in Tehran among the secular middle class with whom they now were in contact nearly every day. The transformation was a noticeable one and reflected aesthetic standards that rejected dark and long coverings in favor of short, tight, and colorful ones and a sheer and loose headscarf on the head that showed their styled hair underneath. The government's attempts to control women's clothing in public through arrests and fines and its imposed definition of respected Muslim femininity (as modest in appearance and dressing in loose, dark, and long clothing) means that Iranian women's badhejabi and their colorful, immodest, and stylish appearance are, in many ways, manifestations of their defiance against the government's imposition of its moral order. This analysis is shared by many scholars, including Khosravi (2013), Mahdavi (2009), and Bayat (2013). As Olszewska argues, such analysis of resistance has limitations: "Cultural dispositions—the consumption of certain products, the profession of certain aesthetic tastes and ideological beliefs, or the practicing of certain lifestyles—are endowed with values as status attributes and may be used as chips in the high-stakes game of social mobility" (2013: 843). Hashemi's (2020) ethnographic study of the lower-class youth in Iran demonstrates that the poor and working classes spend a great deal of effort to "save face" and escape the stigmatization of their identity by appearing middle class. The style adopted by the marginalized clients of ALLY was as an emulation of the cosmopolitan trend in Tehran among the upper and middle classes, whose sense of fashion and understanding of hejab are formed by their transnational ties and exposure to Western fashion and beauty trends. The entanglement of feminist discourses (women's defiance toward imposed norms of femininity) with middle-class norms of respectability (adopting the latest fashion trends) meant that the clients' transformation in appearance could be read as the expected conversion from *zan-e sonati* (a traditional woman) to *zan-e modern* (a modern woman).

I witnessed many daily efforts to accurately perform the norms of respectable middle-class femininity through the aforementioned style of clothing and makeup. The women's transformed appearance, I was told, had made some visiting donors doubt the financial need of the clients. For many of these women, the distance between the norms of self-representation in their communities and the norms of respectability at ALLY was one to navigate skillfully. Knowing that secular and middle-class norms of self-representation were rejected within their home communities, many clients embodied middle-class discourses of respectability part time. The other group of young women who maintained their new appearance in their home communities often struggled with acceptance and respect, and their sexual morality was questioned due to their immodest appearance.

Mina's remark about Zahra's appearance was to remind her that her transformed look would pose a challenge outside ALLY if she were to seek out the help of a local Imam. Zahra, who had found the clergy's influence to be the only realistic solution to the problem of waste disposal in her neighborhood, said, in an indifferent tone, that she would wear a chador when meeting the Imam. Barmak, a young college-educated man in his twenties, taught courses on community development and creative writing and was always interested in engaging clients in important conversations about morality and social attitudes. That day, I was taken aback by how Barmak was quick to reject Zahra's willingness to wear a chador as unethical. He was quick to argue that "one doesn't need to be a hypocrite to do something good." Soon, I noticed that I was not the only one to feel this way, as clients furiously jumped in to convince Barmak that navigating spaces with conflicting norms is not an instance of hypocrisy. Ahoo, a seventeen-year-old client, reminded Barmak that she wore her chador because of her father but took it off as soon as she left home each day. She asked Barmak, in a defiant tone, if he found it right to call her a hypocrite. Ahoo was clearly offended by Barmak's comment. I had heard him make a similar statement in another class about "those women who wear their makeup in the subway and are different people at home." For Barmak, remaining true to one's beliefs and values despite potential opposition was an important indication of empowerment and autonomy. For these marginalized women, however, such privileged ethical bounds meant risking further invisibility and stigmatization. "It's not hypocrisy," Ahoo repeated after every claim made by Barmak, with a tone that suggested her confidence was turning into frustration. Mina, uninterested in the conversation, reminded Zahra that she could wear the chador out of respect for the Imam and to simply make him hear her. Zahra, also looking frustrated, said that the "hejab thing" did not really matter to her and that she would wear a long manto and cover her hair to meet with the Imam. "I'm not sure anymore, I might be wrong," Barmak responded, sounding puzzled after nearly an hour of heated discussion.

It was not difficult to see Ahoo's perspective and to realize the necessity of conforming to the norms of respectability to maintain social status. Seeing her own acts as simultaneous practices of compliance and resistance, Ahoo would not let anyone define her efforts to build a dignified self as an act of hypocrisy. Instead, aware of the conflicting social systems of values, she realized the thin line between defiance and becoming an outcast. As Holly Wardlow (2006) has argued, unfettered acts of resistance can bolster hegemonic structures when stigmatization throws one's very status as a person into question. Yet, Barmak's argument also carried the assumption that women's new look at ALLY reflected their "true" and autonomous self. Assuming that the secular lifestyle adopted by clients reflected their newfound freedom from the pernicious control of their families ignores the dynamic social and political forces (urban youth culture, class and ethnic discrimination, the hegemony of liberal feminism, etc.) that were formative of the subjectivities that appeared as defiant and autonomous. In fact, the ease with which the young women changed their modes of self-expression at ALLY and at home and their nonchalant attitude toward wearing a chador to meet the Imam demonstrated an ambivalence toward these changing modes of self-representation. Hashemi's (2020) research on lower-class youth in Iran demonstrates that public performances of normative modesty in conservative communities, while perceived as submissive behavior, can allow marginalized youth to articulate agentic selves by increasing their moral capital and carving a socioeconomic space. The establishment of a good reputation in their communities, in fact, would lead to small social and economic gains.

Hashemi's respondents did not experience the kind of tension that we assume Iranian youth do due to contradictions between their "performative front" and their "private self," neither did they understand their strategic performance as a form of deception. In fact, striving to be judged positively through self-editing enabled them to feel true to themselves by building a social character that "live[s] in a good way" (Hashemi 2020: 154). While Iranian youth, following the revolution, have experienced a figurative split between their public and private selves and the notion of saving face in the West has negative connotations of covering one's "true self," the process of self-editing is not unique to Iran or the poor. All cultural systems demand conformity to socially acceptable norms that may or may not coincide with what people choose for themselves (Hashemi 2020). In fact, aspects of the public and private self may overlap as sanctioned codes of conduct are internalized and seen as an important part of the self (Hashemi 2020).

While maintaining a conservative look in their neighborhoods could increase their stock of moral capital, outside their home communities, ALLY's clients could see that gaining access and belonging to middle-class social spaces demanded a different mode of self-representation and that this transformation could grant them social status and opportunities for more income. Some clients, in fact, repeatedly complained about the special treatment certain clients received for looking and acting in ways that pleased ALLY's teachers and administrators. While I did not notice such discriminatory behavior, this common perception among clients reveals the pressure felt at ALLY to project an empowered persona. As explained in previous chapters, embodying a secular middle-class habitus was perceived by ALLY's staff as a sign of empowerment and progress. Adopting middle-class norms of respectable femininity as well as conservative discourses of modest femininity allowed for the cultivation of symbolic economies capable of granting clients a dignified status in the two distinct spaces they frequented. While navigating contradictory discourses of respectability, clients resisted the dominant accounts that would further stigmatize them as deceitful or submissive for inhabiting conflicting social systems. Hence, the young women's appearance and style cannot be simply examined as a manifestation of their defiant predispositions, the repression of their will by their conservative families, or their liberal gender and sexual norms. Adding class and social status to this analysis offers greater insight into clients' agency and their motivations for modeling their middle-class teachers in lifestyle or maintaining a religious look in their communities.

Performing Privilege

I had not seen Nasim for two days. The week before, she had asked me to help her write a proposal for ALLY's managing team to request funds for conducting a workshop on "violence against women" in her neighborhood. After taking the same workshop at ALLY, she was feeling compelled to share her knowledge on the subject with women in her community and later in Afghanistan, to which she and many other Afghan women spoke of yearning to return one day. Having crafted a proposal with her, I was excited to hear about the managing team's decision. After lunch, I finally saw Nasim coming out of the social workers' office with teary eyes and in a neck brace. I could not ask what happened, as she was being led upstairs by a group of social workers. I went to a class where I knew I would find Samira, one of Nasim's close Afghan friends. "We fought in the subway with a crazy woman, she picked a fight with us and called us *harze* [whore]!" Samira said laughingly, alleging that the woman kept calling them "sluts" and then pulled Nasim' hair, injuring her neck. I did not probe her more, but I was quite confident that she was not telling me the whole story. After a few minutes, I was able to piece that day's events together: That day, the Afghan women were more distant and reserved, and I remembered overhearing the conversation of a group of Iranian girls having lunch at the table next to me. In whispers, they discussed an incident that entailed a women yelling out "Afghani *ha-ye Kasif* [you dirty Afghanis], *Harchi mikeshim az dast-e shomast* [all our problems are your doings]." I realized Nasim had become a victim of another hate crime against Afghans in Iran, which she confirmed when I spoke to her after class. I was confused about why Samira had hidden the biggest piece of the puzzle from me. When I heard Samira tell the story in another class and again focus on the gendered nature of the attack (being called a whore) and not its ethnic nature (being also called a dirty Afghani), I knew there was more to it.

An unwillingness to disclose one's ethnic or national identity was only an issue among the incoming Afghan clients of ALLY. Those who were part of ALLY for years knew that ethnic discrimination was rejected at ALLY—although some clients had accused certain staff members of being prejudiced. The longer they stayed at ALLY, the more comfortable Afghan women were with discussing their ethnic marginalization, as was the case for Nasim, Samira, and their cohort. As I showed in Chapter 6, Afghan clients shared their experiences of ethnic discrimination and victimization openly in some classrooms, reminding the staff and Iranian clients of their ethnic privileges. Yet they also performed middle-class Tehrani norms of accent and speech, speaking Dari only among themselves and in private settings. Their performances of femininity (choice of attire and makeup) and class (shopping and consumption patterns) would often intertwine with those of ethnicity (accent and dialect). Yet, at times, the young women's performances of middle-class Tehrani femininity entailed a particular privileged demeanor and modes of speech that ignored class and ethnic inequality. Samira's refusal to disclose the ethnic nature of Nasim's victimization was similar to many other instances of careful, well-crafted performances of privilege I had witnessed that would allow clients to embody a dignified habitus. This performance of privilege often entailed refusing to share one's ethnic and class marginalization by emphasizing the gendered aspect of their victimization. Here I argue that clients' rhetorical and discursive strategies can be understood as the cultivation of certain cultural dispositions as markers of higher status—attempts to signify a privileged status by not seeing class or ethnic inequality, as their teachers often did not.

The interaction of another group of women illustrates this strategic performance. Following a passionate discussion about the public harassment of Afghan women, Mona, one of the Iranian clients, shared her own story of being disrespected in public, claiming that such experiences were not unique to Afghan women. "One day, I was on the subway, and two women started fighting. I jumped in to say something," Mona said, "and one of the women yelled out: *You* shut up! Who do you think you are to open your mouth?" Mona described her experience to claim that public harassment and dismissal are experiences shared by many women, not just Afghans. The teacher asked Mona to reflect on what had triggered the woman's disrespectful reaction. Hesitant to respond, Mona said, "Hmm . . . I don't know, but I didn't used to wear makeup back then and I didn't try to look nice." Mona's working-class appearance, still evident despite her efforts to wear makeup, had likely been the cause of her rude public dismissal. Her references to not wearing makeup and not looking nice also reveal her awareness of the importance of performing a respectable middle-class feminine persona in public if one is to be granted a voice, yet she associated the experience with her lack of a proper feminine performance rather than classism. Ziba, another Iranian client, interjected to share a similar story, revealing how she and her family were mocked in public when wearing chadors for "looking different." It seemed to me again that Ziba's insecurity about wearing a chador reflected the experiences of lower-class *chadori* women in upper-class spaces, since working-class neighborhoods are still marked by black chadors, stereotypical displays of humble classes and religious piety. "Looking different" for wearing a chador was an invisible reference to one's exclusion for not embodying respectable secular middle-class femininity in Tehran, where being modern, cosmopolitan, and fashionable defined who belonged and who was pushed to the margins. The discursive dismissal of class inequality and the association of public degradation with "problems of women" can be best understood when exclusionary discourses of class and ethnicity are examined. These discursive strategies can allow impoverished women to refuse to bolster their marginalization by acknowledging it. It was, after all, their middle-class teachers who similarly and regularly refused to see the ethnic and class dimensions of women's struggles by constructing universal conceptions of womanhood and patriarchy. By doing the same, clients could dissociate from the stigma of being poor and construct their selves as dignified (yet oppressed) women.

Given Iran's long history of monarchic rule and elaborate court rituals, "status recognition remains encoded in, and a crucial part of, language, comportment and social etiquette, persisting after the revolution to an 'extraordinary degree'" (Olszewska 2013: 850). Even though the revolutionary government emerged with the claim of establishing Islamic economic justice and guarding the dignity of the *mostaz'afin* (dispossessed) and framed the pursuit of profit as exploitative and evil, Iran has become characterized by a neoliberal political economy that encourages profit-making investments, reduces social welfare, and privatizes resources and social services. In the process, the Islamic revolutionary discourse has changed, as evidenced by its capitalist and consumerist culture (Olszewska 2013). Class and status are major occupations in everyday discourses in Iran (Olszewska 2013; Khosravi 2008), and the consumption of expensive Western brands remains the key attribute of being recognized as ba-kelas. Meanwhile, the lower classes in Iran with aspirations for higher status encounter snobbery, prejudice, and humiliation at the hands of the upper class. As argued by Hashemi (2020), for the lower class, the risk of losing face hinges on being exposed as poor. In this context, posturing through manipulation of one's physical appearance, mannerisms, and modes of speech is an effective means of hiding one's stigmatized social identities and building a dignified habitus as a form of symbolic capital. The experiences of Mona and Ziba reveal the consequences of losing face in public when one fails to present oneself as "respectable." Associating their experiences of victimization with their poverty when retelling their stories of exclusion would have exposed their stigmatized identity. Given the shame associated with poverty, I noticed the young women's efforts to save face in front of one another by creating a hierarchy among themselves in terms of their access to resources, knowledge about what is in fashion, and references to the relatively higher status of their neighborhoods.

It is worth noting again that many of the clients had a clear awareness of their ethnic and class struggles and often problematized the privilege of teachers who ignored the structural effects of inequality. But demanding respect, in public and at ALLY, required constructing universal accounts of oppressed womanhood and presenting themselves as women untouched by inequalities that separated them from the middle-class women they aspired to appear as. They evoked class inequality and economic justice in certain contexts while continuously aspiring to a higher status by performing middle class, bodily and discursively, in other settings. For instance, when asked about their impression of ALLY and its objectives, the young women noted how the organization had helped them to "gain confidence in being a woman," how they needed to "know their rights as women," and how ALLY had shown them that "it's not like the past with patriarchy, when only men had rights; women can enter the society as well." What struck me each time I heard such accounts is the seemingly purposeful dismissal of poverty, racism, or the immigration laws that had created the level of marginalization that brought these women to ALLY. After all, the middle-class female staff there did not need the same services offered by the organization and had already "entered the society" alongside their male counterparts.

The history of women's rights activism in Iran has allowed women to rightfully associate their underachievement with the oppressive and patriarchal policies of the Islamic government rather than personal shortcomings. The biopolitical management of women's bodies by the state, gender segregation of certain work and educational spaces, and the persistence of misogynistic laws have been largely and publicly discussed since 1979. Speaking out loud about women's oppression has become an acceptable and expected signifier of an educated and progressive woman. This manner of speech is particularly embraced by women's empowerment programs, which encourage such a feminist outlook. Sharing their ethnic or class stigmatization, however, only reinforced women's stigmatized identities, particularly in a context where staff had adopted a liberal feminist discourse that did not equally problematize class inequality and ethnic oppression. As such, clients frequently abandoned their intersectional feminism in favor of performing middle-class modes of speech (e.g., referring to the poor in the third person or sharing their desire for "helping the poor"), speaking highly of education, and discussing gender oppression solely in terms of patriarchal cultural norms or laws. The Afghan clients similarly distanced themselves from the stigma of their ethnicity and poverty by making statements such as "not all Afghans are poor and dirty," pointing to the respectability of those Afghans who have embraced the norms of the Tehrani middle class. As Olszewska's research on Afghan refugees in Iran also demonstrates, a microprocess of class differentiation was taking place when those Afghans with newly acquired cultural capital and middle-class cultural dispositions were distancing themselves from those who were deprived of both cultural and financial capital. While resisting exclusion by countering stereotypes, the young women avoided one system of power while assenting to another and creating other hierarchies to carve out a dignified status. An examination of these women's approaches only in terms of gender performances, their feminist sensibility, or class strategies fails to account for the subjective ambivalence of people who engage in these acts (Ortner 1995) or the internal hierarchies within subaltern groups.

This reveals that separating resistance from compliance is in fact more difficult than many studies on resistance tend to argue (Ortner 1995).

Performing Entitlement

My mental picture of overtly grateful young women who felt they owed their livelihood to the kindness of a charity organization was crushed on the first day of my ethnographic fieldwork, when I was told by Marva that the girls have proven to be *por tavagho* (demanding). "I don't like *delsoozi* [pity] for the girls; they don't need it and it only makes them por tavagho!" Marva explained as she described her initial feelings of delsoozi when she began her work at ALLY and learned about the girls' startling problems. She said those feelings made the girls expect too much and think they were the only ones who had problems. "Now I tell them everyone has problems!" Marva said firmly. I was shocked as I listened to Marva's cold remarks, as I knew with certainty, and only after a short while of watching her interact with the clients, that she cared deeply about them and their struggles. Soon, I saw with my own eyes what Marva was referring to, as I encountered many unhappy young women who continuously complained about the classes, the teachers, the behavior of the staff, the quality of the food and services offered at ALLY, the decisions made by the administrators, and the lack of allocation of resources to the areas of their interest. I described some of these complaints in Chapter 5, when I examined clients' frustration with the privileged approach of the staff to empowerment. Of interest here are the language and tone with which such complaints were expressed by the subaltern women who were seeking resources at an organization like ALLY.

Many of the criticisms were perceived as *ghor zadan* (nagging) by the staff. Rather than pleading with the staff or "managing their expectations," as Marva expected the clients to do, the young women complained in a tone that reflected a sense of privilege and entitlement. I had heard other employees speak similarly of the growing "self-centered" attitude of the young women, who believed they were entitled to more and more resources from the organization. I could see that making sense of clients' growing negative attitude had become an everyday interpretive task for the staff; I heard them attempt to explain such behavior by referencing the women's young age and their "typical teenage attitude." Others explained this behavior as a form of confusion experienced by women who had only been granted a voice for the first time at ALLY. Many argued that such behavior was understandable and served as practice for developing more articulated critiques of their social environment.

Vijayendra Rao and Paromita Sanyal have examined the role of poverty and its attendant habitus as they shape deliberations in spaces where "various unequal groups come together in a highly stratified social context to exercise their voice" (2010: 147). In their study on public meetings in Indian village democracies, where villagers made decisions regarding budget allocations, Rao and Sanyal (2010) demonstrate how the discursive style of the upper-caste members of the villages was different from that of the poor, low-caste villagers, who employed a fawning and pleading tone with demonstrations of helplessness. Rao and Sanyal show how groups' varying economic, social, and cultural capital determine "who speaks, what they say, and how they speak" (2010: 152). In this sense, we can identify a link between culture and poverty not through the "culture of poverty" theories of the 1960s but by seeing the connection of economic and educational deprivation with cultural capital and discursive style.

While shaped by inequalities of power, ALLY was a space that could give rise to a community of citizens with a newly discovered voice. The staff repeatedly encouraged the young women to use their voice, to be *jasoor* (courageous), and to demand their rights. This space allowed clients to discard, albeit momentarily, the stigma of their marginalized identities and to slip into the identity of citizens with dignity who could demand rights and services. While the process of complaining and making demands seemed ordinary on the surface, it enabled marginalized groups to claim a sense of equal recognition as dignified members of society (Rao and Sanyal 2010). Clients' complaints about the quality of food and the behavior of some staff and their request for more decision-making power over the allocation of resources were expressions of the politics of dignity—a demand to be recognized as social and political equals deserving of improving their material well-being.

The boundary-testing actions of the poor are skills developed and cultivated in spaces where they can discover new chances of participation (Rao and Sanyal 2010). At ALLY, "nagging" and "complaining" remained the central character of clients' expression of discontent and means of enforcing change at the organization. The demanding attitude of the clients and their refusal to accept anything other than full respect and a position of mutuality with the staff—an attitude likely not tolerated outside of ALLY—were performances of privilege and entitlement as a means of demanding a dignified status. All these small and seemingly insignificant attitudes can add up to tangible and significant outcomes in the high-stakes game of status performance and mobility (Olszewska 2013: 860). Annette Lareau's study (2011) shows how middle-class children learn to assume a position of equality and mutuality in relation to authority figures, which enables them to demand and receive services in various institutions, particularly schools. The growing entitled attitude of ALLY's clients was developed within a space keen on cultivating a middle-class habitus in the young women (see Chapter 5) and in the context of a "women's empowerment" program that encouraged participants to "demand their rights." As shown in Chapter 6, the young women continued to problematize inequality by explaining it as a form of injustice in which those who are privileged (staff) are complicit. In doing so, they questioned the dominant perceptions of themselves as cases of pity or charity who relied on the generosity of benevolent NGO actors. Rather than asking, they demanded quality services as rightful recipients of social services in an unjust society.

The young women in my study performed middle class by adopting a secular and fashionable style of dress and makeup and a feminist language that emphasized women's universal and cultural oppression. Performing middle class through a rhetorical dismissal of class and ethnic inequality and an assertive mode of relationship with the staff based on mutuality was common among subaltern women, both Iranian and Afghan, who wished to benefit from, albeit temporarily, taking on a dignified habitus. In this chapter, I have placed my observations in conversation with more recent studies on class and ethnic inequality in Iran that encourage an intersectional analysis of gender, where inequalities of gender, race, class, and citizenship are not treated as separate categories of analysis. Rather than examining individual motivations behind each mode of self-representation, I have revealed the institutional discourses that necessitate certain modes of self-representation for building a dignified status in a highly stratified society. By doing so, I have aimed to demonstrate the significance of adding class, ethnicity, and nationality to our examination of the transformation many participants embody in women's empowerment programs.

Conclusion

> Moving, we confront the realities of choice and location. Within complex and ever shifting realms of power relations, do we position ourselves on the side of colonizing mentality? Or do we continue to stand in political resistance with the oppressed, ready to offer our ways of seeing and theorizing, of making culture, toward that revolutionary effort which seeks to create space where there is unlimited access to the pleasure and power of knowing, where transformation is possible? The choice is crucial.
>
> —BELL HOOKS, "Choosing the Margin as a Space of Radical Openness"

In 2016, as I worked on the initial drafts of these chapters, I came across the United Nations International Children's Emergency Fund's (UNICEF) campaign for International Women's Day. The campaign entailed releasing what was referred to as a "harrowing" video to "highlight the horror of underage marriage" in an effort to "help eliminate" it (Blott 2016). The bride in the video, a blonde girl in her early teens, is dressed in a white wedding gown while being pampered and prepared for her expensive wedding ceremony in a high-end club. The young bride is shown in snapshots as being occupied with her coloring book as her teddy bear lays on her wedding veil. Walking alone down the aisle, passing teary-eyed family and relatives, she is married to an older man and innocently looks him in the eyes, unaware of the horrific fate that will soon follow. The predatory hand of the groom moves gently on the shoulders of the young child, reminding the audience of the "grim reality faced by millions of girls around the world" (Blott 2016). Various online articles spoke of the power of this video in highlighting the horror of child marriage by replicating a high-end Western wedding.

As I watched the video, I wondered why raising awareness about underage marriage in the Global South required erasing the race and the class of the young girls to whom the video attempts to bring attention. I thought about the implications of this erasure for feminist efforts that are keen on refusing to acknowledge the connection between child marriage and poverty, when the persistence of the practice among the most impoverished populations of the Global South points to its strong linkage with economic and political instability, conditions shaped and maintained by the centuries-long racial-colonial Western domination. The colonial mentality of such international feminist efforts channeled toward "educating" the non-white people of the Global South about the horrors of their cultural practices—horrors so easily recognizable in the "civilized" Western eyes—continues to dominate international institutions and their women's empowerment campaigns. As I examined ALLY's program and its emphasis on education and consciousness-raising, I knew it was important to delineate the deep entanglement between Iran's middle-class liberal feminism and the globally circulating women's empowerment agenda that continues to problematize gender oppression irrespective of its intersecting class, racial, and global political dimensions.

It is no doubt that *women's empowerment* has become the buzzword of our era. The term is widely used by transnational institutions such as the UN and the World Bank, by local and grassroots initiatives such as ALLY, by corporations that claim to empower women by exploiting their labor, and even in commercials that sell beauty products. However, the phrase has come under scrutiny due to its commonplace and paradoxical use by diverse and contradictory institutions that have conflicting agendas (Parpart, Rai, and Staudt 2002). Discussions of co-optation have compelled scholars and activists to question the comfort taken in the popular notion of empowerment and to examine more critically the assumptions underpinning women's empowerment programs. In this book, I have outlined the complex ways middle-class and ethnic discourses of respectability entangle with liberal feminist discourses of "progress" and "backwardness" and place the blame of gender oppression on "cultural poverty." As activists design and implement empowerment programs, they inadvertently bring an array of disciplinary discourses into their emancipatory agenda. As they model UN programs and draw from women's rights packages to define the constitutive elements of empowerment, these organizations allow liberal assumptions about agency being a rejection of culture and tradition to dominate their assessment of progress. As they experience class as a relational construct and perceive poverty through a deficit model, they construct the poor as being in need of guidance by the enlightened middle class.

Depending on the definition of the term *power*—on which em(power)ment programs are founded—the agenda of an organization can take a variety of directions. In most modern definitions, empowerment implies the ability to exert *power over* people, resources, and institutions (Held et al. 1999). Empowerment is also defined as the ability to *make things happen*, which is why it has become the watchword for transformative and progressive agendas seeking to create more egalitarian and equitable systems (Parpart, Rai, and Staudt 2002). Other scholars (Battiwala 1994; Kabeer 1999) have questioned Marxist and liberal definitions that emphasize power over resources and the processes of decision-making. In a feminist analysis of power that goes beyond formal and institutional definitions, these scholars define empowerment as "more than participation in decision-making; *it must also include the processes that lead people to perceive themselves as able and entitled to make decisions*" (Rowlands 1997: 14).

In the 1970s and more so in the 1980s, the gender and development approach highlighted the role of culture and socioeconomic inequalities in women's subordination and their subsequent disempowerment. This approach, however, was largely determined by Western notions of development (Hirshman 1995). In *Development, Crises, and Alternative Visions: Third World Women's Perspective*, Gita Sen and Caren Grown (1987) show that poor women's subordination in the Global South is not the result of a backwardness or underdevelopment from which they could be rescued by progressive projects and programs. The root of the problem, they argued, is in the fundamentally exploitative global relations of power enforced by Western governments and international institutions that portray women's subordination as rooted in their cultures rather than the effects of militaristic neoliberalism.

Government-sponsored women's empowerment programs, however, continue to offer courses on family, health care, food, nutrition, sewing, and crafts, which are reformist and conservative rather than transformative (Ityavyar and Obiajunwa 1992). Critics of these programs argue that without linking the topics that are covered to the dynamics associated with patriarchy, sexuality, colonialism, and power, the knowledge transmitted is not likely to be empowering (Stromquist 2002).

The failure of top-down, mainstream, and state-led development programs resulted in the adoption of alternative models of empowerment that emphasize learning from the poor, engaging in direct democracy, and grassroots participation within local communities. Women-led NGOs like ALLY that cater to adult women are key examples of grassroots mobilization around gender issues. These NGOs attempt to question patriarchal ideologies and to provide women with safe spaces to collectively question their social status. By providing workshops on topics relevant to women's advancement, such as domestic violence, legal rights, reproductive health, and politics, these organizations have claimed to provide women with a variety of empowering opportunities. My analysis of the unacknowledged class and ethnic discourses that shaped ALLY's program is meant to reveal how, even within grassroots and local initiatives with emancipatory agendas, regulatory discourses shape the definition of empowerment and position middle-class women as the enlightened saviors of poor women. Within a women's empowerment program, a defiant attitude toward patriarchal cultural norms without a similar interrogation of the subjugating discourses of class and ethnicity can disempower subaltern women whose investment in their own survival is perceived as "lacking a sense of social responsibility," whose progress is measured by *performing* middle-class femininity, and whose experiences of class and ethnic marginalization become invalidated by universal and reductive accounts of gender oppression.

This study aligns with more recent studies in the women's development literature (see Merry 2006; Lewis and Mosse 2006; Sharma 2008; Levitt and Merry 2009; Thayer 2010; Radhakrishnan 2015) that are concerned with examining the impact of neoliberal discourses on local initiatives. These studies investigate the responses of local actors to global discourses, the adaptation and translation processes involved, and the relations of power and privilege inside development programs.

My study connects the women's development literature with that on transnational feminisms to reveal the hegemony and the shortcomings of a liberal and secular feminist framework in ALLY's program that was translated by cosmopolitan and middle-class NGO workers with access to the global stage. I have shown that cosmopolitan activists' liberal conception of feminism constructed religious women as disempowered others by assuming that rejecting culture and religion is necessary for developing an autonomous personhood. With its emphasis on individual rights, the organization failed to provide subaltern women with a framework of gender justice that would find currency in their communities, resulting in the further stigmatization of clients who experienced a backlash when utilizing this liberal framework to advocate for themselves. The relationship between the cosmopolitan and local elite over the practicality of advocacy for sexual autonomy among marginalized women revealed a contentious dynamic central to postcolonial contexts whereby Western cultural products are translated as universal values by cosmopolitan actors and are contested by local elite, who emphasize the importance of context and resonance. By showcasing the challenges of implementing ALLY's liberal and secular feminist program, I hope to encourage activists to consider the value of a justice-enhancing feminist practice and a nonideal universalist approach (Khader 2019b). This transnational and anti-imperialist feminism recognizes the ethnocentrism in assuming that traditions outside the West are inherently patriarchal and that Western cultural forms are the only moral and viable choice for women. This imperialist outlook is the reason why missionary feminists are unable to recognize how wearing hejab can be empowering or how an Islamic feminist framework can better empower some Muslim women to seek justice in their social environment. Justice-enhancing feminist practice recognizes the nonidealness of social conditions and the significance of the context and historical specificity that shape those conditions. This approach recognizes women's intersecting class and ethnic struggles and examines priorities and strategies for reducing and eliminating sexist oppression instead of committing to an ideal of equal rights in the face of its theoretical and practical shortcomings. Without radically transforming global economic and political structures that reproduce class and racial hierarchies, a definition of feminism as equality between men and women can only privilege white bourgeois women. "Which men do women want to be equal to? Do women share a common vision of what equality means?" (hooks 1984: 18).

I have also argued that the potential and outcome of women's empowerment programs should not be solely measured by their unspoken regulatory practices or their overstated emancipatory objectives. In examining the transformation ALLY's clients experienced, I have revealed the limitation of theorizing women's transformed lifestyle as an indication of the development of a liberal outlook when the symbolic economy of adopting a cosmopolitan lifestyle among poor and ethnic minorities is overlooked. Meanwhile, marginalized clients resist and defy the stigmatizing effects of culturally reductionist accounts of gender oppression that undermine transnational structural injustices. For instance, clients utilized the intellectually nurturing space of ALLY to articulate an intersectional critique of the organization's program, to form class and ethnic solidarities, and to enforce an understanding of class and ethnic privilege on NGO workers. Future research can benefit from exploring the potential of subaltern resistance for transforming the world of the middle-class and cosmopolitan activists who often perceive education and consciousness-raising as unidirectional.

Despite more attention being paid to women's development programs implemented in South Asia, Africa, and Latin America, the growing number of women's empowerment programs designed by states or NGOs in the Middle East have not gotten similar theoretical or empirical attention. Studies on gender in the Middle East continue to focus on Islamism, governments' patriarchal gender policies, or women's political campaigns. In this book, I have examined the impact of the state's repressive policies on the advocacy practices of ALLY, particularly as they shaped ALLY's capabilities-oriented approach to identity politics. However, I hope to have shown that focusing on state policies when examining women's lives leaves out important sites and contexts for examining gender relations and feminist discourses. Women-led NGOs and women's empowerment programs are dynamic sites not only for studying the transnational processes of translation and contestation of globally hegemonic discourses in local settings but also for examining the interplay between gender, class, and ethnic subjectivities in contexts where the NGO directors and their clients are of vastly different class and ethnic backgrounds.

Any analysis of feminism and gender inequality in Iran that remains ambivalent regarding the role of class, ethnic politics, and transnational connections in shaping feminist agenda or the everyday practices of women fails to account for the lives of the majority of poor, working-class, shahrestani, immigrant, refugee, and non-Persian ethnic groups of women whose struggles cannot be analytically separated from class, ethnic, and imperial oppression. While the perspectives of the secular, middle-class, and educated Tehrani women like the staff and administrators of ALLY remain at the center of scholarship on feminism in Iran, I hope that this book offers an alternative perspective by revealing the standpoint of subaltern women for whom empowerment is grounded within struggles for social and economic justice rather than a liberal conception of autonomy and choice, as hegemonic feminist models presume.

Epilogue

As I finish writing this book, nine years after I first began this study, I realize that much has changed in Iran. The hard-liners' control over all branches of the government has led to increasing state violence and various religious-fundamentalist impositions. Rampant corruption among state officials, high inflation, severe economic stagnation and unemployment—exacerbated by U.S. sanctions—privatization and the erosion of state welfare, and the mismanagement of natural resources have made life increasingly precarious for people in Iran, including my research participants, who sadly did not remain immune from the state crackdowns on NGOs and charities.

A glimmer of hope amid the sorrow is the mass uprising that erupted following the state killing of a young Kurdish woman, Jina (Mahsa) Amini. Jina's severe beating in state custody by the morality police over improper hejab and her subsequent death ignited public outrage and a civil unrest that rapidly spread across the country. At Jina's crowded funeral, in her hometown of Saqqez, and later in demonstrations that spread across eighty cities and towns, women furiously and defiantly ripped off their headscarves while dancing on the streets, as crowds of men and women cheered them on. The decades-old Kurdish slogan of *"Jin, Jiyan, Azadi"* [Woman, Life, Freedom], chanted during Jina's funeral in Iran's province of Kurdistan, soon became the rallying cry during the protests across the country.

Much has been speculated about the significance of this movement as potentially the first-ever feminist revolution, one that has placed women at the center of struggles for democracy, freedom, and dignity for all. By constructing a collective claim to life, manifested in the slogan of "Woman, Life, Freedom," this movement has demonstrated an extraordinary ability to mobilize broad solidarity between various segments of society. Defiance against compulsory hejab in these protests is not merely about hejab but also the many layers of injustice and violence enacted by the state. The movement, in fact, has shown an intersectional character by denouncing not only the structural oppression of women but also its ties to the structural oppression of religious and ethnic minorities. After all, Jina's Kurdish and Suni identities were what led to speculation about her particularly violent mistreatment and why the first protests erupted in the Kurdish region of Iran, with its long history of marginalization and revolutionary resistance.

While Jina's death marked the beginning of the uprising, since then, numerous women, men, and children have been killed, injured, and imprisoned, and some executed by a state desperate to repress the largest and most inspiring uprising the country has witnessed since the 1979 revolution. In all state crackdowns, ethnic minorities have been subjected to the most violent repression, such as the drone attacks and shelling of Kurdish regions and the massacre that took the lives of ninety-three individuals in Zahedan as the police fired live ammunition on protesters and into a Suni mosque during worship services. State narratives that emphasize protecting Iran's "national unity" and "territorial integrity" have long been weaponized against ethnic-minority groups such as the Baluch, Kurds, and Arabs, who are forever suspected of instigating separation by simply claiming their identity. The long history of Persian-centrism has not only facilitated the state's assimilation policies and structural discrimination against ethnic minorities but also has contributed to a culture where the recognition of ethnic struggles is perceived as divisive and a threat to the movement's unity. The erasure of the Kurdish voice and perspective by both Iranian diaspora media and international media is evident in the omission of the Kurdish origin of the now globally popular slogan "Woman, Life, Freedom" and the lack of recognition for the role Kurdish women played in this revolution.

Compounding matters, numerous groups outside and inside Iran have attempted to appropriate and co-opt the movement's message and outcome. The images of women's unveiling, burning headscarves, and flipping turbans have rightfully worried those who fear that the Western (mis)representation of the movement would embolden neocon warhawk politics and promote interventionist, Islamophobic, and savior attitudes. Meanwhile, well-funded conservative oppositional groups in the diaspora continue their attempts to restore the monarchy by investing in satellite channels that give considerable airtime to Reza Pahlavi, the son of the former Shah and dictator whose ascendency to power in 1953 was facilitated by a CIA-orchestrated coup. By showcasing the images of unveiled and fashionable Iranian women in the years prior to the revolution, their television programs romanticize Iran's past and position unveiled women as the symbol of the nation's restorable lost freedom. Their attempts to hijack the revolution, however, have been met with a popular slogan chanted on the streets: "Death to the oppressor, whether Shah or Rahbar [supreme religious leader]."

The transformative potential of this uprising remains in the coalition of variously oppressed social groups as well as activists' success in building an intersectional and anti-imperialist feminism. During contentious times, the tendency to erase the diversity of identities and struggles in the name of unity can be strong, and the demands of the most marginalized groups, such as ethnic and sexual minorities, are often silenced to avoid "divisive" politics. Given the enormity of this historic moment, the need for reflexivity and constructing a revolutionary discourse that does not reproduce class, ethnic, sexual, and religious hierarchies is crucial, as is the recognition that the freedom of women is tied to the freedom of Afghans, Kurds, Azeris, Baluchis, and Arabs from all forms of oppression, local and global.

Acknowledgments

The journey leading to the publication of this book has been filled with many wholesome encounters and extraordinary people. My deepest gratitude goes to my research participants, who graciously welcomed me into their world and whose courage, resilience, and humility will always remain an inspiration. They have made my career possible and enriched my world in innumerable ways.

I am greatly indebted to my mentor, S. Crawley, for the invaluable guidance and support they have extended to me over the years and for their encouragement as I developed this project. I am also grateful to Rob Benford for his kind and endless support and to Vrushali Patil, whose insightful scholarship has inspired my work. I would like to express my sincere appreciation to Marilyn Myerson. Her kindness, generosity, and patience were a saving grace during my first years of graduate studies as an international student.

I would like to thank my editor, Ryan Mulligan, for his words of encouragement and thoughtful feedback and Shaun Vigil for believing in this book. People who leave great marks on our work often remain unnamed. I would like to express my appreciation to the anonymous reviewers of my work whose enthusiastic support and generous feedback guided this project. I would also like to acknowledge the University of South Florida's Dissertation Completion Fellowship and the University of Tampa's Research Innovation and Scholarly Excellence Grant for funding and supporting this project at different stages.

I am forever indebted to my parents, Mahnaz Moradi and Mohammad Bahreini. I remain in awe of my mom's resilience and am always inspired by her strength and love. My dad's unwavering love and support are gifts I carry close to my heart. Finally, I would like to thank all my loved ones who supported me during the crucial years of writing this book, especially my friend, Manuel, for always believing in me and cheering me on.

Appendix

Theory, Method, and Politics

As a feminist ethnographer, I reflected greatly on how my ethnicity, class, gender, and education could shape my research and how those identities were perceived by my research participants. While my gender, age, and the fact that I had only left Iran five years prior to my fieldwork could establish me as an insider, I knew that my identity as a middle-class Tehrani woman who lived in the United States had already solidified my status as an outsider among the impoverished ethnic minority clients of ALLY. After a few initial encounters, it became clear that the women's conversations around me would change when they realized I was not one of the clients, and it would change even further when they realized I did not live in Iran, a signifier of class status and privilege that would distance me from them greatly. By performing *approachability* and *credibility* (Lofland et al. 2006), I attempted to build rapport with my participants to navigate this simultaneous outsider and insider status. Ethnographers often highlight similarities to develop rapport and negotiate personal connections with participants (Berbary 2014). To build credibility, I intentionally downplayed my privileged class status by dressing modestly and simple—alternating between two black *manto* throughout months of data collection. I did so to gain cultural credibility among the clients and not draw further distance between us with the flamboyant performance of privilege and class that is commonly practiced by the middle and upper class in Iran. While recognizing approachability and credibility as performances, I concur with Sarah Mayorga-Gallo and Elizabeth Hordge-Freeman (2017) that they are also racialized, gendered, classed, and placed on the body of researchers by participants. Therefore, I recognize that despite all the efforts on my part, being known as a doctoral student who lived in the United States had already demarcated my status as that of a privileged outsider.

I maintained *approachability* (Mayorga-Gallo and Hordge-Freeman 2017) by being easy to talk to and answering all questions with patience and humor. To be accepted among Afghan participants as an Iranian, I knew it was critical to make clear my views on the ethnic discrimination experienced by Afghans in Iran. I had, in fact, noticed the skillful and subtle interrogation of my views by clients during the first weeks of my fieldwork. Establishing trust and intimacy was challenging, and I did so slowly, with trial and many errors. I could see that my status and place of residence were why I was welcomed among many young women, who saw me as a source of information about the outside world. I often found myself responding to the eager and curious questions of the clients about living in the United States and even offering information and advice about immigration to those clients (and some staff) who were keen to leave Iran. The young women who had aspirations for university education and learning English often asked for my help with their English courses or with writing proposals or interviewed me for their projects.

Although being approachable and eager to help enabled me to build connections with my participants, my rapport with clients was most consolidated when I acknowledged as valid their discontent and frustration with certain aspects of ALLY's program and recognized those organizational narratives that troubled and irritated the young women. For instance, as I show in Chapter 6, staff's attempts to deny their privilege had led to many tensions between the two groups. Hearing the clients, legitimizing their grievances, and acknowledging my privilege were authentic practices that led to building rapport with my informants. Due to these attempts, I noticed a change in the young women's response to my presence after a few weeks of fieldwork. I noticed that they opened up more about their views and life experiences, allowed me to be present in conversations they often hid from the staff (e.g., mocking the staff, criticizing classes), and persuasively invited me to join their classes to the extent that not attending would cause resentment. While at times the young women asked for my views as someone who had lived abroad, in most cases, it seemed they simply wanted me to hear what they had to say.

While there were status differences between me and ALLY's clients, many of the staff members and I shared a similar class, ethnic, and educational background. Those on the managing team either lived or had the experience of previously living or studying abroad. Our similar backgrounds helped me build *professional credibility* among the staff and establish myself as a worthwhile investment of time (Mayorga-Gallo and Hordge-Freeman 2017). I was most welcomed among two groups of staff: One was a group of young teachers who identified as activists and taught courses on community development. I attended their classes regularly, for the clients there openly discussed their views on a range of social issues. The other group was the management team, who I admired for their courageous efforts to run a feminist project in Tehran. My periodic observations and critiques of how the organization was run seemed greatly appreciated by the founder and the program director. I had many personal conversations with a range of staff, and while I shared my views when they were solicited, I chose to mostly remain an observer and a listener, learning from and acknowledging the many challenges they faced daily.

Like many ethnographers who have researched marginalized populations, I grappled with ethical questions and dilemmas. I knew my participants' poverty, lower levels of schooling, and ethnic marginalization could place them in danger of exploitation and coercion. Ethnographers are instructed to obtain informed consent to mitigate these harms. While I followed all the protocols mandated by the Institutional Review Board (IRB), I could not ignore that the processes of informed consent are often designed to serve and protect institutions and sponsors rather than vulnerable groups (Grady et al. 2017). Informed consent, while necessary, can give researchers an illusion of ethical conduct, for it cannot impede the common harm inflicted on marginalized communities through paternalistic ethnographic research that pathologizes and exotifies marginalized groups (Yarbrough 2020). As I had grounded my work within the postcolonial feminist literature, the implications of conducting research on the lives of the subaltern were not lost on me. Here I was, a middle-class Tehrani woman, going back to Iran after five years of graduate studies in Western academia to "go native" in my own land and study marginalized and disadvantaged women whose last resort was the nongovernmental organization at which I was going to do fieldwork. While I had assured the IRB that my research had *minimal risk* to the young women attending the organization, I had yet to assure myself that my social and intellectual positioning would not inflict another trauma on the collective experience of subaltern women in academic scholarship. While the inclusion of marginalized populations in research introduces many ethical concerns, so does their exclusion, underrepresentation, or misrepresentation in academic studies.

To address such ethical challenges, I have approached this fieldwork as a form of "solidarity research," which recognizes research as a political act informed by a politics of solidarity with oppressed groups (Yarbrough 2020). I was keen on avoiding the long legacy of academic research that misrepresents marginalized women of the Global South as ignorant and with a "false consciousness." By drawing from Dorothy Smith's (2005) *Institutional Ethnography*, I treated the young, impoverished women as experts of their own lived experiences with valuable insight that could inform academic research and policy. Feminist standpoint theory claims that marginalized women can add to human knowledge by revealing distinct relations of power that are missed by those in positions of power and privilege. Black feminists, for instance, have identified the privilege of White middle-class women in feminist theorizing and have challenged the use of *woman* and *gender* as unitary and homogeneous categories that reflect an imagined essence of all women (Collins 1990; Crenshaw 1991; Davis 1981; hooks 2000). In my study, I considered how the varying standpoints of my research participants were shaped by their privileged or marginal identities. I studied the views of the marginalized clients in relation to the relatively privileged workers of the organization with the hope that the "diversity of life experiences refracts ideas through a new prism, increases the likelihood of more valid conclusions, and more useful policy recommendations" (Yarbrough 2020: 73).

Theoretically, I have placed this project within the standpoint theory, postcolonial feminism, and institutional ethnography to make it an intellectual and political project. It is intellectual because it makes visible the institutional discourses and relations of power in which my informants participated as they simultaneously confronted them. It is political because it aims to depart from the scholarly work on women in the Global South in which, according to Gayatri Spivak (1985), subaltern women's voices remain unheard and occluded by the hegemony of privileged theoretical and conceptual constructs. Emerging in the 1970s and 1980s, the standpoint theory brought to feminist, scientific, philosophical, and political discussions a fresh perspective and anxiety-producing dilemmas that pertain to the relation between power and knowledge (Harding 2004). Beginning from the claim that knowledge is socially situated, standpoint theory takes a position against Western, androcentric science and its universalist claims for being able to transcend particular locations and human perspectives.

Nancy C. M. Hartsock (2004) claims that privileging certain standpoints over others is at the heart of the feminist standpoint theory because, as a political project, it favor positions capable of social transformation by offering possibilities for envisioning more just social relations. Chela Sandoval (2004) argues that certain standpoints are "better," because if they are "self-consciously recognized by their inhabitants," they can transform individuals into resistant, oppositional, and collective subjects. Patricia Hill Collins (2000) similarly sees the standpoint of the oppressed as a space for the formation of an "oppositional consciousness." There are perspectives on society through which certain oppressive relations cannot be seen. A standpoint carries with it the contention that the ruling class and gender have a material interest in that deception. A standpoint is a position in which those relations are *made* visible. Hence, "the vision available to the oppressed groups must be struggled for" (Hartsock 2004: 37).

Yet, standpoint theory has been criticized by those scholars who question its plausibility for all contexts. Uma Narayan (2004), for instance, questions the epistemic advantage given to marginalized groups as holding a "double vision" capable of creating oppositional consciousness. Mere access to two different and incompatible contexts, Narayan suggests, does not necessarily guarantee a critical stance or the choice of subversive practices. Certain kinds of oppressive contexts and practices, she argues, might prevent people from developing the tools with which they can locate the causes of their misery in larger social arrangements, see their misfortunes as more than personal, or develop desire for any radical change. Thus, "epistemic advantage" and "double vision" as sources of insight are treated in this book with caution and not reified into metaphysics. While I have amplified the critical voice of ALLY's subaltern clients and their ignored yet brilliant resistance to culturally reductionist liberal feminist discourses, it would be remiss to conclude that clients' marginalization, deprivation, and trauma had not seriously impacted their intellectual and emotional responses. Consequently, I have treated my participants as "multiple, heterogeneous, and frequently contradictory or incoherent, not unitary, homogenous, and coherent as they are for empiricist epistemology" (Harding 2004: 134).

Standpoint theory has also been criticized for carrying in it the "metonymic fallacy of the intellectual" (Pels 2004). As it is similar in architecture to Marxian epistemology, standpoint theory is criticized for being caught in a singular conflict between primary and secondary identities, "offering similar opportunities for an identity swap and for the resultant 'absent presence' of intellectual spokespersons" (Pels 2004: 280). Critical theorists have created dualistic fields of contest—bourgeois versus proletariat, men versus women, White versus Black—and in so doing, they have created the duality of dominant versus dominated. Arguing that in the contest between the two, one needs to begin from the standpoint of the latter, critical theorists tend to make invisible a third position, which is the position from which they themselves speak (Pels 2004).

The position of the intellectual is that of a contradictory social location. Intellectuals identify with the oppressed but do not find that marginal standpoint suffice unless they are *intellectualized* by the "outsiders within," when marginal standpoints are pushed to "pass through theory, which evidently requires the guiding presence of the professionals of theory themselves" (Pels 2004: 281). Donna Haraway cautions us that there is "a serious danger of romanticizing and/or appropriating the vision of the less powerful while claiming to see from their positions" (1991: 191). The problem lies in marginal intellectuals' unwillingness to calculate the interests and advantages that define their "in betweenness" as they choose to prioritize their class, gender, or racial identities above their identities as marginal intellectuals "and, in so doing, erase the inequalities that separate them from the groups with which they politically and emotionally identify" (Pels 2004: 285). Dick Pels suggests that the position from which the marginal intellectual should speak is the position of *alienation* or the *dominated dominant* (Bourdieu 1991) rather than that of *oppression* or *exploitation*.

Hence, it is important that I make visible my position as that of the intellectual, the dominated dominant. My project, inspired by bell hooks (2000) and other standpoint theorists, is one written from the margin, a space of *radical openness*, with words that *emerge from suffering* yet *carry the scent of oppression*, in the language that is not of the marginalized people I speak of here but of those who dominate them, the language that is *a place of struggle*.

Notes

Introduction

1. I use the terms *girls* and *women* interchangeably to refer to ALLY's clients. The distinction between *dokhtar* (girl) and *zan* (woman) implies not only an age difference but also one's marital status, with the term *dokhtar* referring to young women who have not been married. Clients and staff often referred to clients as *dokhtar-ha* (girls), as many were unmarried and in their teen years.

2. The names of the organization and participants have been changed to protect their identity, and where it did not violate the essence of the analysis, I have changed information regarding participants' private lives and roles at the organization to further protect their confidentiality.

Chapter 1

1. *Manto* (manteau) is a trenchcoat-style covering women are expected to wear in public to comply with the government's hejab requirements.

Chapter 2

1. *Shahrestani* refers to people from provinces other than Tehran. The term is at times used in a derogatory tone by Tehranis to make status distinctions.

2. In 1934, Reza Shah changed the name of the country from Persia to Iran. For historical accuracy, I have used the term *Persia* when speaking of the pre-1930s period.

3. In *Persian Pictures*, published in 1894, Gertrude Bell describes her visit with three veiled women of the nobility in the following terms: "We left them gazing after us from behind their canvas walls. Their prisoned existence seemed to us a poor mockery of life as we cantered homewards up the damp valley, the mountain air sending a cheerful warmth through our veins" (cited in Naghibi 2007: xix).

4. *Chador* is a large piece of cloth covering the whole body, leaving only the face and the hands exposed.

5. The statement was famously made by Ayatollah Khomeini.

6. *Maghnaeh* is a loose and long head cover with one opening for the face.

7. The term *badhejab* refers to women who wear "improper" hejab or dress in public. Government regularly targets badhejab women through fines and jail time.

Chapter 4

1. Behzisti is Iran's State Welfare Organization.

2. A pseudonym for a nongovernmental organization in Tehran that caters to undocumented Afghans.

3. A paramilitary volunteer militia in Iran that engages in activities such as internal security, repressing dissent, law enforcement, and social service (often) in exchange for social benefits.

Chapter 5

1. See Marcia Abramson, "Autonomy vs. Paternalistic Beneficences: Practice Strategies," *Social Casework: The Journal of Contemporary Social Services* 70, no. 2 (1989): 101–105; and Kelly LeRoux, "Paternalistic or Participatory Governance? Examining Opportunities for Client Participation in Nonprofit Social Service Organizations," *Public Administration Review* 69, no. 3 (2009): 504–517.

Chapter 6

1. Literally means the value of milk given to the bride as an infant. The tradition of shirbaha involves giving the family of the bride a certain amount of money. The value of milk symbolizes the effort spent in preparing a girl to grow up and should be compensated when the fruit of the effort is transferred to the groom and his family. The tradition is mostly abandoned in Iran, especially among the middle and upper classes, and should not be mistaken for "buying the bride" (Moridani 2005).

Chapter 7

1. I use *they/them* pronouns when referring to Hiva even though I did not speak individually with Hiva about their gender identity and Farsi is a gender-neutral

language without gender pronouns. Given Hiva's nonbinary gender expressions, I use these pronouns to recognize their genderqueer identity.

2. The Khorasan province in northeastern Iran borders Afghanistan. In fact, until the mid-eighteenth century, much of today's Afghanistan was part of the Khorasan region of the Iranian empires, and the intermingling of people lasted way past the territorial separations (Olszewska 2015).

3. *Pesar nama* can translate as "masculine-presenting" or "tomboy."

References

Abrahamian, Ervand. 2009. *A History of Modern Iran*. Cambridge: Cambridge University Press.
Abramson, Marcia. 1989. "Autonomy vs. Paternalistic Beneficence: Practice Strategies." *Social Casework: The Journal of Contemporary Social Services* 70, no. 2: 101–105.
Abu-Lughod, Lila, ed. 1998. *Remaking Women: Feminism and Modernity in the Middle East*. Princeton, NJ: University Press.
Adelkhah, Fariba. 2000. *Being Modern in Iran*. Translated by Jonathan Derrick. New York: Columbia University Press.
Adelkhah, Fariba, and Zuzanna Olszewska. 2007. "The Iranian Afghans." *Iranian Studies* 4, no. 2: 137–165.
Afray, Janet. 2011. *Sexual Politics in Modern Iran*. Cambridge: Cambridge University Press.
Agamben, Giorgio. 1995. *Homo Sacer: Sovereign Power and Bare Life*. Stanford, CA: Stanford University Press.
———. 2005. *State of Exception*. Translated by Kevin Attell. Chicago, IL: University of Chicago Press.
Ahmadi, Arash. 2012. "Web Users Angry at Iranian Bid to Expel Afghans." *BBC News*. 4 May 4, 2012. https://www.bbc.com/news/world-middle-east-17954943.
Ahmed, Leila. 1992. *Women and Gender in Islam: Historical Roots of a Modern Debate*. New Haven: Yale University Press.
Amin, Camron Michael. 2008. "Globalizing Iranian Feminism, 1910–1950." *Journal of Middle East Women's Studies* 4, no. 1: 6–30.

Amuzegar, Jahangir. 2004. "Iran's Unemployment Crisis." *Middle East Economic Survey* 47, no. 41: 93–109.

Andrews, Abigail, and Shahrokni Nazanin. 2014. "Patriarchal Accommodations: Women's Mobility and Policies of Gender Difference from Urban Iran to Migrant Mexico." *Journal of Contemporary Ethnography* 43, no. 2: 148–175.

Bahramitash, Roksana, and Shahla Kazemipour. 2006. "Myths and Realities of the Impact of Islam on Women: Changing Marital Status in Iran." *Critique: Critical Middle Eastern Studies* 15, no. 2: 111–128.

Bahramitash, Roksana, and Jennifer C. Olmsted. 2014. "Choice and Constraint in Paid Work: Women from Low-Income Households in Tehran." *Feminist Economics* 20, no. 4: 260–280.

Barden, Margot. 1995. *Feminists, Islam, and Nation: Gender and the Making of Modern Egypt*. Princeton, NJ: Princeton University Press.

———. 2005. "Between Secular and Islamic Feminism/s: Reflections on the Middle East and Beyond." *Journal of Middle East Women's Studies* 1, no. 1: 6–28.

Battiwala, Srilatha. 1994. "The Meaning of Women's Empowerment: New Concepts from Action." In *Population Policies Reconsidered: Health, Empowerment and Rights*, edited by S. Gita, A. Germain, and L. C. Chen, 127–138. Cambridge, MA: Harvard University Press.

Bayat, Asef. 1997. *Poor People's Movements in Iran: Street Politics*. New York: Colombia University Press.

———. 2007. "Radical Religion and the Habitus of the Dispossessed: Does Islamic Militancy Have an Urban Ecology?" *International Journal of Urban and Regional Research* 31, no. 3: 570–590.

———. 2013. *Life as Politics: How Ordinary People Change the Middle East*. Stanford, CA: Stanford University Press.

Benford, Robert, and David A. Snow. 2000. "Framing Processes and Social Movements: An Overview and Assessment." *Annual Review of Sociology* 26: 611–639.

Berbary, Lisbeth A. 2014. "Too good at Fitting In: Methodological Consequences and Ethical Adjustments." *International Journal of Qualitative Studies in Education* 27, no. 10: 1205–1225.

Bettie, Julie. 2014. *Women without Class: Girls, Race and Identity*. Oakland, CA: University of California Press.

Blott, Unity. 2016. "Child Bride Is Seen Preparing for Her Big Day to a Grown MAN in 'Wedding' Video to Highlight the Horror of Underage Marriages." *Daily Mail,* March 8. https://www.dailymail.co.uk/femail/article-3481796/Child-bride-seen-preparing-big-day-grown-MAN-video-highlighting-horror-underage-marriages.html.

Bourdieu, Pierre. 1986. "The Forms of Capital." In *Handbook of Theory and Research for the Sociology of Education*, edited by J. Richardson, 241–258. Westport, CT: Greenwood.

———. 1990. "Structures, HABITUS, Practices." In *The Logic of Practice*, edited by P. Bourdieu, 52–79. Stanford, CA: Stanford University Press.

———. 1991. *Language and Symbolic Power*. Cambridge: Polity Press.

———. 1997. *Pascalian Meditations*. Translated by R. Nice. Stanford, CA: Stanford University Press.
Bunch, Charlotte. 1995. "Transforming Human Rights from a Feminist Perspective." In *Women's Rights, Human Rights: International Feminist Perspectives*, edited by J. Peters and A. Wolper, 11–17. New York: Routledge.
Chant, Sylvia. 2006. "Re-Thinking the Feminization of Poverty in Relation to Aggregate Gender Indices." *Journal of Human Development* 7, no. 2: 201–220.
———. 2008. "The Feminization of Poverty and the Feminization of Anti-Poverty Programs." *Journal of Development Studies* 44, no. 2: 165–197.
Chatterjee, Partha. 1995. "The Disciplines in Colonial Bengal." In *Texts of Power: Emerging Disciplines in Colonial Bengal*, edited by P. Chatterjee, 1–29. Minneapolis: University of Minnesota Press.
Chatty, Dawn, Gina Crivello, and Gillian L. Hundt. 2005. "Theoretical and Methodological Challenges of Studying Refugee Children in the Middle East and North African: Young Palestinians, Afghan, and Sahrawi Refugees." *Journal of Refugee Studies* 18, no. 4: 387–409.
Chin, Christine B. N. 2013. *Cosmopolitan Sex Workers: Women and Migration in a Global City*. Oxford: Oxford University Press.
Choudry, Aziz, and Eric Shragg. 2011. "Disciplining Dissent: NGOs and Community Organizations." *Globalizations* 8, no. 4: 503–517.
Chubin, Fae. 2014. "When My Virtue Defends Your Borders: Political Justification of Nation and Order through the Rhetorical Production of Womanhood in the 1979 Islamic Revolution of Iran." *Women's Studies International Forum* 42: 44–55.
Collins, Patricia Hill. 2000. *Black Feminist Thought: Knowledge, Consciousness, and the Politics of Empowerment*. New York: Routledge.
Crenshaw, Kimberly. 1991. "Mapping the Margins: Intersectionality, Identity Politics, and Violence against Women of Color." *Stanford Law Review* 43: 1241–1299.
Davis, Angela. 1981. *Women, Race, and Class*. New York: Vintage Books.
Eagleton, Terry. 1985. "The Subject of Literature." *Cultural Critique* 2: 95–104.
Ehsani, Kaveh. 1994. "'Tilt but Don't Spill': Iran's Development and Reconstruction Dilemma." *Middle East Report* 191: 16–21.
Eisenstein, Hester. 2017. "Hegemonic Feminism, Neoliberalism and Womenomics: 'Empowerment' Instead of Liberation?" *New Formations* 91: 35–49.
Esfandiari, Haleh, and Robert S. Litwak. 2007. "When Promoting Democracy Is Counterproductive." *Chronicle of Higher Education* 54, no. 2: B7–B9.
Evans, Susan. 2005. "Beyond Gender: Class, Poverty and Domestic Violence." *Australian Social Work* 58, no. 1: 36–43.
Felski, Rita. 1995. *The Gender of Modernity*. Cambridge, MA: Harvard University Press.
Ferree, Myra Marx. 2003. "Resonance and Radicalism: Feminist Framing in the Abortion Debates of the United States and Germany." *American Journal of Sociology* 109, no. 2: 304–344.

Fluri, Jennifer. 2012. "Capitalizing on Bare Life: Sovereignty, Exception and Gender Politics." *Antipode* 44, no. 1: 31–50.
Fraser, Nancy. 2009. "Social Justice in the Age of Identity Politics: Redistribution, Recognition, and Participation." In *Geographic Thought: A Praxis Perspective*, edited by G. Henderson and M. Waterstone, 72–89. Oxon: Routledge.
Frye, Marilyn. 1983. *The Politics of Reality: Essays in Feminist Theory.* New York: Crossing Press.
Garbarino, James. 1999. *Lost Boys: Why Our Sons Turn Violent and How We Can Save Them.* New York: Free Press.
Gilens, Martin, and Benjamin Page. 2014. "Testing Theories of American Politics: Elites, Interest Groups, and Average Citizens." *Perspectives on Politics* 12, no. 3: 564–581.
Gilligan, James. 2001. *Preventing Violence.* London: Thanes & Hudson.
Goffman, Erving. 1974. *Frame Analysis: An Essay on the Organization of Experience.* Boston: Northeastern University Press.
Golash-Boza, Tanya. 2015. *Immigrant Policing, Disposable Labor and Global Capitalism.* New York: New York University Press.
Gonzales de Olarte, Efrain, and Pilar Gavilano Llosa. 1999. "Does Poverty Cause Domestic Violence? Some Answers from Lima." In *Too Close to Home: Domestic Violence in the Americas*, edited by A. R. Morrison and M. L. Biehl, 35–51. Washington, D.C.: Inter-American Development Bank.
Grady, Christine, Steven Cummings, Michael Rowbotham, Michael McConnell, Euan Ashley, and Gagandeep Kang. 2017. "Informed Consent." *New England Journal of Medicine* 376, no. 9: 856–867.
Haraway, Donna. 1987. "A Manifesto for Cyborgs: Science, Technology, and Socialist Feminism in the 1980s." *Australian Feminist Studies* 2, no. 4: 1–42.
Harding, Sandra. 2004. "Introduction: Standpoint Theory as a Site of Political, Philosophical, and Scientific Debate." In *The Feminist Standpoint Theory Reader*, edited by S. Harding, 1–16. New York: Routledge.
Harris, Kevan. 2012. "The Brokered Exuberance of the Middle Class: An Ethnographic Analysis of Iran's 2009 Green Movement." *Mobilization: An International Quarterly* 17, no. 4: 435–455.
Hartsock, Nancy C. M. 2004. "The Feminist Standpoint: Developing the Ground for a Specifically Feminist Historical Materialism." In *The Feminist Standpoint Theory Reader*, edited by S. Harding, 35–54. New York: Routledge
Hashemi, Manata. 2020. *Coming of Age in Iran: Poverty and the Struggle for Dignity.* New York: New York University Press.
Held, David, Anthony McGrew, David Goldblatt, and Jonathan Perraton. 1999. *Global Transformation: Politics, Economics, and Culture.* Stanford, CA: Stanford University Press.
Heyes, Cressida. 2016. "Identity Politics." *The Stanford Encyclopedia of Philosophy* (Summer), edited by Edward N. Zalta. Available at http://plato.stanford.edu/archives/sum2016/entries/identity-politics.

Hirshman, Mitu. 1995. "Women and Development: A Critique." In *Feminism/Postmodernism/Development*, edited by M. Marchand and J. L. Parpart, 42–55. London: Routledge.

Hoodfar, Homa. 1997. "The Veil in Their Minds and On Our Heads: Veiling Practices and Muslim Women." In *The Politics of Culture in the Shadow of Capital*, edited by L. Loe and D. Lloyd, 248–279. Durham, NC: Duke University Press.

———. 2004. "Families on the Move: The Changing Role of Afghan Refugee Women in Iran." *Hawwa: Journal of Women of the Middle East and the Islamic World* 2, no. 2: 141–171.

———. 2007. "Women, Religion and the 'Afghan Education Movement' in Iran." *Journal of Development Studies* 4, no. 2: 265–293.

———. 2010. "Health as a Context for Social and Gender Activism: Female Volunteer Health Workers in Iran." *Population and Development Review* 36, no. 3: 487–510.

hooks, bell. 2000 (1984). *Feminist Theory: From Margin to Center*. Boston, MA: South End Press.

———. 2004. "Choosing the Margin as a Space of Radical Openness." In *The Feminist Standpoint Theory Reader*, edited by S. Harding, 153–160. New York: Routledge.

Israel-Cohen, Yael. 2012. *Between Feminism and Orthodox Judaism: Resistance, Identity, and Religious Change in Israel*. Leiden, NL: Brill.

Ityavyar, Dennis A., and Stella N. Obiajunwa. 1992. *The State and Women in Nigeria*. Jos, NG: Jos University Press.

Jaggar, Alison. 1985. *Feminist Politics and Human Nature*. Totowa, NJ: Rowman and Allanheld.

Johnson, Kevin R., and Bernard Trujillo. 2011. *Immigration Law and the U.S.-Mexico Border, ¿Sí Se Puede?* Tucson: University of Arizona Press.

Johnston, Hank. 2005. "Talking the Walk: Speech Acts and Resistance in Authoritarian Regimes." In *Repression and Mobilization*, edited by D. H. Johnston and C. Mueller, 108–137. Minneapolis: University of Minnesota Press.

———. 2006. "'Let's Get Small': The Dynamics of (Small) Contention in Repressive States." *Mobilization: An International Journal* 11, no. 2: 195–212.

Kabeer, Naila. 1994. *Reversed Realities: Gender Hierarchies in Development Thought*. London: Verso.

———. 1999. "Resources, Agency, Achievements: Reflections on the Measurement of Women's Empowerment." *Development and Change* 30: 435–464.

Kamat, Sangeeta. 2003. "The NGO Phenomenon and Political Culture in the Third World." *Development* 46, no. 1: 88–93.

Kandiyoti, Deniz. 1988. "Bargaining with Patriarchy." *Gender & Society* 2: 274–290.

———. 2005. *The Politics of Gender and Reconstruction in Afghanistan*, Occasional Paper 4. Geneva: UNRISD.

Keddie, Nikki R. 1981. *Roots of Revolution: An Interpretive History of Modern Iran.* With a section by Yann Richard. New Haven, CT: Yale University Press.

Khader, Serene J. 2019a. "Global Gender Justice and the Feminization of Responsibility." *Feminist Philosophy Quarterly* 5, no. 2.

———. 2019b. *Decolonizing Universalism: A Transnational Feminist Ethic.* New York: Oxford University Press.

Khoja-Moolji, Shenila. 2018. *Forging the Ideal Educated Girl: The Production of Desirable Subjects in Muslim South Asia.* Oakland: University of California Press.

Khosravi, Shahram. 2008. *Young and Defiant in Tehran.* Philadelphia: University of Pennsylvania Press.

Khurshid, Ayesha. 2015. "Islamic Traditions of Modernity: Gender, Class, and Islam in a Transnational Women's Education Project." *Gender & Society* 29, no. 1: 98–121.

Kitschelt, Herbert P. 1986. "Political Opportunity Structures and Political Protest: Anti-nuclear Movements in Four Democracies." *British Journal of Political Science* 16: 57–85.

Lagarde, Marcela. 1990. *Los Cautiverios de las Mujeres: Madresposa, Monjas, Putas, Presas y Locas.* Mexico City: Universidad Nacional Autónoma de México.

Lareau, Annette. 2011. *Unequal Childhoods: Class, Race, and Family Life.* Berkeley: University of California Press.

Lawler, Stephanie. 2005. "Disgusted Subjects: The Making of Middle-Class Identities." *The Sociological Review* 53, no. 3: 429–446.

LeRoux, Kelly. 2009. "Paternalistic or Participatory Governance? Examining Opportunities for Client Participation in Nonprofit Social Service Organizations." *Public Administration Review* 69, no. 3: 504–517.

Leve, Lauren G. 2007. "'Failed Development' and Rural Revolution in Nepal: Rethinking Subaltern Consciousness and Women's Empowerment." *Anthropological Quarterly* 80, no. 1: 127–172.

Levitt, Peggy, and Sally Merry. 2009. "Vernacularization on the Ground: Local Uses of Global Women's Rights in Peru, China, India, and the United States." *Global Networks* 9, no. 4: 441–461.

Lewis, David, and David Mosse. 2006. "Encountering Order and Disjuncture: Contemporary Anthropological Perspectives on the Organization of Development." *Oxford Development Studies* 34, no. 1: 1–13.

Lofland John, David Snow, Leon Anderson, and Lyn Lofland. 2006. *Analyzing Social Settings: A Guide to Qualitative Observation and Analysis.* 4th ed. Belmont, CA: Wadsworth Thomson.

Mackenzie, Catriona, and Natalie Stoljar. 2000. *Relational Autonomy: Feminist Perspectives on Autonomy, Agency, and the Social Self.* Oxford: Oxford University Press.

Maghbouleh, Neda. 2017. *Limits of Whiteness: Iranian Americans and the Everyday Politics of Race.* Stanford, CA: Stanford University Press.

Mahdavi, Pardis. 2009. *Passionate Uprising: Iran's Sexual Revolution*. Stanford, CA: Stanford University Press.

———. 2012. "Questioning the Global Gays(ze): Construction of Sexual Identities in Post-Revolution Iran." *Social Identities* 18, no. 2: 223–237.

Mahmood, Saba. 2005. *Politics of Piety: The Islamic Revival and the Feminist Subject*. Princeton, NJ: Princeton University Press.

Malikzadeh, Mahdi. 1992. *Tarikh-e Enqelab-e Mashrutiyat-e Iran*. 7 vols. Tehran: Elmi Press.

Massell, Gregory J. 1974. *The Surrogate Proletariat: Moslem Women and Revolutionary Strategies in Soviet Central Asia, 1919–1929*. Princeton, NJ: Princeton University Press.

Mayorga-Gallo, Sarah, and Elizabeth Hordge-Freeman. 2017. "Between Marginality and Privilege: Gaining Access and Navigating the Field in Multiethnic Settings." *Qualitative Research* 17, no. 4: 377–394.

McAdam, Doug. 1982. *Political Process and the Development of Black Insurgency, 1930–1970*. Chicago, IL: University of Chicago Press.

McAdam, Doug, John D. McCarthy, and Mayer N. Zald, eds. 1996. *Comparative Perspectives on Social Movements: Political Opportunities, Mobilizing Structures, and Cultural Framings*. Cambridge: Cambridge University Press.

McAdam, Doug, Sidney Tarrow, and Charles Tilly. 2001. *Dynamics of Contention*. Cambridge: Cambridge University Press.

McLaren, Margaret A. 2019. *Women's Activism, Feminism, and Social Justice*. New York: Oxford University Press.

———. 2021. "Decolonizing Feminism Through Intersectional Praxis On Serene Khader's Decolonizing Universalism." *Metaphilosophy* 25, no. 1: 93–110.

Mehran. Golnar. 2002. "The Presentation of the 'Self' and the 'Other' in Post-revolutionary Iranian School Textbooks." In *Iran and the Surrounding World: Interactions in Culture and Cultural Politics*, edited by N. Keddie and R. Mathee, 232–253. Seattle: University of Washington Press.

Merry, Sally E. 2006. "Transnational Human Rights and Local Activism: Mapping the Middle." *American Anthropologist* 108, no. 1: 38–51.

Mills, Sara. 1998. "Postcolonial Feminist Theory." In *Contemporary Feminist Theories*, edited by S. Jackson and J, Jones, 98–112. Edinburg: Edinburg University Press.

Moghadam, Valentine. 2002. "Islamic Feminism and its Discontents: Toward a Resolution of the Debate." *Signs* 27, no. 4: 1135–1171.

Moghadam, Valentine, and Elham Gheytanchi. 2010. Political Opportunities and Strategic Choices: Comparing Feminist Campaigns in Morocco and Iran. *Mobilization: An International Quarterly* 15, no. 3: 267–288.

Monsutti, Alessandro. 2005. *War and Migration: Social Networks and Economic Strategies of the Hazaras of Afghanistan*. New York: Routledge.

Moridani, Bijan. 2005. *The Persian Wedding*. Tarzana, CA: Inner Layers.

Naghibi, Nima. 2007. *Rethinking Global Sisterhood: Western Feminism and Iran*. Minneapolis: University of Minnesota Press.

Najmabadi, Afsaneh. 1991. "Hazards of Modernity and Morality: Women, State, and Ideology in Contemporary Iran." In *Women, Islam, and the State*, edited by D. Kandiyoti, 48–76. Philadelphia: Temple University Press.

Narayan, Uma. 2004. "The Project of Feminist Epistemology: Perspectives from a Nonwestern Feminist." In *The Feminist Standpoint Theory Reader*, edited by S. Harding, 213–224. New York: Routledge.

Nunstad, Knut G. 2003. "Considering Global/Local Relations: Beyond Dualism." In *Globalisation: Studies in Anthropology*, edited by T. H. Eriksen, 122–137. London: Pluto Press.

Oliver, Pamela, Gerald Marwell, and Ruy Teixeira. 1985. "A Theory of the Critical Mass. I. Interdependence, Group Heterogeneity, and the Production of Collective Action." *American Journal of Sociology* 91, no. 3: 522–556.

Olszewska, Zuzanna. 2013. "Classy Kids and Down-at-Heel Intellectuals: Status Aspiration and Blind Spots in the Contemporary Ethnography of Iran." *Iranian Studies* 46, no. 6: 841–862.

———. 2015. *The Pearl of Dari: Poetry and Personhood Among Young Afghans in Iran*. Bloomington: Indiana University Press.

Ong, Aihwa. 2011. "Translating Gender Justice in Southeast Asia: Situated Ethics, NGOs, and Bio-Welfare." *Journal of Women of the Middle East and Islamic World* 9: 26–48.

Ortner, Sherry B. 1995. "Resistance and the Problem of Ethnographic Refusal." *Comparative Studies in Society and History* 37, no. 1: 173–193.

———. 2005. "Subjectivity and Cultural Critique." *Anthropological Theory* 5: 31–52.

Osanloo, Arzoo. 2006. "Islamico-Civil 'Rights Talk': Women, Subjectivity, and Law in Iranian Family Court." *American Ethnologist* 33, no. 2: 191–209.

———. 2009. *The Politics of Women's Rights in Iran*. Princeton, NJ: Princeton University Press.

———. 2012. "Rights and Other Remedies, A Comment on David Engel's Article on Rights Consciousness." *Indiana Journal of Global Legal Studies* 19, no. 2: 495–505.

Parpart, Jane L., Shirin M. Rai, and Kathleen Staudt. 2002. "Rethinking Em(power)ment, Gender and Development: An Introduction." In *Rethinking Empowerment: Gender and Development in a Global/Local World*, edited by J. L. Parpart, S. M. Rai, and K. Staudt, 3–21. London: Routledge.

Pels, Dick. 2004. "Strange Standpoints, or How to Define the Situation for Situated Knowledge." In *The Feminist Standpoint Theory Reader*, edited by S. Harding, 273–290. New York: Routledge.

Petchesky, Rosalind F. 2002. "Human Rights, Reproductive Health, and Economic Justice: Why They Are Indivisible." In *The Socialist Feminist Project: A Contemporary Reader in Theory and Politics*, edited by N. Holmstrom, 74–82. New York: Monthly Review Press.

Portocarrero Lacayo, Ana Victoria. 2014. "Service Is Not Servitude: Links Between Capitalism and Feminist Liberal Conceptions of Pleasure-Case Stud-

ies from Nicaragua." *International Journal of Politics, Culture, and Society* 27, no. 2: 221–239.
Povey, Tara. 2016. "The Impact of Sanctions and Neo-Liberalism on Women's Organising in Iran." *Social Sciences* 5, no. 3: 26–40.
Pratt, Geraldine. 2005. "Abandoned Women and Spaces of the Exception." *Antipode* 37, no. 5: 1052–1078.
Radhakrishnan, Smitha. 2015. "'Low Profile' or Enterpreneurial? Gender, Class, and Cultural Adaptation in the Global Microfinance Industry." *Word Development* 74: 264–274.
Rao, Vijayendra, and Paromita Sanyal. 2010. "Dignity through Discourse: Poverty and the Culture of Deliberation in Indian Village Democracies." *ANNALS of the American Academy of Political and Social Science* 629: 146–172.
Reader, Soran. 2007. "The Other Side of Agency." *Philosophy* 82, no. 4: 579–604.
Rostami-Povey, Elahe. 2004. "Trade Unions and Women's NGOs: Diverse Civil Society Organisations in Iran." *Development in Practice* 14, no. 1/2: 254–266.
——. 2007. *Afghan Women: Identity and Invasion.* London: Zed Books.
Rowlands, Joe. 1997. *Questioning Empowerment: Working Women in Honduras.* Dublin: Oxfam.
Salami, Qolamreza, and Afsaneh Najmabadi, eds. 2005. *Nehzat-e Nesvan-e Sharq.* Tehran: Shirazeh Press.
Sameh, Catherine. 2014. "From Tehran to Los Angeles to Tehran: Transnational Solidarity Politics in the One Million Signatures Campaign to End Discriminatory Law." *Women's Studies Quarterly Special Issue on Solidarity* 42, no. 3/4: 162–184.
Sandoval, Chela. 2004. "U.S. Third World Feminism: The Theory and Method of Differential Oppositional Consciousness." In *The Feminist Standpoint Theory Reader*, edited by S. Harding, 195–210. New York: Routledge.
Santos, Boaventura de Sousa, Joao Arriscado Nunes, and Maria Paula Meneses. 2007. "Introduction: Opening Up the Canon of Knowledge and Recognition of Difference." In *Another Knowledge Is Possible: Beyond Northern Epistemologies*, edited by B. S. Santos, x–xxxix. London: Verso.
Sen, Gita, and Caren Grown. 1987. *Development, Crises, and Alternative Visions: Third World Women's Perspective.* New York: Monthly Review Press.
Shahrokni, Nazanin. 2019. *Women in Place: The Politics of Gender Segregation in Iran.* Berkeley: University of California Press.
Sharma, Aradhana. 2008. *Logics of Empowerment: Development, Gender, and Governance in Neoliberal India.* Minneapolis: University of Minnesota Press.
Sharma, Shubhra. 2011. *"Neoliberalization" as Betrayal: State, Feminism, and a Women's Education Program in India.* New York: Palgrave Macmillan.
Sheykhi, Mohammad Taghi. 2007. "Youth Housing Conditions in Tehran: Profiles and Challenges." *Journal of Social Sciences* 15, no. 2: 153–160.
Smith, Dorothy. 2005. *Institutional Ethnography: A Sociology for People.* Lanham, MD: AltaMira Press.

Snow, David A., and Robert D. Benford. 1988. "Ideology, Frame Resonance, and Participant Mobilization." *International Social Movement Research* 1: 197–217.

Snow, David A., Burk Rochford, Steven K. Worden, and Robert D. Benford. 1986. "Frame Alignment Processes, Micromobilization, and Movement Participation." *American Sociological Review* 51, no. 4: 464–481.

Spivak, Gayatri Chakravorty. 1985. "Can the Subaltern Speak?" In *Colonial Discourse and Post-Colonial Theory: A Reader*, edited by P. Williams and L. Chrisman, 66–111. New York: Columbia University Press.

Stromquist, Nelly P. 2002. "Education As a Means for Empowering Women." In *Rethinking Empowerment: Gender and Development in a Global/Local World*, edited by Jane L. Parpart, Shirin M. Rai, and Kathleen Staudt, 22–39. London: Routledge.

Sullivan, Zohreh T. 1998. "Eluding the Feminist, Overthrowing the Modern? Transformation in Twentieth-Century Iran." In *Remaking Women: Feminism and Modernity in the Middle East*, edited by L. Abu-Lughod, 215–242. Princeton, NJ: Princeton University.

Tabari, Azar. 1980. "The Enigma of Veiled Iranian Women." *Feminist Review* 5, no. 1: 19–31.

Tamadonfar, Mehran. 2001. "Islam, Law, and Political Control in Contemporary Iran." *Journal for the Scientific Study of Religion* 40, no. 2: 205–219.

Tarrow, Sidney. 1994. *Power in Movement: Social Movements, Collective Action, and Politics*. Cambridge: Cambridge University Press.

Thayer, Millie. 2010. *Making Transnational Feminism: Rural Women, NGO Activists, and Northern Donors in Brazil*. New York: Routledge.

Varzi, Roxanne. 2006. *Warring Souls: Youth, Media, and Martyrdom in Post-Revolution Iran*. Durham, NC: Duke University Press.

Vondracek, Fred W., and Vladimir B. Skorikov. 2011. "Leisure, School, and Work Activity Preferences and Their Role in Vocational Identity Development." *The Career Development Quarterly* 45, no. 4: 322–340.

Wadlington, Elizabeth, Fabian Elizondo, and Patrick Wadlington. 2012. "Working with Adolescents More Productively." *Academic Exchange Quarterly* 16, no. 2: 1096–1453.

Wardlow, Holly. 2006. *Wayward Women: Sexuality and Agency in a New Guinea Society*. Berkeley: University of California Press.

Wedeen, Lisa. 2007. "The Politics of Deliberation: Qat Chews as Public Spheres in Yemen." *Public Culture* 19, no. 1: 59–84.

Yarbrough, Dilara. 2020. "'Nothing About Us Without Us': Reading Protests against Oppressive Knowledge Production as Guidelines for Solidarity Research." *Journal of Contemporary Ethnography* 49, no. 1: 58–85.

Yeganeh, Nahid. 1993. "Women, Nationalism, and Islam in Contemporary Political Discourse in Iran." *Feminist Review* 41, no. 1: 3–18.

Index

abortion rights, 31
abuse in family, 16, 64, 71
adaptation of globally generated ideas, 59, 60, 76
administrators, 3, 16, 61; as cosmopolitan elite, 3, 54, 57, 62–78; education and training of, 19, 61, 63; indicators of empowerment used by, 19, 62; objectives and agenda set by, 13; promotions for international donations, 19; relations with government agencies, 20; research approach to, 11, 20, 22, 164–165; and staff relationship, 22, 57; and *Vagina Monologues* performance, 55–57
advocacy, 3, 4, 12; capabilities approach to, 12, 66, 79–95; historical aspects of, in Iran, 33, 40, 41; as national security threat, 43
Afghan-free zones, 46
Afghan immigrants, 3, 26, 44–49, 64; challenges faced by, 121; in community development course, 115, 117; definition of empowerment, 3; discrimination experienced by, 46, 47, 48, 128, 143, 164; education of, 39, 48–49; hate crimes against, 142; Islam as empowering for, 39; oppositional ethnic solidarity of, 127–128; performing middle class, 44–45, 49, 143, 146; as research participants, 164; rights of, 129; sexual assault and rape of, 65, 123, 128; sexual harassment of, 45, 128; speech and language of, 44, 45, 143; stigmatized identity of, 49, 146; undocumented status of, 17, 46; vulnerability of, 17–18, 48
Afghanistan, 6, 45, 84–85
Agamben, Giorgio, 11, 83
agency, 11–12, 52, 66–69, 130; in community service, 115; in global women's rights packages, 61, 68; indicators of, 66–67, 68–69, 153; and religion, 19, 51, 61, 67–69; and sexuality, 58; and tradition, 19, 61, 68–69
Ahmadinejad, Mahmood, 27, 40, 41, 88
ALLY: empowerment programs of (*see* empowerment programs); as fictitious name, 169n2; founder of, 1–3, 14–16; growth of, 16; hiring process

ALLY (*continued*)
in, 68; internal dynamics in, 2–3, 70; organizational structure of, 15–16; as radical, 76–77; referrals from police to, 92; research approach to, 3–4, 20–23, 163–167
Amini, Jina (Mahsa), 158–159
anti-imperialist feminism, 6, 7, 9, 10, 37, 155
anti-traditionalism, 7–8, 9, 10, 11, 63
approachability and credibility of researcher, 163–164
Article 24 of Iranian constitution, 38
Article 26 of Iranian constitution, 19
art programs, 12, 79–80, 83–84; client view of, 97, 98, 106, 108; cultural capital in, 105–106
Ataturk, Mustafa Kemal, 31
autonomy, 6, 7–8, 71–72, 130; and agency, 52, 66–69; indicators of, 140; liberal conception of, 157; sexual (*see* sexual autonomy); as value in empowerment program, 19, 66

badhejab, 53, 135, 138, 158, 170n7
Barden, Margot, 63
bare life, 11, 12, 81, 82–86
Basij, 91, 170ch4n3
Bayat, Asef, 40, 42, 81, 138
Behzisti (state welfare organization), 20, 82, 170ch4n1
Bell, Gertrude, 170ch2n3
Bettie, Julie, 136
bios, as qualified and proper form of life, 83, 84, 85
boundary-testing actions, 148–149
Bourdieu, Pierre, 104, 105, 136
boyfriends of clients, 68, 69, 71, 111, 124, 134
Brazil, feminist movements in, 58, 61, 99

capabilities approach, 12, 79–95, 156; in advocacy for bare life, 82–86; for gradual cultural change, 89–93; and identity politics, 85, 89, 93–95; in inaccessibility of rights, 86–89

capitalism, 7, 144
Central Intelligence Agency, 35, 160
chador, 33, 50, 133; description of, 170n4; for meeting with Imam, 139, 140; public mocking of, 144
change, cultural, long-term approach to, 89–93
children: educational opportunities for, 46, 49, 107–108; investment in, for social change, 90, 91; labor of, 42, 92, 108, 127; marriage of, 124, 151–152; middle class, assuming equality, 149; rights of, 73, 86, 92, 127
circumcision, female, 89
class issues, 4, 5, 7, 96–115. *See also* middle class; deficit model in, 107, 153; intersection with gender and ethnicity (*see* intersectionality of gender, class, and ethnicity); and oppositional consciousness, 13, 116–130; and staff–client relationship, 13, 96–115, 116–130; in urban structure of Tehran, 24–25, 28; in volunteer work, 112–115
class mobility, 11, 13, 49, 133, 135; cultural capital for, 100, 103, 104, 107
clients, 14–16, 21, 169n1; Afghan (*see* Afghan immigrants); as agents of change, 91; anger and hostility of, 117, 118, 119; as bare life, 11, 81, 82–86; capabilities of, 79–95 (*see also* capabilities approach); class issues affecting staff relationship, 13, 96–115, 116–130; complaints of (*see* complaints of clients); conservative and religious, 49–51; daily commute of, 17, 18, 98; indicators of empowerment (*see* indicators of empowerment); Iranian, 17, 49–51, 143–144; as local subaltern, 44–54, 63; oppositional consciousness of, 13, 116–130; practical realities for, 74–75, 105, 106, 108, 112, 140; research approach to, 3–4, 20–23, 163–167; sexual autonomy of (*see* sexual autonomy); sexual education programs for (*see* sexual education programs); social abandonment

Index / 185

of, 15, 83, 91; as stigmatized, 82–83; us versus them divide affecting, 122; in vernacularization process, 63
clothing, 31, 32–33, 44–45, 49, 50; agency in decisions on, 68, 69; chador in (*see* chador); consequences of choices on, 72; in gender expression, 132, 133; hejab in (*see* hejab); manto in, 15, 50, 140, 163, 169ch1n1; in performing middle class, 13, 104, 133, 138, 149; in resistance expression, 13, 133, 135, 138; in respectability, 138–141; in symbolic economy, 13, 133, 136, 138–141; unequal access to, 121
Collins, Patricia Hill, 166
communication skills, 101–102, 106, 112. *See also* speech and language
community development course, 64, 96–97; client objections to, 50–51, 96–97, 109, 112–115, 127; norms of respectability affecting project in, 137–142; privileged view in, 50–51, 116–118, 119, 127, 139–140; volunteer work required in, 113–115
complaints of clients, 3, 21–22, 98–99, 110; on art programs, 97, 106; boundary-testing actions in, 148–149; in community development class, 50–51, 96–97, 109, 112–115; expressed in meetings, 14, 15; on length of program, 110; in performing entitlement, 147–150; on religious attitudes of teachers, 50, 51, 67–68; staff response to, 98–99, 106, 110
complementarian gender roles, 9, 38
Conference of the Women of the East (1932), 32
confidentiality of research, 169n2
consciousness-raising, 18, 64–65, 69, 81; perceived as unidirectional, 156; sexual autonomy in, 70, 71; social change in, 92
consent of research participants, 165
constitutionalism, 30, 34
constitution of Iran, 19, 37–38
consumerism, 26, 28, 53, 145
contentious talks, 87

cosmopolitan elite, 3, 12, 54, 57, 62–78, 155
creative writing classes, 17, 105, 131–133, 134
credibility and approachability of researcher, 163–164
criminalization of premarital sexual relationships, 40–41, 71
critical mass framework, 12, 90–91
cultural capital, 12, 49, 99–100, 103–110, 136, 148
cultural poverty, 63, 124, 148, 153
culture, 8, 9, 61; and authentic reform, 3, 12, 70; of defiance among youth, 28, 51–52; ethnocentrism concerning, 155; intersection with class and ethnicity, 69–70, 125, 126, 129, 134; local norms in (*see* local norms); long-term approach to change in, 89–93; patriarchal attitudes in, 123–126 (*see also* patriarchal attitudes); reductionist explanations based on, 9, 124, 125, 126, 154, 156

Dari language, 44, 143
dating, local norms on, 111–112
deficit model, 99–100, 107, 153
democracy, 94
Development, Crises, and Alternative Visions (Sen & Grown), 153
development programs, 129–130, 153–155, 156
discrimination, 46, 47, 48, 128, 132, 143, 164
divorce, 31, 32, 33, 38
dropout rate, 98

economic independence, 7, 32, 41, 100–101, 106
education, 17, 39, 48–49; community development course in (*see* community development course); as component of empowerment, 16–17, 18, 66, 107–108; in Pahlavi regime, 31, 32, 34; and resistance in middle class, 53; sexual education programs in (*see* sexual education programs); of staff

education (*continued*)
and administrators, 18–19, 20, 50, 61, 63; as unidirectional, 156; university entrance exam in (*konkoor*), 121; vocational training in (*see* vocational training)
Egypt, 63, 89
empowerment programs, 1–5, 16–20; administrators of (*see* administrators); agency in, 61, 66–69, 153; alternative models of, 154; anti-traditionalism in, 7–8, 9, 10, 11, 63; in bare life, 81, 82–86; capabilities approach in (*see* capabilities approach); class issues in (*see* class issues); clients of (*see* clients); communication skills in, 101–102, 106, 112; complaints in (*see* complaints of clients); components of, 16–17, 65; consciousness-raising in (*see* consciousness-raising); cosmopolitan and local elite in, 12, 62–78; cultural capital in, 12, 99–100, 105–106, 107; cultural change in, 89–93; daily commute to, 17, 18, 98; definitions of empowerment in, 3, 13, 19, 65, 66, 153, 154; dropout rate from, 98; economic independence in, 7, 100–101, 106; education in, 16–17, 18, 66, 107–108; entitlement in, 147–150, 153; family resistance to, 17, 109; glocal analysis of, 13, 55–78; government surveillance of, 3, 19–20, 43, 86–87; grassroots and local initiatives in, 154; and inaccessibility of rights, 86–89; indicators of success in (*see* indicators of empowerment); intentions of developers, 59; international sources of funding, 19–20, 44, 58, 59, 61; interpersonal skills in, 102–103, 104–105, 108; as justice-enhancing practice, 9, 13, 155; in liberal feminism, 152–153; local subaltern view of, 63; objectives and goals in, 64, 65, 66, 91, 100, 107, 156; performing middle class in (*see* performing middle class); practical realities in, 74–75, 105, 106, 108, 112, 140; and religion, 67–69, 73–74, 77–78, 155; research methods on, 3–4, 20–23, 163–167; in rural and urban areas compared, 106; sense of propriety in, 10–11; sexuality in, 19, 55–59, 62, 70–78; staff of (*see* staff); time required for, 12, 17, 18, 98, 101, 102, 108–110; universal frameworks for, 77; vocational training in (*see* vocational training)
entitlement, 147–150, 153
equality, 6–7, 9, 155–156; class issues in, 123, 129; and complementarian gender roles, 9, 38; and empowerment, 3, 10, 18, 123, 129; ethnic issues in, 129; and gender oppression (*see* gender oppression); in global women's rights package, 59–60; in Islamic Republic, 38, 39, 95; and patriarchal attitudes, 18, 132; and performing entitlement, 148
Esfandiari, Haleh, 41
ethical issues in research, 20–21, 22, 165–167
ethnic identity, 3, 4, 13; intersection with gender and class (*see* intersectionality of gender, class, and ethnicity)

face covering (*rubande*), 32
family, 7, 16, 17, 38; abuse and violence in, 16, 64, 71; early marriage in, 111, 112; economic independence of women from, 7, 100–101; income and labor from women needed in, 17, 18, 98, 109; patriarchal attitudes in, 123–124; religious cultural context of, 68, 72–73; resistance to ALLY program in, 17, 109; teachings in conflict with norms of, 68, 72–73
Family Protection Laws, 36, 38
Farsi, 44
femininity, 131, 132, 133, 152; middle-class respectable, 135, 144; Muslim, 138; performance of, 143, 144
feminism: anti-imperialist, 6, 7, 9, 10, 37, 155; anti-traditionalism in, 63; autonomy in, 6, 7–8; class and ethnic

politics in, 4; definition of, 7, 155–156; in history of Iran, 29–41; and imperialism, 6–7, 9, 10, 36, 37, 152, 155; indigenous, 5; individualism in, 6, 7; Iranian, 135; Islamic, 8, 39, 74, 155; middle class, 135; missionary, 6, 9, 155; neoliberal, 6; secular (*see* secular feminism); transnational, 6–10, 11, 155; Western (*see* Western feminism)
Feminist Theory: From Margin to Center (hooks), 6
feminization of responsibility, 7
Ferree, Myra Marx, 77
Fluri, Jennifer, 84–85
Freire, Paulo, 3
funding, international sources of, 19–20, 44, 58, 59, 61

García Márquez, Gabriel, 51
gender: complementary roles related to, 9, 38; and identity, 131–132, 170–171n1; intersection with class and ethnicity (*see* intersectionality of gender, class, and ethnicity); reforms related to, 31, 32, 33, 34, 35; segregation based on, 32, 39, 48, 146; and sexual norms, 18, 34, 40–41, 62; and social problems, 124
gender justice, 12, 39, 72, 77, 155
gender oppression, 6, 7, 8, 9; class and ethnic issues in, 7, 63, 126–127, 129, 134; classroom discussions on, 132, 134; and cultural poverty, 63, 124, 153; patriarchal attitudes in, 8, 146; reductionist accounts of, 9, 124, 125, 126, 154, 156; speaking out about, 146; staff view of, 19, 78, 125; universal account of, 9, 33, 145, 149, 154
gender politics, 5, 11, 31, 38
Gilens, Martin, 94
Global North, 9, 59, 61–62
Global South, 10, 58, 59, 61–62; misrepresentation of women in, 165; subordination of women in, 153; underage marriage in, 152
global value packages, 16, 62; women's rights in, 12, 59–60, 61, 68, 153

glocal analysis, 13, 55–78
Gramsci, Antonio, 43
Great Britain, 33, 35
Grown, Caren, 153

hair styles, 44, 50, 133, 136, 138, 170n6
Haraway, Donna, 167
Harris, Kevan, 52–53
Hartsock, Nancy C. M., 166
Hashemi, Manata, 135, 138, 140, 145
Hashemi-Rafsanjani, Akbar, 26–27
hate crimes, 142
Hazaras, 45
head covering (maghnaeh), 50, 170n6
health care component of empowerment program, 16, 17
hejab, 38, 68, 69, 135, 155; improper, 53, 135, 138, 158, 170n7; noncompliance with, 15, 40, 53, 159, 169ch1n1, 170n7; in norm of respectability, 138
helplessness feelings, 11, 71
High Council of Women's Organizations, 35
historical aspects, 24–41, 51
homo sacer ("bare life"), 11, 83
homosexuality, 31, 73; and LGBTQ movement, 80, 81
Hoodfar, Homa, 39, 42, 48
hooks, bell, 6, 151, 167
Hordge-Freeman, Elizabeth, 163
housing poverty, 100

identity: of Afghan immigrants, 49; of cosmopolitan and local elite, 63; in forced unveiling, 33; gender, 131–132, 170–171n1; Iranian, 47; middle class, 12, 107; Muslim, 30; and performing entitlement, 148; relational, 7, 38, 40, 88; stigmatized, 82–83, 85
identity politics, 42, 80–82, 87; capabilities approach in, 85, 89, 93–95, 156; innominate, 81–82; universal conceptions of rights in, 81, 88
imperialism, 5, 7, 38, 47; and feminism, 6–7, 9, 10, 36, 37, 152, 155
inaccessibility of rights, 81, 86–89
India, 148

indicators of empowerment, 61, 66–69, 106–107, 136; agency, 66–67, 68–69, 153; economic independence, 7, 100–101, 106; lifestyle, 156; performing middle class, 10–11, 12, 13, 109, 140, 154; sexual autonomy, 19, 62, 70–78, 134; staff and administrator view of, 19, 62, 136

individualism, 6, 7, 19, 38

informed consent of research participants, 165

innominate identity politics, 81–82

Institutional Ethnography (Smith), 165

intellectuals, 49, 122, 134, 167

intentions in empowerment programs, 59

International Monetary Fund, 26, 27

international sources of funding, 19–20, 44, 58, 59, 61

interpersonal skills, 102–103, 104–105, 108

intersectionality of gender, class, and ethnicity, 4, 10, 149–150, 156–157; for Afghan clients, 142–143, 146; capabilities approach in, 81, 83, 85; and clients as bare life, 81, 83, 85; in forced unveiling, 33; in justice-enhancing practice, 155; for local subaltern, 63; oppositional consciousness in, 129; in performing middle class, 145–146; in power and empowerment, 13, 152–153, 154, 155; staff awareness of, 119, 125, 146; structural inequalities in, 69–70, 126, 145, 156; symbolic economies in, 49, 134, 136–137; theories of, 85; and universal conception of womanhood, 144, 145

interviews in research, 20, 21

Iran: authoritarian and democratic practices in, 94; constitution of, 19, 37–38; government restrictions on NGOs, 19–20, 41; history of, 24–41; Kurdish women in, 158–160; name changed from Persia to, 169ch2n2; nuclear program of, 28; recent violence in, 158–159; rights talk in, 40, 88, 95; sanctions of U.S. on, 27–28, 158

Iranian clients, 17, 49–51, 143–144

Iranian identity, 47

Iran-Iraq War, 26, 53

Iraq, 6, 26, 53

Islam: and empowerment of women, 39, 66; and feminism, 8, 38–39, 66, 74, 155; identity in, 30; universal education in, 39, 48–49

Islamic Republic: Afghan immigrants in, 44–49; education in, 39, 48–49; establishment of (1979), 26, 36–37, 45; middle class defiance and resistance in, 51–54; modernization efforts in, 53

Islamization, 28, 48

Johnston, Hank, 87

justice, 8–9, 13; economic, 127, 144, 145, 157; and empowerment, 22; gender, 12, 39, 72, 77, 155; social, 23, 27, 157

justice-enhancing practice, 9, 13, 155

Kabeer, Naila, 7

Khader, Serene J., 6, 7, 8, 9

Khatami, Mohammad Reza, 27, 39–40

Khoja-Moolji, Shenila, 66

Khomeini, Ayatollah Ruhollah, 26, 34–35, 37–38, 170n5

Khosravi, Shahram, 28, 51–52, 133, 138, 145

knowledge, 58–59, 136

Kurdish women, 158–160

labor: of children, 42, 92, 108, 127; immigrants as cheap source of, 46, 47–48; in rural areas, 25, 36; unpaid, volunteer work as, 115; of women needed in family income, 17, 18, 98, 109

Ladies' Center, 32

Lagarde, Marcela, 58

land reforms, 25, 36

language. *See* speech and language

Lareau, Annette, 149

Lawler, Stephanie, 107

legal status of immigrants, 17, 46, 83
Leve, Lauren G., 129–130
Levitt, Peggy, 59–60, 62, 74
LGBTQ movement, identity politics in, 80, 81
liberal democracy, 94
liberal feminism, 5, 6, 7, 152–153; administrator commitment to, 57; agency in, 11–12, 52, 54, 69; anti-traditionalism in, 10, 11, 63; of cosmopolitan elite, 62, 70, 77; history in Iran, 29; indicators of empowerment in, 13, 19; and international funding, 19, 58, 77; response of Afghan women to, 49; sexual autonomy in, 62, 69, 70; shortcomings of, 155; staff view of, 13, 18–19, 62, 63, 146
lifestyle, 13, 133, 138; and empowerment, 156; in performing middle class, 13, 49; in symbolic economy, 13, 133, 134–137
Litwak, Robert S., 41
local elite, and cosmopolitan elite, 12, 62–78, 155
local norms, 5, 18, 72–73, 76–77; dating and marriage in, 111–112; gender and sexual, 18, 34, 40–41, 62; and global women's rights packages, 12, 59–60; and glocal analysis, 13, 55–78; modesty in, 51, 133, 135, 138, 140; patriarchal attitudes in, 40, 123–126; and practical realities for clients, 74–75, 140; resistance and compliance decisions on, 52, 139–140, 147; of respectability (*see* respectability, norms of); staff grounded in, 3, 57, 61, 62, 77; and vernacularization process, 60
local subaltern, clients as, 44–54, 63

Mahdavi, Pardis, 40, 51, 81, 134, 138
Mahmood, Saba, 8, 52
makeup and appearance, 50, 133, 139, 143–144, 149
mannerisms, 10, 104, 105, 109, 145
manto (trench-coat type covering), 15, 50, 140, 163, 169ch1n1
Maoist movement, 129

marriage, 68, 69, 111–112; of children, 124, 151–152; historical aspects of, 31, 32, 33; shirbaha tradition in, 125–126, 170ch6n1
Mayorga-Gallo, Sarah, 163
McLaren, Margaret A., 9
Mehran, Golnar, 47
Merry, Sally, 59–60, 62, 74
message framing, 60
middle class, 51–54, 107, 135, 154; femininity in, 135, 144; habitus of, 10–11, 12, 105, 141; identity in, 12, 107; performing as (*see* performing middle class); respectability norms in, 13, 49, 133–134, 135, 141, 144; staff in, 3, 13, 61, 62, 98–99, 108, 116–130, 137
military service, mandatory, 120–121
missionary feminism, 6, 9, 155
modernization: in Islamic Republic, 53; in Pahlavi government, 31, 33, 34, 35–36, 39
modesty, 51, 133, 135, 138, 140; and forced unveiling, 33; and sexual morality, 139; symbolic economy in, 141
Mosaddegh, Mohammad, 35
motherhood, status of, 30

Naghibi, Nima, 29
Narayan, Uma, 166
National Front, 35
nationalism, 30, 48
National Organization of Women, 35
neocolonialism, 8
neoliberalism, 6, 7, 8, 129–130; economic policies in, 26, 27, 28, 100, 144; militaristic, effects of, 153
Nepal, 129–130
nongovernmental organizations: in Ahmadinejad presidency, 41; ALLY as (*see* ALLY); and cultural change, 92, 93; empowerment programs of (*See* empowerment programs); government restrictions on, 19–20, 41; in identity politics, 42; international sources of funding, 19–20, 41, 44, 58, 59, 61; in Khatami presidency, 40; rescue narratives of, 84–85; secular

nongovernmental organizations (*continued*)
  feminism in, 39; self-censorship of, 41; social services provided by, 41–42; and vernacularization process, 60
norms, local. *See* local norms
nuclear program, 28

Obama, Barack, 27–28
oil revenues, 25, 26, 27–28, 41
Olszewska, Zuzanna, 47–48, 51, 133, 134, 135, 138, 146
oppositional consciousness, 13, 116–130, 166
oppositional speech acts, 87
Orientalist feminist discourses, 66, 77
Osanloo, Arzoo, 40, 88, 95

Page, Benjamin, 94
Pahlavi, Ashraf, 35
Pahlavi, Mohammad Reza Shah, 25, 28, 33–36
Pahlavi, Reza Shah, 25, 31–34, 36, 160, 169ch2n2
participant observation, 21
Passionate Uprising (Mahdavi), 51
paternalism, 99
patriarchal attitudes, 8, 65–66, 123–126, 146; and femininity, 131, 132, 135; long-term cultural change in, 90, 91; organized protests against, 133; and religion, 74, 135; of staff, 18–19, 57, 76
Patriotic Women's League, 32
Pedagogy of the Oppressed (Freire), 3
Pels, Dick, 167
performing entitlement, 147–150
performing middle class, 12, 13, 100–110, 132; by Afghan immigrants, 44–45, 49, 143, 146; and entitlement, 147–150; as indicator of empowerment, 10–11, 12, 13, 109, 140, 154; and private self, 141; and privilege, 142–147; respectability in, 133–134, 135, 144; secular appearance in, 133, 140, 141; symbolic economy in, 131–150
performing privilege, 142–147, 149

Persia, 29–30, 169ch2n2, 170ch2n3
Persian Pictures (Bell), 170ch2n3
police, 33, 45, 47, 92, 128
political opportunity structure, 87
Portocarrero Lacayo, Ana Victoria, 58
postcolonial studies, 43–44
potentiality, 11, 12, 84, 89
poverty, 6, 15, 145, 148, 153; of Afghan immigrants, 46, 64, 126; cultural, 63, 124, 148, 153; family income and labor from women needed in, 17, 18, 98, 109; housing, 100; marriage practices in, 111, 112, 126, 152; performing middle class in, 100–110; and privileged views of staff, 2, 51, 98, 120–121, 126, 127; resistance to volunteer work in, 114; and structural inequalities, 64, 66, 78, 124–125; and violence, 105, 124–125
power, 74–75, 125, 153, 154; definitions of, 13, 153; and privilege of staff, 98–99, 123; research approach to, 22, 165–167
premarital counseling, 111, 112
premarital sexual relations, 13, 40–41, 69, 71, 134–135
Prison Notebooks (Gramsci), 43
private and public self in performing middle class, 141
privilege, 36, 154; classroom activity on, 116–118, 119; performance of, 142–147, 149; research approach to, 22, 165–167; of staff, 2, 12, 13, 98–99, 106, 116–130, 137, 143, 164; of teachers, 50–51, 116–118
proper life, 10–11, 84, 85

racism, 7, 47
Rao, Vijayendra, 148
rape. *See* sexual assault and rape
Reader, Soran, 52
reforms: culturally authentic, 3, 12, 70; gender, 31, 32, 33, 34, 35; land, 25, 36
relational identities, 7, 38, 40, 88
religion, 8, 9, 38–39, 62; and agency, 19, 51, 61, 67–69; and conservative appearance, 50; and empowerment,

67–69, 73–74, 77–78, 155; and patriarchy, 74, 135; teacher attitudes on, 50, 51, 67–68
rescue narratives, 84–85
research methods, 3–4, 20–23, 44, 163–167, 169n2
resistant contention, 87
respectability, norms of, 13, 49, 133–134, 135; in community service project, 137–142; contradictory, 141–142; in middle class, 13, 49, 133–134, 135, 141, 144
Rethinking Global Sisterhood: Western Feminism and Iran (Naghibi), 29
revolution of 1979 in Iran, 36–37, 45, 88
rights, 42–43, 71–72, 129; of children, 73, 86, 92, 127; inaccessibility of, 81, 86–89; as national threat, 43, 87, 88; politicized rhetoric of, 87; state surveillance of movements for, 43, 87; universal conception of, 6, 54, 73, 74–75, 81, 83, 88
rights talk in Iran, 40, 88, 95
Rouhani, Hassan, 40
rural areas, 25, 36, 106, 129, 134

al-Saltaneh, Taj, 32
Sandoval, Chela, 166
Sanyal, Paromita, 148
"saving face" practices, 135–136, 138, 141, 145
scientific domesticity, 30, 31
secular feminism, 6, 7–8, 11, 155; administrator commitment to, 57; of cosmopolitan and local elite, 69–70; history in Iran, 30, 38–39; indicators of empowerment in, 19, 54; staff view of, 62, 63
secular nationalism, 30
security, national, women's rights as threat to, 43, 87, 88
Sen, Gita, 153
sexual assault and rape, 2, 65; of Afghan women, 65, 123, 128; blaming client for, 18; in family, 64, 71

sexual autonomy, 10, 12, 54, 58, 155; in economic independence, 41; as empowerment, 19, 62, 70–78, 134; family affecting, 68, 70–73; practical implications of, 70–71, 77; in secular lifestyle, 134–135; unintended consequences of, 71–72
sexual education programs, 58, 70, 71, 78; in conflict with local norms, 73, 76; in universal framework, 77; *Vagina Monologues* performance in, 18, 55–57, 75
sexual harassment, 33, 45, 128
sexual relations, 13, 68, 69, 76; as expression of resistance, 13, 51–52, 134–135; local norms on, 18, 34, 40–41, 73, 76; motivations in, 69, 134–135; premarital, 13, 40–41, 69, 71, 134–135; in secular lifestyle, 134–135; stigma associated with, 82–83
sex workers, 82, 83
sharia law, 31, 37
Sharma, Shubhra, 59
Shia Muslims, 45
shirbaha tradition, 125–126, 170ch6n1
Smith, Dorothy, 165
social abandonment, 15, 83, 91
socialization of rebellious youth, 52
social services, 16, 41–42
solidarity research, 165
speech and language, 101–102; of Afghan clients, 44, 45, 143; gender pronouns in, 170–171n1; in performing entitlement, 148; in performing middle class, 11, 103–105, 106, 108, 109, 132–133, 146, 149; in performing privilege, 143; as symbolic capital, 145; in writing class, 133, 134
Spivak, Gayatri, 43, 166
staff, 13, 16, 18–19, 20; and administrator relationships, 22, 57; class issues affecting client relationship, 13, 96–115, 116–130; client complaints about, 21–22, 98–99; in community development class, 50–51, 112–115; concerns about government

staff (*continued*)
  surveillance, 86, 87; definition of empowerment of, 19; indicators of empowerment used by, 19, 62, 136; as local elite, 62, 76; as locally grounded, 3, 57, 61, 62, 77; men as members of, 103, 120–121; as middle class, 3, 13, 61, 62, 98–99, 108, 116–130, 137; patriarchal attitudes of, 18–19, 57, 76; power of, 98–99, 123; as privileged, 2, 12, 13, 98–99, 106, 116–130, 137, 143, 164; research approach to, 20, 21–22, 164; secular views of, 68; sex education programs for, 55–57, 58; tensions and conflicts with clients, 2, 13, 21–22, 96–115, 116–130; us versus them divide affecting, 122; and *Vagina Monologues* performance, 1, 56–57
standpoint theory, 165–167
states of exception, 83
stigma: capabilities approach in, 12, 83, 85; of ethnic and national identity, 49, 83, 132, 146; identity politics in, 80, 85; of lower economic class, 25, 138, 144, 145, 146; of marginalized identity, 83, 148, 156; of social status, 82–83, 85
structural inequalities, 8, 9, 90, 124–125; in intersection of gender, class, and ethnicity, 69–70, 126, 145, 156; poverty in, 64, 66, 78, 124–125
subaltern, 43–54, 63
subjectivity, 3, 5, 52
surveillance by authorities, 43, 87, 94
symbolic economies, 13, 43, 49, 131–150, 156

Taliban, 45, 49
teachers: client resistance to, 50–51, 96–97; of community development course, 50–51, 96–97, 112–118, 127, 139–140, 164; education of, 50; and oppositional consciousness of clients, 116–130; privileged view of, 50–51, 116–118; on religious beliefs, 50, 51, 67–68; research approach to, 164

Tehran: class divisions in, 24–25, 28; history of, 24–25, 30, 32; indicators of empowerment in, 106; liberal and secular feminism in, 69; location of ALLY in, 1, 18, 25, 43, 44, 163; middle class in, 44–45, 134, 138, 143; migration to, 25, 26, 44; research approach in, 3–4, 20–23, 44, 163–167; respectability norms in, 133–134, 144, 146; response to sexual education in, 56, 70–71; slum areas of, 25, 43; staff of ALLY from, 67, 118, 122; upper class in, 25–26, 28, 30, 41; urban culture in, 24–25; youth culture in, 28, 51–52, 133
Thayer, Millie, 58, 61, 99
time required for empowerment program, 12, 17, 18, 98, 101, 102, 108–110
tokenism, 35–36
tradition, 19, 61, 68–69; and anti-traditionalism, 7–8, 9, 10, 11, 63
translation of globally generated ideas, 59, 60–61, 62, 72, 156
transnational feminism, 6–10, 11, 155
travel time in commuting, 18
Tudeh Party, 34

undocumented status of immigrants, 17, 46, 83
United Nations, 16, 35, 151–152, 153
United States, 6, 35, 41, 45; as oligarchical political system, 94; rhetorical war on Iran, 43, 87–88; sanctions on Iran, 27–28, 158
universalism and universal features: in forced unveiling, 33; in gender oppression, 9, 33, 145, 149, 154; in human rights, 6, 54, 73, 74–75, 81, 83, 88; in identity politics, 81, 88; and imperialism, 6, 29; in liberal and secular feminism, 69, 155; in nonideal approach, 9, 155; in sexuality, 58, 59, 77; in standpoint theory, 166; in suffering, 122; in womanhood conceptions, 33, 144, 145
unveiling, forced, 32, 33, 37

The Vagina Monologues, 1, 18, 55–57, 60, 75
veil use, 29, 30, 31, 37, 135, 170ch2n3; and forced unveiling, 32, 33, 37
vernacularization process, 60–61, 62, 63
violence: Afghan immigrants experiencing, 46, 64, 65, 128, 142; and bare life, 11, 83; in family, 16; in Kurdish region, 158–159; in patriarchal culture, 124; in poverty, 105, 124–125
virginity, value placed on, 69, 73, 135
vocational training, 16–17, 63–65, 103–110; client view of, 97–98; communication skills in, 101–102; economic independence as objective of, 7, 100–101; interpersonal skills in, 102–103
volunteer work as course requirement, 113–115
voting rights, 31, 34, 35

Wardlow, Holly, 140
Wedeen, Lisa, 94
Western culture, 8, 10, 29–30, 47, 155; lifestyle in, 13, 53, 134, 145; in performing middle class, 134, 135; youth adopting, 28–29
Western feminism, 3, 5, 6, 7, 8–9; history in Iran, 30, 36–37, 88; marginalizing effects of, 5; sexuality in, 57, 58–59
Westernization, 3, 25–26, 28–29, 37; in Pahlavi regimen, 31, 33, 36–37
Woman, Life, Freedom *("Jin, Jiyan, Azadi")*, 159, 160
Women's Council, 34
Women's Organization of Iran, 35–36, 37
Women's Party, 34
working class, 107, 134, 144; "saving face" practices of, 135–136, 138, 145
World Bank, 16
writing classes, 17, 105, 131–133, 134

Yemen, 94
Young and Defiant in Tehran (Khosravi), 51–52

Zhenotdel (organization for women), 31

Fae Chubin is Assistant Teaching Professor of Sociology at the University of Tampa.

www.ingramcontent.com/pod-product-compliance
Lightning Source LLC
Chambersburg PA
CBHW020237170426

43202CB00008B/111